DEFY THE WILDERNESS

DEFY
THE WILDERNESS

Lynne Reid Banks

1981

CHATTO & WINDUS

LONDON

Published by Chatto & Windus Ltd
40 William IV Street
London WC2N 4DF

Clarke, Irwin & Co. Ltd
Toronto

British Library Cataloguing in Publication Data

Banks, Lynne Reid
Defy the wilderness.
I. Title
823'.914[F]   PR6003.A528

ISBN 0-7011-2593-4

'My Father Fought Their War for Four Years' from *Selected Poems*
of Yehuda Amichai, translated by Assia Gutman,
is reproduced by kind permission of
Cape Goliard Press; and the poem by Zelda
by kind permission of the author.

Phototypeset by Western Printing Services Ltd, Bristol
Printed in Great Britain by Redwood Burn Ltd
Trowbridge

For those who will not be angry

Then my soul cried out:
Charred lips –
you are on one side,
the world on the other,
all the world on the other side.

ZELDA

AUTHOR'S NOTE

This novel was conceived during a trip I made to Jerusalem in
May, 1980, to research for a book about the First Arab-Israeli War.
Apart from this fact, and certain news stories which occurred
during my visit which have been compressed to fit the time
structure of the book, this work is entirely fictional. Any resemblance of characters, other than politicians, to real people is
coincidental.

CHAPTER 1

She could never hear the phone from her room, which was in the front of the flat. Traffic started up on the main road outside at first light – around 5 a.m. – and the heavy stone walls of the houses, rising straight up from the narrow pavements, caused the racket of the heavy lorries on their way to market to ricochet back and forth like the roar of trains through tunnels. She'd grown used to the worst of it by the second or third day, though if she paused to give ear to it consciously, it seemed incredible that she could sleep or work or even think through it. Today it wasn't nearly so bad because it was a feast day – about like the Sabbath; in any case she was so dead beat after her previous day's work in the boiling heat that she had slept as if poleaxed.

So she knew nothing of the phone ringing until Amnon blundered into her room in his pyjama bottoms, his hair standing up straight and his voice terse with interrupted sleep.

'Ann. Phone.'

'Sorry – '

'Okay.'

He blundered away again. She rolled out of bed and reached for her dressing-gown, but it was too hot to bother with it. The *sharav* which had started three days ago had gathered strength in the night and had managed, if not to permeate the thick walls of the old house, at least to creep round the door or through cracks in the shutters, and was now making itself felt distinctly, even indoors. The tiles under her bare feet were all that felt good as she went through into the kitchen where one of the phones stood on the table.

'Hallo?'

'Ann, hallo, good morning, it's Ruth. Bad news.'

Her heart sank. Befuddled by sleep and the *sharav*, still she guessed at once that today was off.

'It's this damned wind, I suppose.'

'I'm afraid. They're not young any more! And most of them have to come up from Tel Aviv. They've been phoning since early morning to call off.'

Hell. And she'd kept today free. But it wasn't Ruth's fault. And knowing Ruth, she would be disappointed herself, and sorry to let Ann down. Ann joked:

1

'Since early morning, eh? And what is it now, by you?'

'*Mottik*, it's nearly eight o'clock! Don't say I woke you? I thought you were in Israel to work?'

'I am, I am . . . I'm not so young any more either, you know! If all those stalwart Palmachniks are collapsing from the heat, can't I be excused for sleeping in? I had no fewer than four interviews yesterday in different sectors of the city, and I had to do a lot of it on foot.'

Amnon had come into the kitchen in his ancient *abaya*, his eyes still slitty from sleep. She hitched her chair forward so he could get at the fridge for oranges. He'd got into the habit of orange juice for breakfast since Ann had arrived, and started squeezing them. Now he hissed:

'You should rent a car. I told you. You will kill yourself with all this bussing and foot-schlepping in a *khamsin*, you're crazy.'

Ruth was still talking.

'. . . I am so sorry about today. I had some wonderful people for you, a lot of my old comrades, the *cream* . . . marvellous people. You should do your whole book about them and never mind these rotten old ex-terrorists, I say "ex" but that is more than some of them deserve, even if they *are* running everything now – '

'Ruth, don't feel badly, there'll be other days.'

'No, but I planned it so nicely. A picnic at Kastel, the site of some big battles, it would stimulate their reminiscences, I thought. I wanted you to meet them, to see what they're like – the calibre – '

Amnon was putting on the kettle. The gas flame added a little gust of heat to the rising temperature in the room.

'Never mind.'

'It is important to me. I want you to meet the best, not the worst.'

'It's meant to be a book showing all sides.'

'All *Jewish* sides,' Amnon interrupted cynically, cutting oranges beside the sink.

Ann covered the mouthpiece.

'*All* sides. Arabs too.'

'First catch your Arabs.'

Ruth was saying, 'So what will you do today?'

'Try to get some interviews at short notice. One can, sometimes, just by phoning. People are very good about seeing me if they can fit me in, even quite important people.'

'Do you phone their homes? Generals and things?'

2

'I usually leave generals to Liora at the Foreign Press office, along with the big-wheel politicians, but some of the lesser lights I'm not scared to beard in their lairs.'

'Be careful today, though. It's *yomtov*.'

'Yes, I know.'

You never knew who was going to get frosty if you phoned on the Sabbath or a feast day. That was one of the few drawbacks about Jerusalem. You never knew who was religious – the most unexpected people were. And weren't.

'You could come round and be with us, if you wanted.'

Ann wanted. It was a joy to be with Ruth, and her husband Elihu, and their two children. Eli was an artist. They lived in a house in Yemin Moshe, bought after the '67 War when the district was a tumbledown ruin after its ordeal by fire on the edge of no-man's-land, and now worth a fortune, but only on paper. It was small and crammed with the work of Eli's hands. Their back windows overlooked the Valley of Gehenom and the glowing walls of the Old City, and the Jaffa Gate, entrance to the Old City market, Ann's happy hunting ground . . . It would be lovely to go there and pass *Shavu'oth* in peace, and maybe, when and if it grew cooler, to stroll across the Valley to the market with Ruth . . . But then she remembered. Ruth had stopped going to the Old City.

Still, just to be with them would be healing. The thought startled her. Why on earth should she need healing, after barely a fortnight? Absurd! Was she so feeble, so get-at-able? Probably nothing but tiredness, and the *sharav*. It did funny things to one's mood sometimes. She gave herself a physical shake.

'Ruth, I won't, if you don't mind. My time's so limited, I shouldn't waste a whole day, even if it is a holiday.'

'I understand. Well. We are here. Come whenever you can. And I will try to arrange – the picnic at Kastel . . . What about next Saturday? Not this one, we are going to my mother's, but next.'

Ann raked her notebook towards her from across the table where she'd been transcribing an interview the night before. She had a sort of makeshift diary in the back of it, in which she scribbled her appointments. She tended to be inefficient, a fault she could only afford as a novelist. Now that she was wearing (as Peter would put it) her 'journalist's hat', writing a 'real' book dependent upon the co-operation of 'real' people, she must try to be organised. It was an effort.

Next Saturday.

'Ruth – I don't think so – it's good of you, really, I know how busy you are, but – Amnon's driving to Petach Tikva and I'd half decided to go to the kibbutz that weekend.'

'The kibbutz! *Ma pitom*? You've never been back before, any more than I have.'

'Well. It's been fourteen years, after all. The old sores have had time to heal. I'd like to see it again.'

'It – or him?'

'Them. Everybody. The kids I taught – all of it. I dream about it. I won't die happy till I've had another look.'

There was a pause, and then Ruth said, 'Ann, I think you shouldn't.'

'Why not?'

'I just think. Never go back to old places. It always hurts.'

'I don't agree. I like completing circles.'

'Leave this one open. I would. Anyway, your Peter wouldn't like it, would he?'

No, he wouldn't. She would tell him afterwards, when she got home. Of course, she told him everything. She would say, 'Well, Amnon was driving up that way, and I had someone to interview in Tel Aviv, so I just dropped in – ' Just dropped in! A likely tale; she would have to browbeat Amnon into taking her well out of his way, and then cadge a lift out . . . But Peter's notions of the geography, as indeed of everything else about Israel, were hazy to say the least. It was such a small deception for such an immense pleasure! To see it all again – the place itself, the hills behind it, the people – the children. They would be grown up by now, strong and lovely, tall – would they remember their English? She must see those kids again! She'd wanted to for so long, but she'd always been . . . afraid. Yet, now, it seemed to her that if Menachem were there, if he were around, not abroad or anything, it would not hurt either of them (or Peter) to say hallo to him. *Fin de siècle*. Loose ends were abhorrent to her, in life as in books.

A glass of fresh juice was plonked at her elbow and a bare foot simultaneously stepped on hers. A gentle hint that Amnon would like to get to his own telephone. Ann said a fond goodbye to Ruth and bore the glass back to her own room, via the bathroom.

Amnon's flat was huge and rambling, like a version of an old Arab dwelling with rooms leading off a central court. The 'court', which was roofed-over of course, was the living-room, the quietest room in the house and the darkest, having no outer wall or window. As Ann walked through it, she almost fell over a

4

body, asleep on some of the big floor cushions. Although it lay under a sheet (the most anyone could bear when the *sharav* blew) Ann became aware of her own state of undress – a skimpy night-dress picked up cheap from the Co-op the morning she left. Amnon and she were used to each other, like relatives – he had stayed at her flat in London, and she here, till all formality had been abandoned through propinquity. But strange bodies made a difference. She shut the door of her room, which she didn't bother with normally, and put on the coolest dress she had with her, scoop-necked and loose, then dipped her comb into her bedside water glass to run it through her hair for coolness.

There was no mirror in the room, which was not designed as a bedroom, but there were pictures – portraits of Amnon's Russian forebears, whose dark frock-coats and high-necked bombazine dresses behind the glass provided excellent reflections; quite as much as Ann, who had little to be vain about in point of looks, required to pin up her hair and slap on the minimum of make-up she used here. It was a lot less than she used in London. In London, she reckoned women of forty-nine needed some camouflage, for the sake of those who had to look at their ageing faces; but in Israel it was different. How, different? She could not and never had been able to pin it down. It was not just a practical matter of heat, or the marginal improvement of a suntan. It was something to do with not needing disguises, or artifice . . . Be-sides, in her own eyes her face looked better. Looking at it now, framed 'in a glass darkly' by Amnon's grandfather's waistcoat, she thought: *I'm not old yet.* She meant, though she did not formulate it, *I am still attractive. Here*, she felt like adding. It was absurd . . . to think such a thing, to ascribe her strange sense of well-being, her subjectively rejuvenated looks, to the country.

That man yesterday, the old Stern gang member who now, of all things, ran a flower shop – what had he said about 'Eretz Israel', as he called it with a sort of reverent devoutness? That some 'power' emanated from it to its people, and from them back to it, that made it give of its best. Anything they needed, he implied, the Land would provide. She hated all this chauvinist mysticism. She had argued with him hotly, forgetting her con-sciously-adopted new rôle of impartial interviewer. It had been a relief to argue with him about this relatively 'safe' matter; she hadn't dared allow herself to tackle him on his political views, or his violent past, lest she lose her temper.

'So what you're saying, David' (they had gone immediately

onto first-name terms, of course) 'is that since what Israel now needs most is oil, if you, for instance, were given a square kilometre here in Jerusalem – these rocky hills, right here – if you put enough faith and enough spadework into it, oil would come gushing out?'

He smiled his froggy smile. He was somehow, to her dismay, very sweet. Ann's friend and sometime colleague Neville Baum, the London *Gazette*'s man in Israel these five years or more, had called the likes of David 'cuddly little terrorists'. Ann had only just begun, with extreme reluctance, to see what he meant.

'Let me put it this way,' David had replied, unruffled. 'If no oil came out, it would not be the fault of Eretz Israel. It would be my fault for digging where there could be no oil. The Land would do its best for me, if I dug in the right places for the right reasons . . . There is everything here that we need, the Land will yield it up to us when we stop expecting to find everything ready for us on the table. We are spoilt husbands whose wives look after us too well . . . When America stops putting out meals in front of us, we will have to learn to cook for ourselves. As a matter of fact I am certain there *is* oil for us under our Land somewhere to make up for what that traitor gave away to Egypt.'

It was unexpected to hear a man who had been a member of the Stern gang speaking like that about a Prime Minister to whom he should have been slavishly devoted. If Ann had not been taking notes she would have missed that rather good metaphor about the food on the table, through sheer surprise . . . The schisms, the polarities, were not always where one might expect to find them; they split the country across as well as down the middle.

'Oops – excuse *me*!'

Ann spun round. In the doorway was an American female elf with huge eyes like pansies and a blonde bubblecut, in a see-through nightgown.

'Can you point me at the bathroom?'

'If you can bend. Stand with your back to that door. First door on your right. Turn left, turn right and that's it.'

'I'll have to be real kinky! *God*, isn't it *hot*!' She vanished, leaving the door open. A moment later Ann heard a feminine squeal, as, presumably, the elf made a wrong turning and fetched up in the kitchen where her see-through nightie could be seen through by Amnon.

Ann stood at the big mahogany desk and counted her tapes. She'd made a reasonable beginning, considering that the first week had had to be given over to making contacts and laying things on. The first three interviews had been catch-as-catch-can affairs, one with Ruth, who had been a driver in the '48 War, one with an old man she had met at a bus-stop (she was continually having fascinating encounters at bus-stops) and one with Amnon. Amnon, though a mere stripling of forty-two, had vivid memories of the period Ann was interested in; after all, children could be valid participants in wars as much as anyone else – she was not only interested in combatants.

Amnon, as a child in a border kibbutz in the North, had watched the British troops – the Red Berets – coming in to rip up the floor of the dining-room and shovel the muck out of the cow yard to search (successfully) for the arms caches of the Jewish underground army. They had paused only to hand out sweets to the children on their way in, and beat up a couple of kibbutzniks on their way out. The kids ate the sweets, and then climbed on a roof and pelted the British soldiers with the screwed-up papers yelling 'Calaniot!' and singing a little ditty, which, Amnon said, could be freely translated as:

> Fat old Bevin
> Has a baby in his tum
> When the Britishers go home
> It'll pop out of his bum!

Ann had taken that interview down in shorthand because Amnon had suddenly started talking, on the second evening she was there; her notebook was handy and the tape recorder wasn't. She was worried about the shorthand. It was twenty years at least since she had had any real practice. The outlines had flowed from her pencil point, as Amnon rambled on, with deceptive smoothness; but uneasy, half-suppressed memories gnawed at her confidence: dreadful men she had mentally categorised as 'shiny-arsed clerks' in vast antheap blocks in the depths of the City, or Bermondsey, or Camberwell, dictating at breakneck speed uncountable letters beginning, 'dearsirinreplytoyouresteemedcommunicationofthetwentiethult –' She had evolved a single outline to cope with that one. But frequently the gobbledygook that followed would result in hours of unpaid overtime and surreptitious, furious tears falling helplessly upon the undecipherable squiggles . . . She would be forced back upon invention, but her budding creative powers were unequal to the task of filling gaps

7

in letters or reports or contracts dealing with road haulage, tunnel construction, sewage or catering. Sometimes the shiny-arsed clerks would rise in their wrath, and sack her. She dimly recalled marching stiffly away through the 'pool' of giggling, gum-chewing, beehive-topped girls who could read back their every outline with ease; they watched her ignominious departure smugly, their valedictions hanging out of their sly blue-lidded eyes: 'Thought you was cleverer than us, didn't you, Miss Posho, eh? Can't even read yourself back, so good riddance, say hullo to the Queen next time you're passing Buck House . . .'

She had been saved by what she called the Second Coming – the advent of ITV, the second television channel. She became a journalist on one of the weekly magazines which sprouted to cater to the advertising side of this new, commercial, enterprise. She interviewed account executives, ideas men, minor film directors, starlets, and one or two ground-landlords of small outer London playhouses who had seen the way the wind was blowing, and were, with a great show of cultural remorse, putting the bricks and mortar on the market. Later, Ann would sadly watch the guts being torn out of these theatres and do more interviews – producers, camera crews and an assortment of so-called writers, busily turning out jingles and slogans of mind-blowing banality to put across the ad-men's message in the commercials being shot under roofs which had once enclosed nobler endeavours.

She hated it. Not as fiercely as she had hated the antheaps and their denizens and defeats, but fiercely enough. It 'paid the rent', though – a phrase she heard on many lips in those days, and come to despise so much on her own that she stopped using it, quit the magazine and took herself on a private version of the Grand Tour, though in the ungrandest fashion possible.

She contrived this by drawing out every penny she owned from the bank, supplemented by a loan from her closest friend, who happened to be a man fifteen years older than herself (she then being in her late twenties) called Peter Randall. *The* Peter. Her now husband, Peter. Little did either of them know, in those careless, matey, uncommitted days . . . Well. Perhaps Peter had an inkling. He told her later he had always had an eye on her. But Ann regarded him as a sort of father figure at the time, and employed him as such. Exploited him, rather.

This exploitation extended to intimate confidences about her love affairs, weekends (totally pure) in his country cottage when she was fed up with the Smoke, and sundry loans when she was

8

broke. They'd never amounted to more than a few pounds before. Now she touched him for a hundred pounds and he gave it to her without even twitching. That should have told her something because he was half-Scot and 'close', at least with other people. He still was. Not with her, though. Never with her . . .

She wandered across Europe. She'd seen much of it before, on student and post-student tours – always in young company, surrounded by shrieks of mirth, enlivened by fleeting romances: chalets in Austria, converted mill-inns in France, sticky, under-staffed hotels in Majorca . . . Every summer holiday since she started earning her living in the early 'fifties, she'd rushed abroad, looking for something she couldn't find in England, some element of excitement, something to get her teeth into . . . Peter had always found this mildly irritating.

'You've never given your own country a chance,' he would complain. 'The most beautiful place on the face of the earth, and you haven't the wit to appreciate it or even have a proper look – '

'It's boring. It's cold.'

'Ah. *Cold* . . . Well, of course, if you haven't enough hot blood in your veins to keep yourself warm without blazing, burning, boiling sunshine hammering mindlessly at you every minute of the day, I've nothing more to say.' Peter had had more than his fill of heat in the Western Desert in 1943. On his discharge from the army on medical grounds (one piece of shrapnel, too securely lodged for removal, in his shoulder, plus chronic dysentery) he bought his cottage in Suffolk with his gratuity plus an inheritance, and settled down to write obscure books about British insects, and deal in second-hand war books on the side. Nothing and nobody, he vowed, would ever get him abroad again, and so far nothing ever had.

So Ann had pursued her search. It was 1960. London was about to start swinging, but it was, for the moment, in the trough of boringness before the high crest of creative and permissive adventure . . . She hankered for nothing in it as she made her way south, tasting, touching, putting out feelers . . . She didn't recognise it as a search. She supposed it was another holiday, longer and more enterprising than the two-weeks-between-jobs that she had permitted herself before, a voyage of discovery, or at most, of self-discovery. It was to prove far more than that, a strange, tangential turning-point, an explosion blowing her life off-course.

She had several small amorous adventures on her journey –

perhaps inevitably, for this was part of what she was unconsciously seeking: the completion of herself by a special love in a special place. Only they staled in the mouth quickly, exotic dishes made of cheap ingredients; they sprouted like the seeds of her childhood which came in bright, penny packets and bloomed, and were dry and shrivelled at the end of a week. Such rootless, costless amours were against her principles; she not only got little present pleasure from them but suffered disproportionately when they died their trifling, worthless deaths. It was her first lesson in dealing with her adult conscience; it had had no severe trials till then (she had led a morally sheltered life). Recovery was helped by the peripatetic nature of her existence at the time. She gnawed at herself a little for each faded 'romance' and ran on to the next place.

She finally reached the Levant, and there narrowly avoided some adventures not of her choosing, for in 1960 young women travelling alone through Turkey were regarded, even in the cities, as fair game. Once she entered the courtyard of a mosque and narrowly escaped a multiple fate worse than death at the hands (so to speak) of a large group of pilgrims. She was saved by an old man who hobbled out of the mosque, found her backed in terror against a wall and forced a way through to her with surprising strength. Standing beside her he screeched and shook his scrawny fist at the diverted worshippers, stabbing with his stick toward the mosque to remind them of the proximity of sanctity and the unseemliness, in its purlieus, of what they were about. She left Turkey the next day for Greece.

Greece was beautiful. She learnt to drink retzina with relish and slept in youth hostels and nobody took any notice of her, which after Turkey was a relief. She thought for a time that she had found at least part of what she was looking for in those throbbing hot hills, eternally pregnant with the skeletal infants of antiquity. She bought guide books in English and read them in her youth hostel bunk at night, emerging in the morning, knowledgeable and eager, to embark on self-improving excursions . . . But the excitement lay in the gilt of novelty. That having rubbed off, what lay below, for her, was dross.

Sad now, disappointed, as much with herself as with the accumulating muddle of remembered impressions, and getting low-spirited with tiredness, she climbed on board a little white steamer of the Greek Line which was calling at Rhodes and Famagusta on its way to Haifa. She had heard of the magic of

Rhodes, of the fascination of Cyprus; at one or the other she would rest a while, flinging guidebooks aside together with all thoughts of commitment or self-improvement, and just do as she had always done in the past – bake in the sun, swim in the aquamarine sea, and eat, and drink, and gird her loins for a return to the life she had found no compelling reason to break away from.

Rhodes was indeed magical. The ship stayed there for six hours and she did the excursions, swam in the most beautiful bay she had ever dreamt of, bought a plate, and climbed a hill to yet another acropolis. And then, when the guide called, she obediently remounted the donkey, re-entered the bus, re-embarked and sailed on. The magic had proved to be that of a birthday party conjuror, fun while it lasted, enchanting for the hour – but basically mere sleight of hand.

They reached Famagusta. It *was* fascinating. The little gaggle of tourists from the ship was herded about, being shown the Turkish quarter and the supposed sites of Othello's adventures. They had an exotic meal in a Greek restaurant, and a bathe from the nail paring of beach. It was September, and headachey hot. The whole amounted not even to kids' magician magic. Ann mounted the gangplank with the others without even enquiring about the possibility of staying longer.

And thus she found herself in Haifa at the beginning of October.

The hot wind which had caught them unawares in Cyprus had followed them. It was (like the one in Jerusalem today) at the beginning of its third day when the Carmel Hills loomed across the bay through a haze of heat and dust. For the first time Ann wished herself in England – cool, unsqualid England, laved by rain, green, and quiet, and patient.

Haifa was uninviting from the harbour, insupportable from the docks. The Greek ship was not turning round for three days. She was stuck there, unless she could find other transport . . . She crawled ashore, tasting ashes in her mouth, her nose in urgent need of picking, her shins coarse as sandpaper. Her passport crackled as the man stamped it, like old parchment about to fragment. Her ears rebelled against the noise, her skin shrank from the dryness, her energy failed her totally. She hated it in Israel. For all of half an hour, she actually wanted to flee from it and never come back . . . Then, by some uncanny chance, she met a kibbutznik in a little oriental food-bar near the port. They chatted. Something stirred at once, something which kept their eyes fixed upon each other's mouths, even while these were occupied with the unlovely business of eating. He invited her to visit his kibbutz. And that was her undoing.

Or her doing, depending on how such things are measured. If they're measured by inner sureness, a calm slow ascent towards maturity and fixed principles of living and philosophy – then she was undone. If by confusion, turmoil, the probing of strong, dredging fingers of experience into the sludge at the shallow bottom of her nature, then that meeting and all that followed it was the making of her.

Standing now by Amnon's desk, twenty years later, fingering her piles of tapes without seeing them (seeing Menacham, the café, feeling the layer of *khamsin*-borne grit on the counter, tasting, almost, the smoky aubergine salad and the sharp sauce burning her mouth deliciously for the first of so many times) she thought with a sort of rue: I'd used all the superlatives before I got here. All the alliteratives. Fabulous France, incomparable Italy, glorious Greece, celestial Cyprus, romantic Rhodes! Cheap, used-up, worn-out words. Israel was all of them and none of them and far more than any of them to me, and small wonder I could never explain why to Peter, because I have never satisfactorily explained it to myself.

CHAPTER 2

Not for want of trying, though.

How many times since then had she been asked (not infrequently by her own husband, though he was not her husband for some time – she only married in 1970), 'But what *got* you about it? Why are you so obsessed by it? You're not even Jewish!' They all said that, even Jews. As if one needed to be Jewish to feel something overpowering for this place which had been the focus of so much passion. Ann had very little mysticism in her make-up, and not much patience for it either; but her writer's mind, which tended to function through transforming abstractions into images, had sometimes toyed with the idea of this country as a dent in the world's psychic surface, comparable to the Dead Sea, into which the sulphurous residues of so many emotions had gathered that one could not dip even a foot or a hand into it without getting a sensation like a burn. This would explain why some people, with no stomach for being burned, hated it and ran away, shaking (as it were) their stinging extremity; while others felt the strange, agonising clutch of the place, as if they were being pulled under, dipped more and more of themselves, feeling the smart, yet challenged by some inner need to absorb it, and, eventually, if they could bear its heat, relishing it, becoming dependent upon it – making that weird medium their own habitat, like some new kind of creature evolving to fit an emotional environment which to others was intolerable.

But one thing, she thought, staring at the wall, one thing I've always known, or nearly always. There's something here, for me, in my feelings for this place as well as in the place itself, which is . . . dark. Dark words are needed, words not to be found in travel brochures. I've been so happy here. I have cared more here, been more fully alive, than anywhere in the world. It's my place. I have loved it with so much openness, so much straightforwardness; I've allowed myself to feel so much pain in connection with it. I've even welcomed the pain because it's an inevitable part of living on a committed level. Yet there's this darkness which is part of it, part of the attraction. So it must be part of me.

Like the dark pool.

What was that? *Wait* – she snatched at it in the recesses of childhood memory – what was that, *the dark pool*? A fairy tale.

13

With a beautiful fair-haired girl, good and happy in a sunlit world, who was compelled by underworld forces to go every night to a satanic pool in the midst of a forest and kneel on its banks under the stark, dripping trees, to bend so that one long strand of her hair was dipped . . . to wring it out, dip it again, and finally wrap it round her golden head, a contrasting fillip. And there was more – a black snake coiled at the centre of a golden rose, embroidered in golden hairs on the breast of her bridegroom's gown: the ultimate evil, the compulsion to destroy the thing most beloved, the agony of the antidote, the plucking-out of the black hairs, one by one . . . Caught by this suddenly-recollected image, unremembered for many years, Ann stood motionless, struck by some terrible sense of its aptness which was inadmissible to her.

Oh, stop, what's the matter with me? A few short days into an important assignment and I'm succumbing to some ludicrous morbidity . . . Most unlike me. A specialist in affirmation and positiveness, me. Ask anyone – ask them in the kibbutz (if they remember me at all. I hope they remember me, I hope they won't look blank, I want them to welcome me – enough! They owe me nothing but my desertion. I go back at my own risk.)

She needed to shower, but she could hear doors banging now, and voices – American voices. She remembered that Amnon had gone to the airport yesterday while she was about her interviews to meet a small company calling themselves 'The American Pocket Circus', who were to perform in his pocket Festival. No doubt, as was his generous wont, he'd invited them to stay with him. Chaos would now reign, which was a pity, but after all she couldn't even *think* a complaint when she was staying here for nothing herself and saving a small fortune off her publisher's advance . . .

But she couldn't face people, especially pansy-eyed circus elves and God alone knew what else besides (strong men? bearded ladies?), just yet. She sat at the desk and looked at her list. It contained some forty names – from the Prime Minister down. Or up, depending on how you looked at it. Anyone who had played a part in the War of '48 – the first of the wars – was of interest to her. The problem was likely to be keeping the material to manageable proportions, not allowing herself to get swamped . . .

One could get swamped here so easily. Swamped in people's feelings, their pasts, their stories, their politics, their psychoses. In their Jewishness . . .

The Jewishness was, in a sense, forever closed to her, a foreign territory to which she could never get a visa, a different planet, light years from her own. She marvelled that people could delude themselves into thinking they could 'join' just by going through some mumbo-jumbo ritual. You could become a 'practising Jew', you could do that all right, *if* they'd agree to let you in; but what did that amount to? Following the formulas, saying the words . . . even if you were religious, it could only make you some kind of carbon copy. No amount of study or solemn undertakings or dips in the *mikve* could transform you into the genuine article. You might as well paint yourself black and learn a few chants and customs and call yourself an Ibo or a Tutsi. You can't implant tribal memories and emotions into your marrowbones.

What was a Jew? The Jews themselves were forever rowing about it, but to Ann all that was absolutely obvious was that she wasn't one and that there was no way she could change. She'd gone into all that, with Menachem. Not that he cared, but at that time she had wanted to. Not knowing how or why, she had wanted to cross the gulf and come to him, be whatever he was . . . She had loved him enough to jump into the *mikve* if it had been a cauldron of boiling oil, to have learnt the Torah from end to end, to swear to anything, consent to anything . . . remake herself from scratch. Stupidity! The sheer insanity of love . . .

But it was for the kibbutz too. (Though she realised later that they would not have thought better of her for it and rather liked their solitary *shikse* the way she was.) She was hooked, over-ears in love with the whole place and everyone in it, besotted with the single idea of a community of productive Jews proving something to the world. What it was, exactly, she didn't analyse. It was enough that they had left their own worlds (or been deprived of them) and created a new one which seemed to her both beautiful and heroic; its imperfections charmed her more, endeared the place to her, as a slight limp or a crooked tooth makes a person one passionately loves all the more attractive . . . Yet in six years it was to become intolerable, a threat to her individuality, a place to flee from or to sink into and be lost without trace – a place of the most terrible frustration she had ever known, a prison without out bars. Even Menachem couldn't hold her then.

She had discovered she wanted to write. She came to know it there, in the hot coastal plain; creativity, which had smouldered in her for years, flared up now, in her early thirties, blown into a blaze perhaps by the wild wind of her first real love, combined with this permeating chemistry worked on her by the country itself, a white witch-dust thrown on the flame. She wanted to write. The need ate at her. She had things to say now. But they wouldn't give her time. She was teaching their children English and that was, to the kibbutz members, much more important (obviously! – she well understood it) than her unproven and unsubstantiated urges.

She didn't try to persuade them. She tried to write in her spare time. In one room, after a day's teaching, with Menachem exhausted too from his day in the cowshed. She tried and failed. She grew angry with herself, and then with the kibbutz. She paid them back by cutting down on the extra things – English 'magazines' and plays, special stories, English evenings – that she had done for the kids till then. No one noticed except the kids. So when the school year ended, she let it be known that she intended to stop teaching altogether.

The members noticed that all right. Thirty-six lots of parents came to her room, singly and in pairs and sometimes in groups, to beg, cajole and coerce her into changing her mind. She wouldn't. She said she would rather clean the communal lavatories and showers than teach any more. They asked her why – it was months since she had asked for time to write, they'd forgotten. Some had never known. She refused to remind them. The flow of imprecations and callers dwindled to a trickle, and died out. She was left alone with her stubborn, self-defeating decision. She had loved the teaching. Now it was finished.

Menachem did his best. He understood some part of what was behind it all, for he had been witness to her lonely, weary, disorganised struggle in the evenings, and besides, she had told him – in those days she believed one told one's lover everything, shared everything and kept nothing back. But he could not and would not interfere on her behalf, because, deeply as he loved her, he understood the kibbutz better than he understood her need. 'There are kibbutz artists,' he told her, 'who have worked for years, who have been given one day off a week for their art, then two, perhaps eventually even all their time. But they have to prove themselves first. And you are a wonderful teacher . . . That is what you are needed for.'

A crack – amazingly, considering their diverse backgrounds, the first – opened ominously, almost visibly between them, like the presage of an earthquake. The crack was to widen into a gulf so wide and deep they could scarcely touch hands across it when the time came to say goodbye.

16

There came a night when she was sitting in the dining-hall watching the weekly film. There was the usual break to change reels, and the lights came on; she looked round at the *chevrai*, sitting on the hard chairs, chatting and laughing. A voice rang out from the back:

'Shosh! *Haben shelah bokheh* – your son's crying!'

A girl jumped up, still smiling, and hurried out into the scented night, heading for the baby-house. Somebody else came and spoke to Menachem. He patted her arm and went away from her on some kibbutz business; she could see him, through the glass partition in the club-room next door, talking to the farm manager. She had sat there alone beside his empty chair, and looked around, at all the people she had come to know so well, to admire for what they were doing in their self-created world, and to hate for what they were doing to her. And she'd suddenly thought: I love this bloody place. I'd die for its ideals if I had to. And hot on the heels of that thought came another: But if I never saw any one of these people again, I wouldn't grieve. Only Menachem matters to me. Menachem and my writing. My *self*.

That was when she knew she would have to leave, though it didn't happen for months. Months of begging Menachem to leave with her, to try living any other kind of life – here, in Israel, in town, in a *moshav*, anything. Or in England – ? Not that she herself was anxious for that. In any case, he refused. The kibbutz, ultimately, mattered more to him than she did. If she couldn't fit in ('Submit myself, you mean!') that was very terrible for him but he would have to bear it because it meant that they were too different, bascially, to make a life together. If she were unhappy or frustrated in this place that he had helped to build, then it was a rejection of himself. For his part, he said simply, he couldn't live anywhere else; if only because – and here it was again, each man his own definition – only here could he be a complete Jew.

Of course she had not understood at the time, how a man could find his identity through creating a place and a way of life, and feel that abandoning it would destroy him. (Her bruised heart was focussing on a more subjective interpretation – their failure, *her* failure, in six years, to fill a cot in that baby-house.) It was only much later that she understood: through Peter, who, in his totally different style, was akin to Menachem in this. He hadn't created England, but England was his shell, it gave him his form and being, it had written his legend. That might even have been why, after all those years of sexless friendship, she had decided at

17

last to marry him. Because, through studying him in the tender, unstressed way one can study a friend, she found Menachem, the Jew with the kibbutz shell, revealed and comprehended, accepted, and, at last, forgiven. She married Peter – in a sense – on a wave of gratitude, because, all unknowing, he had freed her of Menachem after four iron-cold years of desperate longing for him and of hatred of him for letting her go.

'Come and meet the Circus. And cook breakfast.'

She started violently. Amnon stood in her doorway, dressed, his hair in order, spruce and grinning.

'How many do I have to cook for?'

'Full house. Five. And you and me.'

She sighed and laid down her list and her memories, the latter with some relief.

'Scrambled eggs okay? Have we enough?'

'Vonderful,' he crooned, putting on his best *yecce* accent. 'I *loff* your vet Englissche ecks.'

The Circus crowd were intriguing. Apart from the elf, whose name was Sue-Ella, there was a couple – a tall, lugubrious man who appeared to be wearing sad-clown's make-up even when he wasn't, and his wife, as tall, thin and much more silent than he was – and their child, an androgynous little creature of about seven who, apparently, could walk on stilts and tightropes and swing from trapezes before it could crawl. It was, of course, part of their act, and its name was Dill, or Pickle for short. The fifth member of the team was Dill's attendant, or nanny, or something, a nubile black girl with legs up to her navel whose name – carrying overtones of a demureness at odds with the warm waves of sexuality she exuded – was Mary.

Amnon's roving eyes were swivelling in an effort to fasten upon Mary and Sue-Ella at the same time. Once during breakfast, eaten round a low table in the windowless living-room with most of them sitting on the floor, he knocked over Dill's milk glass in an untypically maladroit attempt to pass the last of the scrambled eggs to both girls at once. Sue-Ella shot out a hand as white and darting as Mary's was black and languid, and collared the prize, while Amnon looked baffled, Dill bounced on his/her cushion with glee and Ann mopped up with her headscarf to avoid the milk running onto the Persian rug.

'Why don't we eat in the kitchen?' she suggested testily. 'Wouldn't that be simpler?'

'Because I want to show off my seraglio room,' said Amnon.

18

'But not at breakfast, for God's sake,' said Ann, making yet another trip round three corners to the kitchen. Amnon followed her out, contrite.

'I'm a *shlemeil*.'

'You can't have little kids eating on Persian rugs.'

'It was me spilled the milk, not Pickle.'

'Or big kids either. Show off your seraglio room, indeed! Just because it's got a few mattresses on the floor, and some bits of copper and brass – '

'And the wall-hangings,' he reminded her eagerly, getting under her feet while she buttered hot pita and got more yellow cheese out of the fridge.

'Wall hangings notwithstanding, tomorrow we eat in here on a proper table over a tiled floor.'

'They may not be here tomorrow, anyway. Well, maybe tomorrow yes, but after that I must find them their own place. Sleeping arrangements will get complicated. One can see that there are cross currents.'

'Huh?'

'Mary. The black one. She is not with the company only to look after Dill's needs.'

'Oh come on, Amnon, we're not all like you. That tall emaciated fellow doesn't look the type to run a harem.'

'Do you mean he is a homo?'

'A – ? Of course not, that's his wife and child, isn't it?'

'If he is not a homo,' said Amnon firmly, 'then he is the type to run a harem, like all of us, given half a chance.'

He grew somewhat abstracted.

'And he has made a good start, I must say – one blonde, one black – like in my nice book of erotic photos – I wonder if he – ?'

'Oh sure. One in front and one behind and that skinny great wife on top. Try to keep your libidinous imaginings under control, Amnon. Here, take this plate and remember when you pass it round, wives and children first, odalisks and houris last.'

He went, obediently. Unpredictable, over-sexed, manic-depressive that he was, she was devoted to him . . . He was what she privately termed a nowty little man, short, compact and well-muscled as a welterweight boxer, with stiffly-curled red hair and thickly-freckled face and small, neat, strong, wandering hands . . . Not that they had ever wandered in her direction, naturally enough; she was far too old for him – not just the seven years of chronology, but at least three times that (she felt) in maturity. She often mothered him, and he would play along, letting her scold him and retaliating with mock sheepishness or minor torments of a deliberately schoolboy type.

Despite all this horseplay and his calisthenic approach to women, he was a remarkable man. He had spent his post-army years on the fringes of the fairly rudimentary Israeli theatre. Then in July 1967, shortly after the Six-Day War, when he was twenty-nine, he had gone scouting round East Jerusalem, then newly 'liberated' (he invariably used that expression, with heavy overtones of scorn and irony, about all the occupied territories beyond the old Green Line). Not far from the American Colony he found what he was looking for – an old, partly ruined but still sturdy and evocative Arab building. Once a restaurant, it had been abandoned by its owner and was now held by the Custodian of Abandoned Arab Property. Amnon took one look at this sorry wreck of a place – 'Filled', as he put it in typically scatological fashion, 'to the dome with lumps of Jerusalem stone cemented by lumps of shit' – and set his heart on it for a theatre of his own.

It took two years to obtain permission to put it in order and use it as a theatre. He ran into every conceivable obstacle, the main one, to his ever-deepening fury, being that nobody in authority saw the slightest point in establishing any kind of cultural centre in the midst of Arab Jerusalem. 'The Jews won't cross into the Arab sector,' he was told, 'and the Arabs won't go to a theatre run by a Jew.' His right-wing acquaintances accused him of cultural treachery for siting his theatre in an Arab area; his left-wing friends abused him for stepping across the Green Line for any reason whatsoever, thereby helping to ratify the decision of the Government to annex the eastern part of the City in the teeth of the United Nations and the world community. Only Amnon's stubborn determination to have his own enterprise, and to have it in that particular building, carried him finally through the veritable barbed-wire entanglements of bureaucratic, ideological and just plain officious red tape, to victory at last.

It took him two more years to clear the rubble and rebuild. He tried to use a mixed work force of Arabs and Jews; but by that time there were fewer and fewer Jews at the sharp end of the building trade, and the Arabs were, on the whole, unreliable. This caused delays. Then he had to find materials which suited the site and satisfied his somewhat eclectic tastes. For instance, he refused to use the ubiquitous standard tiling for his foyer. If the great Sherover Theatre, in the Jewish sector, just then being built, was (as his spies informed him) to have a polished marble floor in its vast foyer, Amnon's theatre would go one better. *His* foyer, approximately a tenth the size of that of the Sherover, would have flagstones of an idiosyncratic and unmatchably beautiful apricot stone, found only in a certain West Bank quarry. *His* stage might not be blessed with a proscenium as wide as Drury Lane or enough fly- and wing-space to mount the Ring Cycle in all its splendour, let alone revolves and traps and orchestra pits and all the folderols the Sherover would have. (After all, Mr Sherover was paying.) But it would have something unique – a circular stage set in the middle of the small vaulted auditorium, with performers making entrances along a trio of cat-walks through the audience, which would sit in three sections of banked seats. The inner walls were of the original bare rough-dressed stone, with scalloped pillars supporting the vaulted roof, providing excellent basic scenery and acoustics.

At the back of the building was a courtyard, open to the sky, where once customers had sat puffing their narghiles and sipping coffee as they slid their backgammon pieces about. This he planted with three young olives and a fig tree. When he learnt that the other theatre would be holding art exhibitions in its purlieus, Amnon let it be known that he would exhibit sculpture in his courtyard and hold free concerts on Saturday lunchtimes at which young musicians could try out, and meet expenses by taking up collections.

At this blasphemy, the Municipality withdrew Amnon's hard-won grant. The Mayor had been covertly rather keen on the whole enterprise till then, but he had more important battles on hand than fighting the devout elements of his council on such a side-issue. Reflecting the situation of successive Israeli governments, which traditionally depend for viability on the support of Orthodox politicians, the council had to bow to religious pressure in the matter of Sabbath-breaking. For the next ten years, Amnon had been, officially at least, on his own.

One of the City's deputy mayors, however – a young Oriental Jew called Amatsia Misrahi – supported him to the point where he quarrelled openly with the Mayor, and was booted out of his job. Or resigned. The two events occurred so nearly simultaneously that no one could ever prove which came first, though both sides tried. Amatsia Misrahi reacted by going to Amnon and asking to be taken on as a partner. His chief interest was not the theatrical side as such, or even the business side (though like anyone else he was not averse to making money) but the side of the Green Line the theatre was on.

'Yoni,' he remarked, referring with the customary familiarity to the Mayor, 'insists that this City is now united, but I know, and so does everyone else, that it's not. It takes more than pulling a few barriers down to stick two halves of a divided city together.'

He added that he'd lived in Jerusalem all his life, and yet, till he began to work with Arabs after the Six-Day War as part of his responsibility as Deputy Mayor, had scarcely registered them as people at all – in his childhood they'd been part of the scenery, in his youth simply stereotyped 'enemies'. Now he had begun to know them. 'I won't say I'm in love with them,' he said. 'None of my best friends are Arabs. But they're part of this country. Like it or lump it we've got to live together, and one way to do it – I admit it's a single straw in a squadgy brick of mud – might be to bring a theatre into their sector. Because nothing on earth is surer than that they'll never come to that big white elephant we're building in ours.'

So 'The Two Alephs' as their company was called (after their joint initials) came into being. The first pressing problem was money. That was when Amnon made his first trip to England, on a *shnorring* expedition.

Why not America? 'Instinct,' he would say. 'I knew from meeting American Jews that they're still living in the Dark Ages of the 'thirties and 'forties when all Arabs had horns and tails. I thought, maybe the British have learnt how to be Zionists without lunatic chauvinism.'

That was when Ann and Amnon had met. It was in the home of a Jewish millionaire. Not that Ann moved with any frequency among millionaires, Jewish or otherwise, but she happened to know this one. His name was Sir Matty Golombosch (Amnon referred to him affectionately, behind his back of course, as 'Sir Muddy Goloshes') and he was a rare bird indeed. Not only was he a Jewish millionaire, of which there are a fairly large number, even in Britain. (*Dayenu.*) He was a Jewish millionaire who willingly gave a lot of money away, for of those there is a less large number. (*Dayenu.*) The really unusual thing about him was that he was willing to be persuaded (conditional always upon sensible facts and figures being provided) to give money for projects which were not exclusively concerned with his fellow-Jews in Israel. (*Dayenu.*) His amazing, virtually unique attribute was his ability to see that a project like Amnon's which involved your actual

Arabs – or was intended to involve them, whether they would consent to be involved was, at that stage, anybody's guess – was a Good Thing and worthy of a generous donation with a promise of back-up money when, as he cheerfully warned Amnon was quite inevitable, the whole thing ran into a series of apparently insuperable difficulties and threatened to get bogged down altogether.

'Sweet Sir Muddy,' Amnon enthused to Ann at the time. 'How like him to choose an English idiom so in keeping with his nickname! When we get "bogged down", what more useful to have around than your incredible British institution of goloshes?' And he rushed home to Jerusalem, chanting the chorus from the Passover thanksgiving song: 'Dai, dai, eynu, dayenu, dai-ay-NU pom-pom-pom . . .'

Ann didn't see him again for three years. And as he never wrote letters, on principle, and was not yet fond enough of her to waste costly phone calls as he began to do later, especially when he needed things, she lost touch with the theatre of 'The Two Alephs'. Except when, occasionally, she came across a *Jewish Chronicle*. Then she would turn straight from the headlines to the arts pages, and once in a while would be rewarded with a snippet of information about *Nat'am*. That was the name of the theatre. The *Jewish Chronicle* usually managed to get it wrong, either by accident or design, calling it various things including *Hata'am* (Hebrew for 'taste') and *Natan* (Hebrew for 'Nathan'). But discreet enquiries confirmed an educated guess Ann had hazarded about the real meaning. At that time she had only had one, if very lengthy, *tête-à-tête* with Amnon; on impulse she had invited him to have supper at her flat the night after meeting him at Sir Matty's. But that one conversation, which had dwelt exclusively upon Amnon's overriding preoccupation of the moment, with all its ramifications, had been enough to enable Ann to guess that the name he had chosen for his beloved theatre had been the word he had found written over the entrance when he first saw the building, the Arabic word for 'restaurant'.

She guessed further (and correctly, as it turned out) that this stubborn insistence on keeping an Arabic name had caused him some subsidiary problems. Nor was she surprised, when in 1973 she was at last able to visit Jerusalem and see the place for herself, to discover that the name written on the arched portico was in Arabic only. What did surprise her was that underneath the original Arabic calligraphy, Amnon had also retained the name of the original, Arab, proprietor.

'Who was he?'

'One Abu Daoud. He's our *éminence grise*, our reminder if you like. His name's on the doorpost instead of a *mezzuzah*.'

'As well as a *mezzuzah*.' Ann had seen one of the Jewish prayer containers discreetly let into a crevice in the stone. Amnon looked embarrassed.

'My aunt insisted.'

'Your *aunt*?'

'Yes, my aunt!' he had yelled suddenly. 'My lousy sweet old Aunt Rifka, bless her reactionary old Russian heart! She hired a workman to come like a thief in the night and screw it on there and in the morning I arrived for work and found her standing right outside the doors with her arms folded . . . Oh, why go on? I couldn't do anything. And Amatsia sided with her. Pure atavism in his case. I was outgunned. Now I have to keep explaining to people that it was Aunt Rifka who did it behind my back, it was not me trying to minimise the resistance of my Jewish audience, or lick the behinds of the rabbis of the Municipality.'

'Where *is* Abu Daoud?'

'In Damascus.'

'What if he ever comes back? What will you do?'

'Take him home for coffee in my seraglio room and negotiate. Meanwhile I compensate him. He gets a percentage of the take.'

'I don't believe you! How do you get it to him?'

'Sir Muddy arranges it. No problem.'

'Who else knows you do this?'

'The other Aleph. And my accountant, a staunch left-winger like us. No one else. Whose business? And *you* keep your big mouth shut as well, I don't know why I should trust a *shikse* like you, and a journalist to boot.'

'I'm not a journalist any more, I'm a novelist. I deal in fiction. Your lovely little fact is safe with me.' And she had kissed his cheek which was always, at least after lunch, sandpapery with ginger stubble.

CHAPTER 3

The Circus quintet took off right after breakfast, undaunted by the ever fiercer blasts of the *sharav* which had now filled the normally crystalline air of the city with a myriad atomies of dust, and was, incidentally, drying up the lavatory paper until it reminded Ann of the worst era of Bronco in London's public conveniences.

They had asked Amnon to hire a car for them to visit, of all places on such a day, Massada. Amnon had implored them to wait till the wind changed, but since their schedule of indoor and outdoor performances set in the following day and would thereafter leave them very little free time, they gaily insisted.

Ann could see that Amnon was exasperated by their wilful determination to roast to death, and also financially torn – he would normally have lent them his own car in order to keep down theatre expenses; but as he explained to Ann furiously the moment the door closed behind the party, 'I am not going to let them blow *my* radiator up on a day like this. Let Hertz take the risk. Oh, curses upon them, now I've got to worry all day about Pickle dehydrating to a raisin – not to speak of Sue-Ella fainting straight off Herod's terrace on her sweet little curly blonde head.'

'Well, you made them take enough drink and oranges for a second Siege. And at least Mary won't faint, not with her pigmentation.'

'Mmmm – Guinness and champagne – black and fizzy . . .' Amnon, on his annual talent-hunting trips to Britain, had become a great Anglophil, relishing English idioms, drinks and other native institutions in much the way that Ann relished their Middle Eastern equivalents. He now flung himself down on a pile of Bedouin-embroidered cushions. 'Turn off that top light, for God's sake, it's adding to the heat. Ah . . . that's better! Ann, before you, too, collapse, do me a favour, and go check that those *shmegegs* haven't gone opening windows or shutters in their rooms. Foreigners just don't understand about *khamsin*.'

Ann made a tour of the flat. The Circus obviously thought it was a hotel and everything was in chaos in the two bedrooms. *And* the windows had been flung wide. No wonder the flat was so stifling. Usually it took four days of *khamsin* at least till the heat and dryness fully penetrated the merciful thickness of these

25

walls. Now all was lost – it had got in and there would be no getting it out again. Still, she dragged the heavy metal shutters closed against the furnace-blast and latched the windows. There were no curtains, but at least now the flat was decently dim – the glare, if not the heat and dust, could be denied access.

'You should have told them,' she said as she re-entered the inner room. Amnon was spreadeagled now, not on the cushions or the rug but on the bare tiled area near the door. She all but fell over him.

'Stop running around so much, you are making mé hot. Lie down here on the floor. Spread your arms and legs.'

'Pardon?'

He opened one eye. 'For coolness! Do you think there are no limits to my – what do you call it – lecherousness?'

'Thanks very much,' she said sourly, lying down in the limited space he had left. There was no room to spread anything, so she just lay on her stomach on the tiles with her arms at her sides and her right cheek on the floor. She and Menachem used to do this in the kibbutz, only naked, after their after-work showers . . . An odd thought came to her. If Peter came to Israel – not that anything would persuade him to do so, but *if* he did – would the exigencies of the climate and his natural tendency to seek equilibrium induce him to lie naked on the floor? Or even semi-naked? She smiled against the tiles.

Never. Under all circumstances, she was certain, Peter would be true to what he himself called 'my stereotype'. He would stick, through thick and thin, and certainly through the hottest *khamsin*, to being what he essentially saw himself as, a typical Englishman. Built like one (tall, lean and a little soldierly), dressed like one, speaking, eating and behaving in the ways he believed to be good – good, that is, for an Englishman. There was nothing self-righteous in this. He had no inflated notion of possessing a monopoly of sound practice or correct living. He would have been profoundly disturbed to find, say, a Frenchman, a Spaniard or an American trying to ape the English manner. But it suited him. He fulfilled, steadily and unshakeably, the outline, form and inner patterns of the best of his countrymen as he saw them.

The only distressing aspect of his stereotype – guarded by him with an odd sort of patriotic jealousness – was that he also tended strongly to resent what he felt was the imitation of it by others, foreigners in essence, who had come to share his country. Three generations on British soil were insufficient to give such intruders the right to consider themselves, or behave as, Englishmen. Which of course, in its way, was *part* of his stereotype, a part too fundamental to change. Ann knew, because she had tried. For years, she had tried, not just by arguments but by the sheer weight and pressure of her passion for Israel. With this she had sought to deflect him from a bent to which she had never given a name, because she loved him and was married to him and whatever he was, was part of her. Repudiate as she might those bits she disliked or even those which secretly appalled her, she had chosen him. Her mind, if not totally her body, had accepted him, given him its ultimate 'yes'. Not by a mistake or on an impulse, but after many years of friendship and intimacy. That meant to her that she could no more find an intolerable flaw in him than in herself, because once such a thing was discovered there must follow a personal catastrophe. The atoms of the soul can't be split without immense destruction.

And Peter had accepted *her*. It couldn't have been easy for him, with his stereotype, to accept hers, which was none at all, but just a muddle – no safe predictable set pattern at all but a sort of Frankenstein's monster of bits and pieces, some of them the wrong sizes, grafted together somehow into one person. He had accepted most of them because he loved her and had loved her for years, and was in need (he often told her) of an occasional jolt, like an electric charge, to keep him from getting fusty and stale. 'I'm a bit of an old stick-in-the-mud,' he had often said – until she had ordered him sharply to stop, never to say it again. So then he had to find new ways of telling her that she was necessary to him, that her waywardness, her patternlessness, her inconsistencies, complemented his staid personality, that he liked them.

Most of the time.

The books, the writing – any amount of that, and what went with it: late meals, erratic catering, the cottage untidy; dashings up to the London flat; sudden influxes of visitors; bursts of typing half the night and sleeping late – he was endlessly patient about all that. He would do the shopping and cooking, he would bring her meals to her on trays when she forgot; when they were apart, he would ring her each night at the flat – 'Hallo my love, everything going all right? Me? Don't worry about me! I was looking after myself splendidly till you took over, so don't imagine I need mollycoddling.' (But he loved it when he got it.) He was proud of her, too, and boasted about her talents. He listened to her when she needed to read to someone: his comments were often cogent and never cruel. He welcomed her friends, putting up with their shop-talk, which must have bored him. He would sometimes even watch, with her, the awful television rubbish she relaxed into sometimes when she was tired or dried-up, sitting at her side holding her hand and sharing in those idiot conversations that are half the pleasure of watching entertainment in one's own home where there is nobody to be irritated by one's running commentary.

Her errant socialism was harder for him, but he put up with that (she often felt) because he kept patiently expecting her to grow out of it. They didn't discuss politics much. At election time they made a joke of putting the campaign posters of their respective parties up in their front window side-by-side; once Peter took a thick marker pen, and leaning through the standard roses in the front bed which were his pride, carefully printed 'His' and 'Hers' under the photos of the two candidates. The Liberal came to complain that he felt left out.

But there was one feature of the monster that he couldn't easily take, and that was the grafted-on part about Israel and the Jews. *That* he couldn't comprehend, because to him it was like a deformity, an extra breast or something, some freakish part which didn't belong and which, however hard he tried to hide the fact, repelled and bewildered him . . . That thing in him that she had chosen not to recognise, came perilously close to the surface at times, like an evil face leering at her through the calm mirror of his personality, sending shafts of panic through her.

'They put out high-tension vibrations. They're always so desperately striving.' 'But in Israel they don't have to – strive in that way. That's the point of it.' 'Well, fair enough, but then they start a different sort of striving. Same old thing in a new guise. Wherever they are, somebody else has to make room.' 'Peter, that's not fair! You don't know their history, or you couldn't say that.' 'Well, darling, if I live long enough with you I expect I shall piece it all together. In the meanwhile, would you mind just glancing at the sky? Look at the pattern those rooks make against that poor benighted elm . . . We're supposed to be having a country walk, you know, not driving each other to drink with Subject Normal. I always thought that was a euphemism for sex, didn't you? However did it come to mean the Jews?'

Her life with him in the country had all the makings of an idyll. The cottage was perfected long before her advent, and was beginning to look shabby again after the loving restoration Peter had given it in the fities; there was a garden which they both took pleasure in, and a beautiful area of wilderness between it and the nearest village which made it unnecessary to see anyone they didn't want to see or do anything they didn't want to do. There was nothing restricted or primitive about the place, however; they each had a study and there were all the mod cons anyone could want. She had her own car and her own flat for the freedom they gave. They had a dog and two cats and, more important, a great deal to talk about. They were very comfortable and companionable together and, except for these rather rare conversations (it was unfair of him to call it 'Subject Normal' – for her part she tried never to raise it directly) they seldom quarrelled. Ann had never, for more than a few minutes together, been anything but very glad she had married him. Love, she had learnt, was safer, more lasting and of far more value than being in love could ever be. It provided everything, like the cottage; and it almost never hurt.

. . . 'I'm thirsty.' Amnon – a dry-throated croak from the darkness.

'Me too.'

'So who's going to get up and get a cold drink?'

'Why not you?'

'You're nearer the door.'

'Only just.'

Neither of them moved. The heat passed over them in waves. It pressed them down. Ann thought, I must get up, I must have a cold shower, I must telephone people, not waste the day completely. Aloud, she said, 'Amnon.'

'Have you come back or haven't you gone?'

'You know damn well I can't move. Listen. Where can I get some Arabs to interview?'

'What sort do you want?'

'The same sort that I want Jews. People who took part in the War of Independence.'

'The War of Catastrophe, for them. Aren't names of wars interesting? Did you know Ben Gurion wanted to call it "The War of Renaissance"?'

'Well, whatever it's called . . . I want balance.'

'Is that what your publisher wants?'

'I don't think so. I think he wants a lovely wallow of nostalgia.'

'Ah, yes! For those happy days when the cause was pure and the issues were clear and the Jews were all heroes and nobody'd heard

29

of Deir Yassin, let alone Kibya and Kfar Kassem. When everybody knew there was only one side to be on and all the world agreed . . . How comfortable it must have been then, to be a Jew and to be sure you were right! No wonder those American Jews want to get back to it.'

'Well, *if* that is what he wants,' said Ann slowly, 'and I suspect it is, he's going to get a disappointment. Because this is definitely no time for nostalgia and the purity of arms revisited. This book, if I can manage it, is going to be about the first Arab-Jewish War, *not* the Israeli War of Independence as if nobody else was fighting. But to do what I want I have to have Arabs.'

'Come and stand in the foyer tomorrow evening for the Pocket Circus. With luck you'll get quite a few. They love circuses almost as much as the Jews.'

'But were they in the war?'

'In what capacity?'

'As fighters.'

'*Fighters* she wants – !'

'I'm getting Jewish fighters, I need Arab fighters to balance them. Jewish readers ought not to be confirmed in their notion that all the Arabs ran away. There were, as I understand it, a number of your actual battles, and battles need two sides.'

Amnon rolled over to chill his stomach, and bumped into her legs.

'The fighters,' said Amnon, 'are now mostly to be found in Beirut, in Damascus, and in Cairo. Why don't you pop over to Egypt? You'd find a large number of old soldiers there. Though the generals and things are probably rather old by now.'

'I've already interviewed two ex-generals from our side, both still in their prime.'

'The Jewish officers were mostly very young, the Palmachniks especially – young kibbutz kids in their early twenties. The Arabs didn't get to be officers till they were much older. Kawukji – '

'He's dead, unfortunately.'

'What's unfortunate?' asked Amnon indignantly. 'That bastard nearly killed me when I was a tiny little kid of nine!'

'Kawukji tried to kill you?'

'I know what you're thinking, why should he bother? But he did. He would have succeeded, too, only we were all evacuated. He took our kibbutz to pieces when we'd gone, and crapped in every single room.'

'What an effort! I bet he never got over it.'

'He had more than all that crapping to get over. He lost. But he wasn't that young. I think Tel's dead too, the commander of the Jerusalem sector, under Glubb . . . But Glubb's still going strong. I have an idea that old Neguib, the Egyptian colonel, is still doddering about among the pyramids somewhere. Why don't you go?'

'You want to get rid of me? I've got another three weeks, that's all – it's little enough to collar all the people I want *here* with your telephone and bus systems the way they are.'

'Not a word about our telephones! Try the Egyptian ones, it's quicker to walk from one side of Cairo to the other than phone, so I've heard. As to buses – '

'I didn't mean that. I'm crazy about Israeli buses.'

This, incredibly, was true. It was something that always puzzled her, how the non-queues, the crush, the strap-hanging with both feet braced to give a wide base against the violent halts and swerves, while the radio blared out its strident pop, should seem to her like an exhilarating adventure and not an outrage. One such bus trip would drive Peter beyond all bounds. He hated crowds and he hated to be in physical contact with strangers – any strangers, never mind scores of pushing, sweating, noisy, un-English Jews.

'You could do it easily,' Amnon was saying. 'Amatsia's done it, lots of people do it. You get a visa at the Egyptian Embassy, you get a bus down to Kantara, then you get a taxi across the Canal, then another bus takes you up to Cairo. It's fun.'

'And then what? I couldn't just look Colonel Neguib up in the Cairo directory and phone him the way I did Uzi Narkiss and Chaim Herzog. It would probably take three weeks to even find the "proper channels", let alone proceed up them. No, Amnon, exciting as it sounds, I can't. I've got to stay here for this trip. But I want some Arabs. There must be some on the West Bank.'

'One and a half million, I heard, all of them wishing us in hell.'

'I mean, men who fought in '48.'

Amnon reached out a sly hand through the dimness and began to tickle the sole of her bare foot.

'I wish you'd go and get us a drink. There's a Maccabi in the fridge. We could share it.'

'I won't till you advise me.' She felt too paralysed by the heat even to move her foot away.

'What about that fellow?' Amnon asked after a pause.

'What *fellow*, Amnon? I'm surrounded by fellows. Name

31

names, for God's sake.'

'Why don't you jump?' said Amnon peevishly. 'Don't you notice I'm tickling you?'

'I'm getting to like it.'

'Ah! That's the *khamsin*. You want to watch that, it makes a lot of women very susceptible. Let's have the other foot, then. I'm very good at feet. You know, that big hairy fellow, that mad right-winger. Arabist. I picked you up at his house once. When you were here last year.'

Ann opened her eyes suddenly. A face had appeared behind her eyelids which she didn't particularly wish to see, but on the lofty gloom of the ceiling she could see it still. A square, heavy face with hot yellow eyes and a bull neck, a thick curved nose and a springing matt of dusty, wiry hair.

'Yes,' she said.

'What was his name?'

'Boaz Shachterman.'

'Couldn't he help you? He actually *lives* on the West Bank.'

'He lives just outside Jerusalem.'

'East Jerusalem. Well, south, really. I had to drive half-way to Bethlehem to find the bloody house the night I called for you.'

Ann said nothing. That had been a very strange day. She had not let herself think about it much in the meantime. The man and the events had threatened her somehow; she had tried to forget or even suppress them. Yet Amnon was right. If anyone could help her it was Shachterman. He worked with West Bank Arabs. She knew, from that day, and from other days dating back to her first meeting with him after the '73 War, that very little happened on the West Bank that he didn't know about, and that everybody who was anybody there was his acquaintance. 'I've even got a few friends there,' he had said with heavy irony . . . Strange. They had been together all day and he must have said a lot to her, they had talked a great deal; yet she remembered only a few things – the things that had shocked her, she supposed. Such as when he had said, after a meeting with some Arabs in a café, 'Don't touch them. If you touch them, except to shake hands, they take it as an invitation. Especially if the woman is very attractive.' She could not remember touching anyone but he had insisted that she had laid a hand on one Arab's arm, to make a point in conversation.

She might have done. She was a great toucher (unlike Peter). Shachterman's words had made her ashamed somehow. They had shocked and startled her because she felt as if, whatever the Arab had thought, Shachterman might have seen through the apparently innocent, friendly gesture to what she suddenly realised was her real motive – to show the Arab, and herself, that she felt no differently about him than she would about a Jew, that she spoke to him and treated him the same. She would have touched a Jew's arm at that point, so she touched the Arab's, but there had been self-consciousness in it. She had surely not been drawn to touch that man whom she felt, at a deeper level, to be an alien and an enemy, inimical to all she loved here. It was not a true impulse, the touch, but the result of an intellectual effort.

How much of this Shachterman had understood should not really have mattered to her. Part of the obscure feeling of threat had come from the fact that she had worried about it. Oddly, she had not worried for fear he would think she was, in any sense at all, flirting with the Arab. (If the Arab had thought that, it was just his bad luck, or his conceit.) But the words at the end of Shachterman's remark – 'Especially if the woman is very attractive' – had also troubled her. Though he had not looked at her as he said them, but straight ahead at the empty road unwinding above the steering-wheel that he gripped between his hands.

What the hell else would he grip it with, his teeth? Ann thought angrily. Why, remembering, did she focus abruptly on his hands, why could she see them as clearly as she saw his face, and why on earth did they still make her shiver? She had watched them, covertly, all that day, raising her eyes to his face only when he turned it to her, when she couldn't reasonably avoid looking at it, and even then she had dodged his eyes. Lion's eyes. Sensual, ruthless – possibly even cruel.

But she couldn't find a metaphor for the hands. They were just the hands of a man – a very big man – and there was no visible reason why she should have tried so hard to find a way to describe them to herself. Unless – this occurred to her only now, many months later – she was trying to diminish their power. Wasn't there something in mythology about supernatural forces losing power by being subjected to verbal description? But they had defied her efforts, and lay in her memory now, dark and clenched, full of some fell strength.

'I don't want to get in touch with him.' She heard her own voice, suddenly vehement in the hot darkness.

'Okay, okay, it was only an idea. Not that I blame you. A real fascist, you should pardon the expression.'

She felt unaccountably irritable. 'I don't pardon it. How can Jews call other Jews fascists?'

'Oh, don't get excited, it's far too hot. It's *the* word for everyone's political opponents, that's all. Anyone on the Right, I mean of course. Though there's something in it. Men like your friend what's-his-name, and all too many like him, think their own ends justify any means at all. And they have this exalted idea of the State. You hear them in the broadcasts from the Knesset, talking about "this holy land", "our sacred soil", and even, sometimes, "this holy house" – the bloody centre of government, mark you, where they all shout and rave at each other, calling each other every disgusting name they can think of – and when the insults get too much, they become all pious and say, "How can you address a fellow-Jew like that in *this holy house*?" It makes me spew up. Oh, enough!' he said sudddenly, smacking the ankle he'd been idly stroking and clambering to his feet. 'I need a beer.'

'And I need a shower.'

'After you. Don't take all the hot water.'

'I won't take any of it. God! Will this accursed *sharav* never end? I can feel my brains beginning to dry up.'

'So why come in May of all months?' called Amnon from the kitchen.

'It had to be May or August, and I thought May wouldn't be so hot.'

'Ha ha. August, the heat is just normal. A May *sharav*, and you might as well be in the Sahara. You should know that. You actually lived here.'

'That was fourteen years ago, Amnon,' she said through the blessed rush of water. She'd left the door ajar so they could talk. 'I've had time to forget.'

'In a kibbutz . . . Funny. I can't see you in a kibbutz somehow.'

'I loved it.'

'But did they love you?'

'Yes. They did. Oddly enough.'

'Nothing odd in that, I love you myself, in a perfectly platonic way of course. But odd, a bit, that kibbutzniks should love a sort of foreign body like you, especially in those days before they got used to strangers from every corner of the globe flocking in to eat in their dining-rooms and lie about on their lawns and introduce their kids to sex and drugs . . .'

'And do a lot of their field work for them, don't let's forget.

34

There are definitely two sides to the volunteer movement.' She watched the lather washing down her body, and relished the cold streams of water which were warm by the time they reached her knees.

'Did you work in the fields? Don't tell me!'

'I did. At the beginning, before I began to teach. In the vineyard and the chicken-house. And latterly cleaning out the communal loos.'

That's how they demonstrated their love? Wishing the nastiest task in the place off on you?'

'Not at all. I volunteered. I wanted to do it.'

'Clean the *batei shimush*? Why?'

'They needed it.' She had finished washing. Now she stood under the blissful flow with her face turned up to it, not caring that her hair got wet and heavy and fell down, scattering pins with little plinks in the bath. It was almost worth the horrible heat to feel this relief.

When she emerged from the bathroom she looked at her watch and discovered it was still only ten-thirty. Extraordinary how this unnatural wind-driven heat telescoped time, stretching and shrinking it . . . She shook her wet head sharply. She'd felt so peculiar, lying on the floor with Amnon playing with her foot, thinking of Peter, remembering Menachem and getting both mixed up, somehow, with Boaz Shachterman. It was like being mildly delirious; the east wind tickled the inside of one's brain, stimulating memories, bringing them with a disconcerting sudden rush into the forefront of the mind . . . How clearly she had remembered, just for a moment, Menachem's long body, its brown and white sun-markings as distinct as those on a skewbald horse, lying at her side, his hand on the small of her back or her flank or the nape of her neck, making a hand-shaped pattern of perspiration, the only sweat on her body in that intense dry air . . . She had smelt his breath for a second, mingling with hers, the sweetest breath in the world. It had stirred her blood to get even that remembered whiff of it. Then to start thinking of Shachterman's hands . . . No. She must have been half-comatose to have let that happen. She didn't like her mind swerving like that, half out of control, like a drunken driver, making things happen inside her body as well, or maybe that was just Amnon's casually expert fingers. That little devil could rouse the sensual instincts of a stone. She laughed at herself. Better old Amnon's fingers between her toes than the remembered hand of Boaz

35

Shachterman lurking between the folds of her mind!

She would not phone him, she decided. Not to get an introduction to King Hussein himself.

CHAPTER 4

Re-showered, shaved and dressed, Amnon stood ready to take off for the theatre.

A Jewish feast day brought nearly everything in the New City to a halt; but the Old City, and the Arab sector outside the walls, went its way as usual. Amnon had compromised to the extent of having no actual performances on the eve of a feast; but there would be one tonight, after sunset, when *Shavu'oth* ended. It was not yet the Circus, but a company from Haifa – a small group of young Arabs and Jews who specialised in mixed-language plays which could be enjoyed by 'mixed' audiences. They were called 'Hagesher' – 'The Bridge' – for obvious reasons. Amnon had given them their first indoor engagement, five years ago. Till then they'd been performing in the open, in streets and playgrounds or even, greatly daring, in Arab villages. They were especially popular in Katamon and districts like it where many oriental Jews lived. These had the deepest aversion to the Arabs, having come mainly from Arab countries where relations had steeply deteriorated since the advent of militant Zionism; nevertheless, to everyone's surprise they were among the first to come to Nat'am to see their favourite street performers under a roof. The fact of mingling with the very few Arabs who had ventured to come, in the early days, seemed merely to add spice to the unaccustomed evening out – such people had not been numbered among the large Israeli theatre-going public previously.

But Amnon had been cunning. He had left the Jerusalem Theatre (as the Sherover came to be popularly called) to present the heavy, highbrow stuff, and the big splashy companies, while he concentrated on encouraging local *ad hoc* groups, everything from satirical reviews (mainly directed against the chauvinist Right, which, since the '77 elections, he considered included the Government), through small cast musicals and folk troupes from both communities to fairly broad comedies and a bit of straight drama, with a preference for what grew organically out of local conditions and stresses. He didn't go in for too much experimentation unless it resulted in strong and what he called 'accessible' productions.

In other words, Nat'am was a theatre of the people in the true sense, and as such had become very popular at all levels, and even ran the risk of becoming trendy. Prices were kept low, thanks to Sir Muddy, whose involvement continued unabated. (Despite his many virtues he was still enough of a Jewish millionaire to be unable to resist dropping remarks among his cronies about 'my little theatre in Jerusalem', but he had earned that.)

And lately the Municipality had relented somewhat, and restored a partial grant. Aunt Rifka took full credit for this; but Amatsia probably had more to do with it. As full of low cunning as Amnon, he had prevailed on his partner to book a troupe of dancing and singing Hassidim.

The entire premises had to be koshered for the run, which included the removal from view of all female staff, whether with their bare arms hanging shamelessly out of their dresses or decently robed from head to foot; but Amatsia insisted that was a small price to pay for the publicity and for the broadening of their base.

It could not be claimed that, after the Orthodox lads had rolled up their sidelocks and silently stolen away, the extreme religious element which had broken ranks by attending that show continued to be patrons. But there are almost as many shades of religious opinion and practice in Israel as there are inhabitants, and the line between those who would and those who would not be seen dead in a left-wing, bi-cultural establishment was pushed fractionally in the right direction.

As Ann had already seen 'The Bridge' a few nights before, she refused Amnon's invitation to come again and help fill the house.

'But you're not doing anything tonight – I looked at your diary.'

'Keep your nose out of my diary, please. I intend to get an interview for tonight.'

'Didn't you *like* the show?' he asked plaintively. He always took even implied criticism of his theatre as a personal affront.

She turned down a sticking-up corner of his shirt collar and patted him. 'I loved the show, but I didn't understand a single word of it. Now go on if you're going. I want to sit on the phone.'

'Kicked out of my own flat . . .' he grumbled. 'I'll ring you later. If you can't get anybody, I'll expect you to come and give support. Bookings are lousy because of the weather.'

Notwithstanding the heat he managed to break into a small soft-shoe shuffle in the doorway, and exited *en l'air*, blowing kisses. Two seconds later he was back.

'Now what?'

'If Bob phones – '

'Who?'

'Bob, Bob! King of the Circus Sex Act!'

'Oh, the Sultan. *Nu?*'

' – *If* he phones, or if anybody phones to say some tragedy has happened and they're all hospitalised with sunstroke, get instantly on the phone to me at the theatre.'

'Whereupon you'll brush up your own sex act as a replacement, no doubt. Stop worrying, they've all got hats. Goodbye.'

'Shall I bring us back a watermelon?'

'No. They're too expensive and too heavy. Will you go?'

He bent beside her and presented his cheek.

'Kiss,' he ordered.

She kissed him. He kissed her back.

'Got your key?' he asked. She showed it to him, attached to her silver medallion by a blue elastic-band. 'Oh, very chic! Don't forget to double-lock when you go out. So *ciao*.'

'What's wrong with *shalom*?'

'Who says "*shalom*" any more? Only Americans, and they call it "Shalome".'

'I say it. I refuse to stoop to "*caio*" and "hi". You'll all be saying "tara-well" and "bye-bye" soon.'

'I say "bye-bye" now, I love saying "bye-bye", so English! Bye-bye!'

'*Shalom*. Get lost.'

At last he'd really gone. Now she could get down to work. There were no offices open today, of course. It would have to be phone calls direct to people's homes. She decided to restrict herself to the 'ordinary' names on her list, hoping they were not religious. Well, and if they were, they could always let the phone ring.

She started with a woman she had heard about who had been in a combat unit in '48. Ann had discovered already that contrary to popular legend there were comparatively few women fighters. She wondered how the American public, reared on the myth of Israeli 'girl soldiers', would take to having this oddly-cherished illusion shattered. All those films and stories about girls with rifles pressed to fragile shoulders, ruthlessly sighting along the barrel and pulling the trigger . . . Ann marvelled that men, and women too, enjoyed the idea of such a thing. For her part, it made her quail.

Peter had passed through a sporting phase during her early acquaintance with him. She remembered going out shooting with him once. He had let her hold the gun, fire at a pheasant. He had helped her hold the stock, arms round her from behind . . . she'd almost forgotten. *That* must be why the feeling of it was still there, in her shoulder, in her arms and hands, her eyes . . . the spiked sight wavering, settling . . . Bang! 'Damn. You've winged him. You stay here, I'll finish him off – can't leave him like that . . .' Of course he hadn't expected her to hit it. It had been sitting. He'd been appalled – so unsporting – he'd just let her try for a lark. He went on about it for days. He'd had to wring its neck . . . You couldn't do that to a wounded Arab, lying on the hill where you'd winged him.

She found the number in the English language Jerusalem phone book. It rang about six times, a lot for the size of flats most people had. At last a thick, sleepy voice answered.

''Allo, *mi ze?*'

'Mrs Bat-Hillel?'

'Yuh?'

'Did I wake you?'

'*Wake* me? It's nearly lunchtime, isn't it? Who are you?'

Ann went into her spiel.

'My name is Ann Randall, I'm an English writer. I'm here to collect interviews for a book about the War of Independence. I heard you had an interesting story and I wondered if you'd agree to tell it to me.'

There was a pause, and then Ann heard the sound made by someone blowing out cigarette smoke.

'I've told it already. Too many times.'

'To journalists?'

'To journalists. To book writers. To historians. To *p'sychologues*. To what you like. I've told it till I'm dry.'

Her inflexion was very final. But still, she didn't hang up.

Ann said, 'Are you busy today?'

'No.'

'Could I just see you, to talk? I won't record if you'd rather not.'

'Record? Why do you need to record, can't you make notes?'

'The idea of the book is to use people's exact words. It's an oral history.'

There was a short guffaw.

'You Americans say "oral" about everything now!'

'I'm not an American,' said Ann patiently. 'I'm English.'

'You're *English*! Why didn't you say so in the first place? I took for granted you're American. Well. I've nothing better to do. Why

40

don't you come over?'

'Where do you live?'

'In Rehavia. The not-smart section.'

'I can walk there.'

'In this heat? Mad dogs and Englishmen! Well, it's your own business, but you had better take a taxi, if you can find one.' She gave her directions. 'I should warn you I am in no very nice mood. I went last night to a party in Tel Aviv and I got very angry and that made me drink too much and I drove badly home and I cried all night, what was left of it. Don't worry, I've stopped. But don't expect smiles and stiff lips, what you call, because I don't have.'

'That's all right. Perhaps I can cheer you up.'

The voice turned suddenly harsh.

'I don't want to get cheered up, thank you. If you plan to cheer me up, just don't come.'

Kicking herself, Ann left the flat. There was obviously something wrong with the lady, probably quite badly wrong. Ann really must try not to be too . . . too much as she would be in England. In England, in the unlikely event of a total stranger telling you over the phone that she had got angry, got drunk, driven dangerously and cried all night, you would assume that she was (a) an extrovert, (b) probably an exhibitionist, and (c) that the trouble was likely to be something fairly straightforward like a family row or a professional reverse (what else was there?) – unless, of course, she were a chronic drinker or otherwise abnormal in some way. (Peter: 'Don't get involved, darling. You know nothing about her' – anent an old tramp woman at the cottage door with a sob story. But if he had heard Shula Bat-Hillel – ! He would have said it, even now. He *had* said it, before she left. 'All right, darling, go off and do your job, that's fine. But don't get submerged. I know you! Hold that essential core of your *self* in reserve. No one and no cause on earth has a right to chew away at that.')

She had sensed something in that woman's silences, they had clawed at her along the telephone wire. She needed Ann to come, Ann or anybody. She needed to talk, not about the '48 War perhaps, but about more recent battles. (Last night's party?) How old must she be? Fifty at least. Crying all night . . . Could you still do that, at fifty? Within only one year of the dreaded plimsoll line between – as she had always seen it – middle and practically old age, Ann still thought of it as the time when violent emotions relaxed their power. It would have to be a rather abrupt change in

41

her own case, she thought . . .

The *sharav* tugged and buffetted her, yet the air was too hot to breathe. The streets were almost empty. There were no taxis, very few vehicles of any kind. Jerusalem, unlike Tel Aviv and other more modern towns, goes to sleep on feast days; but then Jerusalem is observant. Even its non-observant denizens – radical anti-clericalists, avowed atheists – observe the observant and pay their holy days grudging respect. It was something Ann found hard to understand. The older she herself got, the more she disliked and mistrusted all brands of militant orthodoxy, and the less need she felt to be tolerant of them . . . Had not she and Menachem been prevented from marrying by the Rabbinate who had refused to perform the ceremony, and by the politicians who had always barred civil marriage in Israel? (It had been tacitly agreed that they would go to England or Cyprus to get married when she got pregnant . . . the kibbutz would not see the need to stand the expense of the trip otherwise.)

Quite recently some journalist had rung Ann in Suffolk, wanting to write something about her and her most recent novel, which had a Jewish hero. 'Are you Jewish yourself?' 'No.' 'Are you married to a Jew?' 'No.' 'No Jewish connections at *all*?' 'No.' *Not now.* 'But no doubt,' the voice had purred on, 'you have a great respect for the Jewish religion.' 'I haven't the slightest respect for the Jewish religion,' Ann had retorted, 'or any other.'

This extreme and categorical statement had surprised her very little less than it had surprised (and evidently shocked) the interviewer. Reflecting on it afterwards, she had suddenly laughed. 'How do I know what I think until I hear what I say?' she had remarked to Peter, who had overheard the conversation. 'I think I have come of age.' 'What do you mean by that?' 'Who was that American who said that he knew he'd grown up the day he realised it wasn't necessary to like sunsets? Well, I've just realised it isn't necessary to pay lip service to reactionary, dogmatic, money-grubbing religious establishments any more than to reactionary dogmatic money-grubbing political ones, in the name of tolerance or liberalism or anything else. Roman Catholicism, Judaism, Islam – all the lot of them. They're all retrogressive, they're all superstitious, they're all self-seeking and they're all awful.' 'What about the good old C. of E.?' 'Less so, but only because it's got less power, which is possibly because its adherents are less fanatical, or more sensible, or marginally better educated on the whole.' 'Darling! You won't turn into an atheist

42

bigot, will you? Or you'll be just as bad as the rest.'

It was not often Peter acknowledged her atheism. In conversation with friends, he could be overheard referring to her, when absolute necessity forced him to, as a 'rather wavering agnostic'. (He did not specify the direction of her wavering.) She didn't correct him because she knew that her godlessness hurt him, not least because he knew where it had come from – it was Menachem who had 'converted' her, or, as she preferred to think, set her free from the lingering ties that impeded her mind and the development of her spiritual independence. Seeing how an atheist community flourished, how much more healthy, sane and unhypocritical, and withal how genuinely *good* most of them managed to be by relying on their sense of mutual responsibility and their humanity, she saw that God is not necessary for a creative, honest, and, by her new interpretation, spiritually rich life. With that recognition, her lifetime's struggles to reconcile an omnipotent loving father figure with the horrors of the world fell off her like weights and shrivelled up at her feet – chimeras, nothings. She was free. Free to fight her own battles, to be as good as she could because that was what worked best. She had never wavered from that position, even though, at times, she had felt her freedom as a weight scarcely less burdensome than the ones she had cast off.

It was a long walk. Somehow after the first five minutes, Ann stopped minding the horrendous heat. In the kibbutz she had learnt to cope with it, and this triumph over her temperate Englishness gave her immense satisfaction. When the temperature is much higher or lower than blood heat, one becomes aware of one's skin as one's borders, a finite barrier between oneself and the air. The skin then becomes very important, and the sweat seeping out of it can be actively enjoyed. Working in the sweltering heat of the chicken-houses, she had learnt to blow on her wrists, or, better still, run them under the low-set taps that filled the drinking troughs. Crouching in the mucky shavings, breathing hot dust and chicken stink, she rejoiced to feel the blood cooling as it passed through those big veins. If she held her wrists long enough under the flow, she felt all the blood in her body being cooled. In the blazing sun of the vineyard, she would lift her arms away from her sides and stand with thighs apart to let what breeze there was act upon her sweat; the contrast then became a sort of sensual treat . . .

Never before or since that time had Ann lived so consciously through her senses. Of course this had its roots in Menachem, the body-poetry of his lovemaking, the varied levels of ecstasy in the nights resonating during the working days . . . Even later when she was given the 'cushy' job of teaching, shut away from the worst of the elements, she would still find herself relishing the way many quite ordinary things looked and felt, the hot scents that came through the screened windows, of pine and cut grass and especially that carnation-sharp fragrance from a certain shrub that bore both red and yellow flowers . . . But any smell would do . . . She used to sniff the blackboard cleaner sometimes. The smell of the chalk came to symbolise her delight in her work. And the children had their own smells. She loved it when they bent over her with their 'copybooks'. In summer they wore nothing but vests and shorts, and their sun-laden skins gave off sweet, childish odours mixed with the clean, hot smell of cotton dried outdoors . . . She wanted to touch them, even hug and kiss them sometimes when they were especially good and showed her, by their achievements, a good image of herself as their teacher, succeeding where others had failed, giving her, through their parents' satisfaction, her place in this community she loved . . . She didn't touch them, except just occasionally their hair, brushing a head with her palm lightly as she passed up and down the aisles. But they were objects of primal sensuality to her just the same. She realised it only now. Forty-nine and childless, she realised it.

She heaved sigh after sigh as she toiled up Keren Kayemet to Terra Sancta, where she must turn off into the conifer-shaded purlieus of Rahavia. She was carrying a hold-all containing her tape-recorder and camera, her precious notebook, her maps, her wallet (not that she'd need any money, nothing was open) and her Woolworth's make-up bag. Her headscarf was on her head. Just the same she was getting sun-struck and was almost on her knees by the time she reached the big stone-faced building she was looking for.

The flat was at the top. She literally crawled the last flight, pressing her hands to the still cool tiled steps. She heaved herself upright, and rang the bell. The door was opened at once.

'I knew it – you walked. You are *meshugga*. Now I must revive you.'

'I'm so sorry! I'd have got a taxi – ' Ann gasped. 'There wasn't one.'

'Then it's my fault, I should have come for you.'

She was all of fifty, but she had a trim, athletic figure and her hair was a natural-looking red with only a little grey at the front. She wore a short house-coat and Japanese sandals. No circus folk had left *her* shutters open. Her flat, deep in the walls of the old house built in the heyday of rich immigrants from Germany, was dark, and still miraculously cool.

'Drink first,' she was saying as she led Ann into the small sitting-room, 'then a shower. Then we'll see about lesser matters.'

Ann was too dizzy and exhausted to answer. Shula Bat-Hillel went away and Ann looked about her, as she always did, automatically data-collecting.

It was the room of a person who has drawn her life – her whole life, fifty years of it – in around her, the way a child tucks its bedclothes in around and under its body to keep out the cold. The walls of it were lined a foot deep in *things* – a mass of them, at first glance indistinguishable in the dim light and in their conglomerate bulk. If there were shelves originally, as a foundation for this almost sculptural life-box, they were now totally obscured by the stacks of files, books, cartons, magazines, display cases full of strange dusty collections, and a welter of other impedimenta which climbed in perilous towers to the ceiling. These false walls were in their turn curtained with another, thinner layer – calendars, pictures, photographs, scraps of embroidery, a fringed shawl – and also more utilitarian objects: a duffle coat on a hanger, hooked to a glass-fronted box of shells and star-fish; a ladder; a clutch of papers in a bulldog clip; a batik; a damp dishtowel. Every available corner of the floor was occupied by houseplants, some of which wove their leafy stalks over all the rest as if rejoicing in this unique trellis; and embedded in all this fascinating mass of dark objects was a huge fridge, and three or four bright oblongs of light – aquaria, filled with the moving pattern made by bubbles and trembling weed and brilliant tropical fish.

Shula came back with an ice-cold bottle of grapefruit juice. Ann drank all of it, feeling herself, as she did so, filling out again, her cells expanding as the liquid reconstituted her. Next she was bundled into a small shower room, where she stripped off and had a cold shower, which gave a similar beneficial effect from the outside. In the kibbutz, she had used to qualify summer weather according to the number of times she had to shower. This was definitely a five shower day.

A hand came round the door holding a loose housedress. 'Put

this on,' she was told. 'Over nothing but talc. It's on the shelf. You can dress again when you leave.'

Ann gratefully obeyed, leaving her pants, bra and dress on a stool. She left her sandals there too. She groped (her eyes were still dazzled by the outside glare) her way back into the small, dim living-room.

'You are better?'

'Much. Totally, really. My God, though!'

'Yes, it's a bad one. Worst I can remember.' Ann laughed. One always said that, about every *khamsin*.

'You mind the mess in here?'

'No.'

'Good.' She lit a cigarette and blew out smoke with that tense, purse-lipped sound that Ann had heard on the phone. 'You want to smoke?'

'I don't.'

'At all?' – incredulous.

Ann shook her head.

'I will never give up smoking. Sometimes it is the only thing.'

'Coffee's like that for me. I couldn't live without coffee.'

'Drink, then. It's real coffee, not Nes. I made it with *hel*. You like *hel*? The Arabs use it.'

'Yes, I love it. I love all the tastes here.'

'The hot ones too?'

'Especially those.'

There was a pause. The two women looked at each other.

'My name is Shula.'

'I know. Mine's Ann.'

'So. You're English.' Shula was looking at her narrowly, appraising her through the smoke and the poor light. 'How old? May I know?'

'Forty-nine.'

'My God! Nearly as much as me!'

She got up abruptly – all her movements were tense and jerky – went to the door and switched on a bright top light. Then she stood looking at Ann's face for a minute before switching off and returning to her stool.

'Where have you been living in this lousy world, to look so young when you are so old?'

'In England mostly.'

'Ah. That explains it.' She smoked and stared. Ann felt uncomfortable. There was undoubtedly a lot of difference in their faces.

Shula's was sallow and covered with hard lines. Her own looked almost unlived-in by comparison.

'I did live here for some years once,' she found herself saying, as if in self-excuse.

Shula shook her head slowly. 'Not long enough,' she said obscurely. And then, 'When? What era?'

Era . . . Only in Israel can one speak of eras in a space of thirty-two years. That was all that modern Israel had existed . . . Yet the word was apposite. There had indeed been eras. Ann knew that; first from Menachem, confirmed by everything she had learnt since. The pre-State era, of course; and then, since the State was declared in '48, there had been quite clearly defined ones: the era of the 'fifties, with its austerity, its upbuilding, its strikes and counter-strikes across the borders; its ingatherings and the first creepings away abroad; its political infighting; Suez and Sinai . . . That was the last real era of pioneering, which she, to her sorrow, had just missed. It was the era she knew least about.

Then the early 'sixties. Her era. Recessions, reappraisals, first real crises of conscience among the intellectuals – and everywhere the sinking-in of the knowledge that the Palestinian problem was going to get worse and not go away. But still – idealism. Hope. Single-mindedness. A sort of blindness *vis-à-vis* the Arabs and anyone else who frowned, up to and including the United Nations. Still massive support in the world; America a bottomless well; the Diaspora one hundred per cent 'pro'. Not too terribly many leaving, although the influx had thinned to a trickle, especially from the much-wooed West. But in the kibbutz, still seventy, eighty, ninety per cent of the post-army generation coming back to settle. And in the country at large, still no drug problem, no organised urban crime; patriotism not yet a dirty word; more upbuilding; pride . . . And still, of course, the perennial Labour Government, though not free from taint and scandal . . . A period, Ann came to think after the great watershed of the '67 War, of blinkered introversion, over-confidence, and a sort of innocence – a lingering national virginity and a kind of *faux-paix*, even within each individual . . .

' '60 to '66,' she said.

'Sandwich.'

'No thanks,' said Ann stupidly.

Shula smiled with one side of her mouth. 'No, no. I mean, that was the sandwich era. When everything looked nice. Long

47

enough after Kibya to have pushed it away, and before we lost the Six-Day War.'

Ann thought she understood the ironic reference to the War, but puzzled about the rest. 'Why Kibya?' she asked. 'Why not Sinai?'

'Sinai? Sinai was not so bad. I was not against Sinai. I was not even against collusion with the British and French – I was against lying about it. Open war is often preferable. It was a cleaner way, in this case, to stop the *fedayeen* than some of the dirty things we did earlier.'

'What dirty things?'

'The big raid on Gaza. And before that, the Lavon affair. You don't call that dirty? – to send espionagists to blow up buildings in Egypt so that the Egyptians will think Americans did it, and break with them? We did that. Well, *we* didn't, because none of us, no ordinary Israeli knew anything about it, not then and not for years after; we were not told what all the world could read in *Time* and *Newsweek*. We were encouraged to yell and cry when the Egyptians put some of our people on trial and executed two of them; but we weren't told what they'd done. It was called ''a security mishap''. We argued for months and years about who ''gave the order'' and we never demanded to know what the order was . . . *That* was dirty. A dirty trick. Also on us . . . It was a bit our own fault, though, for trusting too much our leaders. They were Jews, weren't they? And Ben Gurion told us that *all* of us Jews were good people. He forgot that he'd once called the leaders of the terrorist armies Nazis. He told us after the '48 War that we were all goodniks, those Etzel and Sternists had done their part, just as the Palmach. He let us think their ideologies were as good as our ideologies – what a deep, dirty lie! What a mistake, what a stupid blunder! Unity – that was his cry. Oh, he was ready to shoot them on the *Altalena* in April '48, and he was right to do it, but in '49 he opened his arms to them, rubbing out the lines between them and us, and now look! BG is safe in his grave in Sde Boker while one of those goodniks is the Prime Minister of our country and he is ruining it, that frog-faced evil autist.'

She stubbed out her cigarette angrily and took a long swig of the black coffee, wiping her mouth on the back of her hand.

'God, I have such a hangover! I never drink, you know. Nearly never. Last night I drank. I had to! I got so *furious* I thought I would kill some of them . . .' She gave Ann a sharp, ironic look. 'You perhaps have heard that with me, that is not just, how you

48

call, a figure of speaking. Those Arabs I shot, that you want me to tell you all about it, they were just poor bastards. My fellow soldiers. They were doing nothing to me really, just trying to shoot me before I could shoot them, and so what? That is what soldiers are supposed to do, isn't it? But these men last night, they are doing worse things. They are worse people than those poor fools who ran at me, going down one after another, while I sat behind my heap of stones reloading and reloading and bringing worlds to an end. That is what the Jews say about killing a man, that you kill a world, all his children and their children . . . But these men, last night in Tel Aviv, they won't fall down. They are rising up, and they know it. They are on top now, clinging to the skirts of the ruling party. Well, one expects that from the weak, the opportunists. But not from these men, because they are not of that party, they are of my party – they *were* of my party. They were Palmachniks, like me. Socialists, like me. Now they are no more socialists, they are territorialists, they are nationalists. *Cus umak*, they are *fascists*, those old comrades of mine! Once we knew what fascism was and we knew it was our enemy and we tried to do away with it, even in ourselves. But *now* – they sit there in their nice beautiful homes, with Danish furniture and French food and Dutch tiles and Swedish what-you-want, because what we make in Israel is no more good enough for them.' She broke off and stared rather wildly round the room. 'Do you know I have not one thing in this flat which is from *khutz l'aretz* – imported? Not one thing. But that is not the point, it is just the – ' She stabbed the air with her finger. 'The pointer. The point is that they . . .'

She stopped suddenly. She had been shouting. Ann's ears felt as 'dazzled' as her eyes had, coming into the dark after the glare outside. There was a numbness in the sudden silence, as if she had gone deaf.

Shula sat there perfectly still. She was trying to control herself so as not to weep. The Englishwoman in Ann sat stiff with embarrassment, with an ignoble, but painful, social trepidation. But when two tears actually did roll down Shula's cheeks, when she bent her head suddenly and sniffed and covered her eyes, this alter-ego of Ann's melted. She leaned forward, took the newly lit cigarette away (it had been about to singe the red-grey fringe) and at once Shula reached blindly for her hand and held it hard against the table-top, still covering her streaming eyes with the other.

'You see I don't believe they have all changed their minds,' she

49

said in a muffled voice after a while. 'If they had really changed I would say, well, they are lost souls, that's all. The world has corrupted them, our situation has rotted them. But they still believe in the same things as me really.' She threw back her head violently as if to throw her tears back into their ducts. She sniffed again, deeply, and let go of Ann's hand. 'One of them,' she said, 'a man who was my commander in that first war, a man one could love and respect, and follow to the death, he has a seat now in the Cabinet. He helped to form a new party – you heard about it? "Dash", we call it, *called* it. They knew we were sick of the old leaders and looking for new ones, and some of the best people were on their list, and we voted – God forgive them, we voted for them, and they got fifteen men into the Knesset, *fifteen*! You know what that is? They could have fought, they could have opposed, they could have balanced the religious parties who always join every government providing they're allowed to make our lives narrower and less free . . . But what did they do? You know what they did?' She stared at Ann through wild, red-rimmed eyes.

'Yes. They joined the Government.'

'Some joined, yes, and they split themselves apart, and their party fell into pieces, and all the hopes and promises of a new way, a new start, they threw them away. And there is my old commander, grown fat and ugly, sitting in his soft chair eating cream cakes and drinking foreign brandy and laughing at me. "Don't listen to her!" he said to them when I lost control and began to shout at him. "She is *p'sichi*!" ' She twisted a finger like a gimlet at her temple. 'You know what is "*p'sichi*"? Crazy. I said to him – you want to know what I said? – I said, "I know better than you that I am *p'sichi*. My life is in pieces like your party. But you are a *p'sychologue* and you should know that crazy people must also be listened to. You are afraid to listen because Crazy Shula is telling you the truth." '

She stopped and drank the rest of her coffee. She didn't look at Ann now. She was reliving her humiliation. After a while, she went on:

'The truth that I told them is that I killed men – not dropping bombs as we do now, but face to face – in close-up – that is the worst, when you see them alive, then dead – for something those people shared with me then, a belief that we have a right. That we are fighting, like anybody, for an essential thing, our own place, to be not ruled and pushed around any more by the *goyim*. That

50

our right justified us. *I* never said that we should be just a normal country with our jails full. I didn't kill men to be as lousy as everywhere else. I thought we were better. I thought we were cleaner . . . I killed them clean, kill or be killed. But now, look what we are doing! Now *we* dominate, now *we* hold down, now *we* think we can steal land and water and cut down their trees like they used to cut down ours. We think we can ignore the world, we think God gave us a mandate . . . *Cus umak!* They talk about the Torah! They should read the rest of it and see what our God is like before they use him as our bill of rights!'

Ann got up and made the next lot of coffee, and the next. They talked on and on in the still, tomb-like stone darkness of the kitchen. When they got hungry, around 1 o'clock, Shula reached over without rising, opened the door of the big old-fashioned fridge and fished out a plastic dish of yellow cheese, some *eshel* and a bowl of enormous strawberries. With no break in the conversation (which was more of a monologue) they dipped their teaspoons in the *eshel* – even in the throes of strong intellectual and emotional concentration, they both grinned with sheer physical pleasure as the cool, light, slightly fizzy junket slipped down their throats – gorged themselves on the strawberries and then nibbled endlessly on cheese.

Ann left her tape recorder in her hold-all. This was one of her difficulties. When a person was talking, freely and naturally, as so many did here, talking from a need to talk while she listened from an equally profound compulsion, it seemed an intrusion and an outrage to start flashing machines around which would capture the flow, make it something permanent, possibly regrettable later . . . People tended to dry up when one did that. It was as if they themselves were being plugged into a not altogether benign force. Yet her memory was not to be trusted . . .

At length she got out her notebook.

'Do you mind?'

'No. Yes . . . I don't know. But not the part about my life, my family, all the things that have gone wrong with me . . .'

'Of course not. Unless you think that some of these things are the result of what happened in the war.'

Shula threw back her head and gave her harsh guffaw.

'You stupid! Of course they are! Listen. You can write my opinion now. The Tsars and the Romans had the right idea about soldiers. They seized them – only men of course, but in some ways it's the same thing, not in all ways but some – they took them, and they said, "Now you are a soldier. That is all you are and it is all you will ever be. Because you stay now in the army for thirty, thirty-five years. You don't go home. So just forget about everything else." In Israel we do different. We take young people, everyone, and we train them. We don't talk about killing of course, or teach them to hate – no no, that's un-Jewish, BG forbade the teaching of hatred for the enemy as army policy. Some officers wanted it, but he said, never. Did you know that? In the British army, isn't it so that the sergeant makes the men charge on a dummy in an enemy uniform and stick a bayonet in him with a great blood-hungry yell? I've seen it in the movies. But we don't. We show them how to shoot at targets and how to break down a gun, and we teach them tactics and how to drive tanks and fly planes and all that. Then if a war comes, which usually it does, we send them into battle and they kill Arabs, and some-times each other by mistake, and after it's over we send them back home and say, "Thank you, now make some children." And they make children, like I did, to – well, I'm not saying everyone who has killed people has kids like I did, as a – how you call – antidote to the poison, to heal the trauma that you ended worlds, to create new worlds to make up for that. I'm a woman, don't forget that. Biologically a woman has to make life, not end it, so perhaps it was worse for me – I'm not stupid – I know there are men, good men even, who, if the cause was good, kill and go home and think no more about it. But many who pretend that, they feel as I do inside, they suffer as I did. Because I'll tell you something. Maybe you are waiting to go into battle and you are lying in your bed or under a tree and you breathe deep and feel the air in your lungs and you think it's a pity to die. You pity yourself, and you have a right to. The right you have is that you are innocent, so why should you be killed? But once *you* have killed, you can't think like that any more. That you killed someone, that he no more breathes because of you, that takes away your innocence, it takes away your right to comfort yourself with self-pity. After that you deserve to die and in a deep place you hope you will, because at that time, when you still have those dead men's faces in the front of your memory, you wonder how will you walk away from it all, how will you manage with yourself for the rest of your life, with your head full of those men and who they were and what their wives thought when they heard and how their . . . Well, never mind. That fades. It has to. We are all born with a box

52

of tricks built into our heads to take care of such things. But if you think that a veteran like I was can go away and make children without problems, that from such a parent they can inherit nice red hair and underneath it no wounds in their minds – well, I think you are wrong.'

'Are you saying that a large proportion, or any significant number of men who fought in wars in Israel are so – excuse me – psychologically disturbed – '

'Don't be polite for God's sake! I excuse you! I *am* psychologically disturbed, I am "*p'sichi*", I told you! The difference is, I know about it. It is even, I would say, normal to be disturbed after what I went through, it is not normal *not* to be disturbed. You should be afraid of the ones who are *not* disturbed.'

'Well. So I was asking – if you think most of – '

'Are most young people, in Israel now, children of the '48 fighters, problem children? You want the truth? So stop writing.' Ann stopped. 'Close the book.' She obeyed. 'Now you will not quote me. About this, not. But my answer – my own answer – is that, yes, this generation, many of them are disturbed. Look at them. I don't speak of their beauty, their vigour. Look how they behave, what they do. Many of them are going back to religion. They put back on again the chains their parents, and grand-parents, broke and threw away. It is always a sign, of emptiness, of insecurity, of searching for something they don't find inside them or in their surroundings. Now look again. Those who were blessed with a kibbutz upbringing, the finest in the world – need I tell *you*? You saw it, you felt it – they are leaving in their thousands, to come in to town, to live as hedonists, materialists. They are throwing away what every other group of youth in the world seems to be looking for. Security. Pride. An honest produc-tive life among honest productive people. Freedom from stupid fears and worries about money and illness and how to educate their kids and give them a culture and traditions – they don't even have to be afraid to grow old. And the best is ideals. A belief and a frame. An identity . . . And look at them! The first chance they get, they throw themselves back in the *botz*. Drugs and drink and aggravation and ego and Danish furniture . . . Is that normal? Is that sane?'

Ann was silent. Even six years in the 'sandwich era' had taught her that things were not quite like that. It seemed very sad to her, too, that so many were leaving the kibbutz, but till now she had thought only that it was sad for the kibbutz. As far as the youngsters were concerned, it *had* seemed to her natural, a drift back to the Western norm from heights of idealism too rarefied to breathe in unless you yourself had climbed there, acclimatised yourself through your own will . . .

'And now look a third time,' Shula was saying. 'Look at the West Bank, you should excuse me that I won't call it like *they* call it, like it says on the official maps – "Samaria" and "Judea" . . . What will you find there? Settlements, so called, of young patriots, so called, who believe they are above the law because God gives them a higher right. Well, okay. We have always had our dangerous patriotics like that who say, God is on our side so we don't care who isn't. Our own Prime Minister thinks it. The worry is that other young people, not religious maniacs, look at these crazy settlers and say, well, we don't agree with them, but we admire them. Because at least they are strong in their opinions, at least they act what they believe, at least they *know* what they believe. Even if it is crazy and dangerous, it is better to be like them and hold to ransom the government and the army who don't want to let flow Jewish blood, than be like the rest of us who have forgotten what strong believing is. They, these crazy Gush people, are the inheritors of our pioneering traditions! That is what our young people say. Is it normal to admire crazy people, who steal the land of the Arabs and defy their own authorities and make fools of their own countrymen before all the world? And what else do we find in those areas, those "liberated" areas? Young men doing what *we* would *never* have agreed to do thirty years ago . . . with guns and half-tracks and tear-gas and all of it, patrolling the streets of Nablus and Jenin, not to mention Hebron. We had better not mention Hebron!'

'They're needed in Hebron,' murmured Ann.

'What?' Shula snapped.

'If the settlers are going to be allowed to stay there, they have to be protected against attack.'

It was the first time in the conversation, now three hours long, that she had allowed a journalist's trick to escape her – a little thorn of devil's advocacy, a deliberate provocation. It worked. Too well. She regretted it the instant she saw its effect. Shula reared back her head as if Ann had struck her.

'Now *you* talk like a fascist,' she said. She stood up. 'It's time to end this conversation.'

Ann sat there mutely, looking up at her. Her eyes were quite used to the dimness now and she could see clearly the expression on Shula's face.

'You really mean it. Just for saying that.'

'Just.'

Ann opened her mouth to argue, and then closed it again. She got up silently and went through to the shower-room and got dressed, leaving the housedress hanging behind the door. She would have liked another shower, but . . . The automatic friendliness and informality accorded to her as a stranger when she first arrived had been forfeited. She understood the rules. She accepted them – for the moment.

When she came out Shula was standing in the hall. Her face was now perfectly under control – hard to believe she had wept and clutched Ann's hand and told her so many personal things . . . Ann felt ashamed of her trick and very sorry for it. She would have given a lot to undo it. But she was not totally cast down, because she sensed that what had happened was a quarrel between friends. That she had been, apparently, demoted to the status of a crass intrusive right-wing journalist was no more than she deserved for wanting to see what Shula would say about the Hebron killings, for wanting her to say it a bit louder and with more edge than she would have done believing that Ann agreed with her about it.

'Shalom, Shula. I'll phone you tomorrow.'

'What for? Don't bother. Go away and get yourself some grey hairs. Then maybe we'll have something to talk about.'

Ann grinned ruefully, gave a little nod, and left the flat.

CHAPTER 5

Out in the simmering street again, she stood for a while, unable to decide what to do. It was that same killing walk in reverse to get back to Amnon's. The pragmatist in her could not help reflecting wrily that if she had not carelessly antagonised Shula, she would certainly have driven her home . . . But that wasn't the worst.

She walked slowly away down the hill, but after a few paces regret made her glance back and upward. Shula was standing on her balcony, watching her, her paprika-and-salt fringe blowing back in the seering wind.

On impulse, Ann called up: 'I agree with you about the Hebron settlers!'

Shula put both hands on the stone railing and leaned forward. Her voice came through the siesta-hour quiet with shocking clarity:

'Do you agree with me that they deserved what they got?'

Without waiting for a reply, she drew back, and a moment later her iron shutter clanged behind her.

Ann walked on, her head down. Six Jews dead from grenade blasts and gunfire, sixteen wounded. Civilians, unarmed, walking through the streets of a town on the way from synagogue. And an Israeli woman said they'd asked for it.

Amnon had said, after *his* outburst, 'But of course you couldn't understand.' She accepted this, because she acknowledged herself to be forever an outsider; but it hurt, because she thought she did understand, at least he might have credited her with trying. Certainly she felt within her the horror and confusion behind what both Amnon and Shula, in their different ways, had said. It must be the first time in history that the deep Jewish instinct to be outraged by the murder of Jews by their enemies was inhibited at source, baffled by conflict and turned back upon itself. This confusion, not the event itself, had split the country.

She'd heard about it the night she arrived, from Amnon, who had met her at the airport. He had been almost beside himself with rage and distress.

'I knew it!' he kept saying. 'I said something like this would happen! Just because the West Bankers have been fairly passive till now, does that mean they'll stand for anything? The occupa-

56

tion with the lightest hand in history – yeah, for sure, but just so long as the occupied kept quiet. Now they're being pushed too hard, they're getting organised ... . That wasn't just some *bekachte* little ambush got up by some communist hotheads on the spur of the moment. *That* wasn't a pile of smouldering tyres in the road or a few schoolkids incited to throw stones . . .' They were weaving in and out of parked cars in the dark, pushing the airport trolley bearing her bits of luggage between them. Amnon's hand kept releasing the trolley-handle and clutching her adjoining wrist in spasms, like italics.

'But was it our fault?' Ann asked.

'Of course it was our bloody fault! What are those bastards doing there? "Establishing their God-given right to live anywhere they like in Eretz Israel." A suburb like Kiryat Arba, built cheek against jaw with Hebron – occupied exclusively by religious fanatics – *that's* not good enough for them. No, no, they have to get right inside the town, right in the heart of the Arab area; they have to send their women to squat in an old building that used to be Jewish, in '29 – '

'A date to conjure with – ' Ann reminded him. They found the car. Amnon wrenched open the boot and flung her cases in violently.

'Oh yes, I know. Everything always dates back to a massacre of the Jews. Including Israel. God knows what, in a few years or even weeks from now, will date back to *today's* massacre. We despise the Arabs because they carry on blood-feuds for generations, we say, "Look how they are! They're primitive, they're cruel, they never forgive, they kill each other, what will they do to *us*?" So that makes it okay for us to trample all over their rights and their feelings and expect them to sit quiet forever! Get in!' She got in and he slammed the door on her. Two seconds later he jumped in beside her and started backing the car at hair-raising speed out of the car park, scarcely seeming to glance over his shoulder. Ann clutched her seat and remembered that she had to reaccustom herself to Israeli driving.

'Why didn't the Government act *then*? A year ago, when those crazy American females started their squat? Weizman was responsible, he *said* it was illegal, he *said* it was provocative, but what the hell did he do about it? Nothing, that's what he did! You can't have Jewish soldiers carrying Jewish women, religious ones at that, bodily out of a place they've no business to be in, can you? You couldn't ask Our Boys to do a thing like that. Chasing Arab

57

schoolgirls, that's okay, shooting up Arab youths when they demonstrate, *that's* their honest duty. Moving Arab farmers off their land, chasing Bedu across the borders, shooting infiltrators on sight – '

'Oh, come *on*, Amnon! You can't be such a dove as all that! Of course they've got to shoot infiltrators, look what happens when they don't – Ma'alot, Misgav Am, the bus – '

'All right already!' shouted Amnon, putting the car viciously into forward gear and zooming into the night, nearly dislocating Ann's neck. 'Shoot infiltrators! We've had enough practice. We started off in the late 'forties, early 'fifties, when most of 'em were coming across the border to pick their own fruit – '

'Amnon, come off it. They were hell-bent on sabotage and murder.'

'Some were, some weren't. The armistice lines were drawn so stupid, with their villages on the Jordan side and their land on ours. We'd bought it, we'd fought for it, we'd chased them off it – good. Now we've found a new way, now we just expropriate it, or divert their water so they can't cultivate it. Or let women squat in it.'

'You said they squatted in a Jewish building.'

'Yes, like I'm earning my living now in an Arab building. If Abu Daoud marched into my theatre tomorrow and said, "This is mine, I'm squatting in the foyer till you get out," how fast do you think Our Boys would be round to throw him out?'

He drove on. Ann leant a little out of her window, savouring the sweet, warm air and smelling the Israeli night scents. Olive blossom – more subtle than orange, more nostalgic . . . Oh, if only he wouldn't make me *think*, not just yet! I only want to *feel* it all, say hallo to it quietly before the mental turmoil begins . . . But it was no use. Amnon was wound up like a spring.

'We have to accept it, Ann, if we want them to accept it. In '48 they began it. We beat them, they left, one way or another – ' He glanced at her and raised his eyebrows – 'Finish. We won, they lost, that's war. The Arabs should have thought of it before they attacked us, it's no use crying later. But then *we* began it in '67 – shut up, listen – of course we did – that fool Nasser gave us the opportunity we'd been looking for for nearly twenty years, to lay our hands on Sinai and the West Bank. But now *we* have to face facts. We can't just go on ruling over those people. Or if we decide we will, we mustn't start crying if they fight back. What's shocked me till now is that they have done so little, that we have been able to kid ourselves that our being there is not so bad, that even it's benefiting them, making them "prosperous" – '

'Well, hasn't it?'

Amnon swerved, narrowly avoiding an oncoming lorry.

'You think? Good, you think so. So now wait and see how much they want "prosperous". They want, first, out from under *us*, that's what anyone would want, and the worse we make it for them with our Kadums and our Eilon Morehs and our Hadassahs in the middle of them, flaunting our "Biblical rights", the more they will get onto rooftops and throw grenades at us, and then the more we will cry and do back to them, and the more we will fight among ourselves about what we have to do to hold them, and – oh, never mind talking about it! It makes me sick.'

He blew a long blast on his horn and overtook on a bend. 'And you couldn't understand. How can you understand what it feels like to be a Jew and *not* be persecuted?'

They had driven the rest of the way to Jerusalem in silence. Later, when they arrived, things eased up. He asked her about her plans and she asked him about the theatre and he gave her a meal and after a while he got up and came round the table and put his arm round her and said, 'Sorry.'

'For what?'

'I couldn't help it.'

'It's okay, Amnon. Forget it.'

So they did, until the next night, when they both got back late from their respective work and slumped on the seraglio mattresses in front of the television. They watched the Defence Minister being interviewed and trying to defend his refusal to act earlier to move the squatters out. Amnon was on his knees before the set, urging the interviewer on – 'That's right – go on – you ask him! – Ask him whose fault it is – '

And then came the inevitable pictures of the wounded in hospital, and that was when Amnon, looking at their white, shocked faces and bandages and legs in traction, suddenly flung himself back on his mattress and shouted in a voice of anguish:

'I want to feel sorry for them! I want to hate the shits who did it! But they are the shits – lying there! Oh damn it all to hell! The Jews are the shits now . . .'

Ann walked on through the heat, watching her sandals, pushing them forward, one by one. If you want an oppressor, she thought, choose a victim. Only it's not that simple this time, of course it's not. One of the saddest indicators was that a rational man like Amnon, a humanist, an anti-bigot, could himself become so one-sided, could be pushed by his guilt feelings so far to one extreme . . . He wouldn't listen to any counter-arguments, even the ones that might make him feel better . . . And there were others like him. Shula . . . Ruth . . .

Ruth. That's where she'd go. Yemin Moshe, the district Ruth and Elihu lived in, was marginally nearer than Amnon's. Their door was always unlocked. She could just creep in, if they were resting (Ruth always took the phone off the hook between one and four, while the children napped) fling herself down on their divan and sleep herself till they got up. Then she could use their phone to try to fix up an interview this evening – they might even have some useful suggestions. After that she could relax with a clear conscience and just . . . be with them. *They* usually managed to find something to talk about apart from politics and battles – art, for example. Not that that, too, hadn't got its militant aspects . . . But knitting! Oh, blessed knitting! How could that be a source of contention? It was what Ruth did for a living, to supplement Elihu's fluctuating (usually downward) income. On a huge machine at one end of their small living-room, she turned out amazing and unique creations and sold them to the smarter boutiques. *Yes*, thought Ann, enough of all this burning intensity! We English aren't built for it. I shall go to Ruth and Eli's and have a kip, then drink mint tea, admire the latest bits of knit-couture and let Ruth bore me into a happy stupor about the children . . .

She looked up at the sky. It was the colour of dirty sheep's wool and had the same stuffy, oily look. The trees in the gardens moved tiredly, stirring the dusty air. Ann's throat hurt when she tried to swallow. Her shins and heels were beginning to get painfully rough, and her thighs chafed as she walked.

But despite the discomfort of every movement, the beauty still distracted her. The unique colour and texture of the stone walls, the flowers spilling over their tops, the worn-to-satin desert coloured flags under her feet, the passing shapes of the buildings . . . Hadn't Amos Oz, the novelist, said somewhere that the New City was an act of communal creativity? He'd said, if Ann remembered rightly, that there were four, to be set in the reckoning against any loss of individual Jewish creativity in the Diaspora, as bemoaned by those who accused the Israelis of sacrificing the unique Jewish contribution to culture to become 'a nation of peasants and soldiers'. What were the four? Jerusalem rebuilt; Hebrew revivified; the kibbutz movement of land settlements . . . The fourth escaped her, tantalisingly, because she suspected it had been the most interesting and controversial.

As she walked through the new park, past the Windmill and down the wide, shallow steps into Yemin Moshe, she had the usual difficulty pulling her eyes away from the magnetic view across the valley, of Suleiman's Old City walls and the Jaffa Gate, to the nearer architectural felicities. Despite certain misgivings, it was impossible to resist the charm of this quarter, a charm more often associated with antiquity than with buildings put up in the past ten years . . . So much was written in outrage about what had been built in Jerusalem since '67 – the Wolfson Monstrosities, the 'fortress suburbs', the 'Phal-ton' Hotel and its equally uncircumcised brother, the Moriah . . . But Ann had no inherent prejudices against skyscrapers; on the contrary, if not too slabby (there was an outlying bit of Haifa University, shrieking out of the Carmel Hills, that she longed to dynamite), they could inspire her. She didn't object to skylines jagged with the results of man's entirely proper endeavour to soar, as distinct from horizons smooth with nature's inclination to hug the centre of gravity.

That being so, Yemin Moshe could scarcely fail with her, even though she knew the little villas, crowded in carefully orchestrated disorder along the golden alleys, had been built chiefly to appeal to rich Americans, and was, in consequence, only partly occupied much of the year. Thus it was lacking in some basic reality: it was more like a showplace than a genuine community, as it had been in the days before '67. *Then* its front-line position facing the Jordanian guns across the valley had meant that only the poor would live there, which was how Ruth and Eli had come . . . Though they never said so, Ann realised that they were sometimes very hard up. She wondered how they were coping with inflation at a hundred and thirty per cent. Even Amnon, who got a good salary from Sir Muddy plus a share of any profits, was feeling the pinch . . . Ann remembered that only last year, the freezer section of Amnon's fridge had been stuffed with frozen steaks and turkey schnitzels. This year it contained a solitary packet of peas and three ice-lollies.

What wouldn't she give for an ice-lolly right now! She was relieved to find herself thinking of her stomach, something she did a great deal at home but not nearly so much here. She always managed to lose weight here, no matter how much she ate, and it wasn't just sweating it off, it was . . . well, tension generally, and activity, mental and physical, she supposed, though secretly she suspected it was all part of the thing she had noticed while looking at her face this morning. She was better looking here because she was healthier. At home she ate and drank too much and sometimes Peter would comment on it and hint that she should diet. Her attempts to do so invariably failed, until a trip to Israel was in prospect. Then, mysteriously, she could diet easily, cut out drink almost entirely, live on eggs and cottage cheese, and in two weeks she'd be feeling a new woman, and looking it.

Before she'd left this time, Peter had come upon her in their bedroom, standing in profile before the long mirror, frankly admiring herself. He'd stopped in the doorway and looked at her with an unreadable expression on his face.

'Look how slim I am! I've lost over half a stone.'

'Yes. I see you have.'

Something in his voice made her swing round.

'What?'

'What, what? Nothing. You look very nice. Very – young.'

Danger. Neither of them liked to be reminded that Peter was over sixty. Ann said instantly, 'Well! You wanted me to lose a bit, and I have. Be pleased.'

'But you didn't lose it because I asked you to.'

After a moment she said, 'Yes I did.'

'No. You lost it for the Jews.'

He had turned and walked out, his still straight back somehow expressive of the sadness of unreasoning jealousy, as his voice had been. What was at the root of his resentment exactly? Surely he didn't think that her obsession with Israel, the avidity with which she grasped at every opportunity to run there, was a woodpile which concealed any one particular Jew? No, he couldn't think that, because deception was not part of her nature and not part of their relationship. Even in small, wifely matters – extravagance, a serious breakage, a minor disaster with the car – things she might have meant to hide from him, at least till she picked her moment, she couldn't. She would come out with them the minute she saw him, like a child. 'You're a full-frontal personality,' he told her once, tenderly . . . No. It couldn't be that kind of jealousy. He knew all about Menachem and that since then there had been nobody, that there was never likely to be anybody else, now. Forty-nine . . . A woman didn't start having extra-marital affairs at that age if she hadn't been more or less in the habit of it. Even when her husband was . . . (Ann groped for a word which would not belittle him, even in her thoughts) . . . slowing down a little. She had never expected another Menachem. The main thing, after all, was companionship. Those four terrible years alone had taught her her priorities.

The door of the Gilboas' house was unlocked, as Ann had expected; but there was no somnolent silence within.

The moment she pushed the door open, Ruth, who had been sitting on the divan between two men, jumped up with her face alight.

'A big miracle happened here!' she cried in biblical Hebrew. Everyone stopped talking, which they had been doing more or less simultaneously, and looked towards Ann. Ruth pounced on her and led her forward like a farmer parading his prize milker.

'Who needs a phone?' she said. 'I've been trying to ring you for hours, but we are so attuned, you caught my thoughts and came through the heat at my call . . .'

She smiled her lively, plump smile. She was short and a bit dumpy, with her hair piled on her head and skewered there with long old-fashioned pins which she was forever scattering and then collecting up again, as other women empty ashtrays or plump cushions while they talk. The more excited she got, the more the hairpins flew, and in consequence the more strands of hair escaped, giving her a perpetually scatty, ungrown-up look. She wore owlish glasses over pale blue eyes, and her face, in contrast to her girlish, impetuous manner, was as lined as Shula's, though the lines were not as harsh.

Now she announced: 'Here she is! Ann, meet some of my old comrades. The tough-guys who did not call off! We're going to have our picnic here, and just pretend we are at Kastel – '

Ann was led round and introduced. The names were all the old names – the names the pioneers of the 'forties changed to, from the Carls and Wolfgangs, the Harrys and Simons of their origins. Chaim, Shimshon, Reuven, Ephraim . . . era-signals. Nobody was giving their sons those names a generation later. All Ann's pupils of the early 'sixties had names from the new era; the old ones had begun to have a stale, old-fashioned ring, an echo of the Diaspora. So it was all Yuvals and Yorams and Odeds and Gioras. By now there would be still others . . . Only a few perennials, David, Yonothan, Daniel, survived the changing fashions.

For Ann's part, she warmed at once to the old names. Her own 'comrades', in the kibbutz, had had names like them, and indeed these men might have stepped straight out of a kibbutz. Perhaps they had . . . Certainly they all had what Ann privately categorised as 'the kibbutz look'. It was hard to define without sounding, even to herself, absurdly biased in their favour; but the fact was that although they were all in their fifties and unblessed with anything remarkable in the way of conventional good looks, each of them was, in his way, attractive to Ann. Height and bulk had little to do with this – oddly, for she had a predisposition toward tall men and an aversion to fat ones. But added girth in men with the 'kibbutz look' did not rate as fatness because there was nothing flabby or gone-to-seed about it, nothing to indicate that the man had lost his self-discipline. It was simply a thickening of muscle, an underlining of the stockiness that the shorter ones had always had. In the tall ones, grey hair and the lines on the faces simply enhanced the basic emanation of strength and, in some indefinable way, inner health.

Masculinity, thought Ann as she shook hands with them one by one. *That is the essence of it.* They radiated it, and Ann could not help but bask. Not one Englishman in a thousand that she saw or met gave her such a sense of her own womanliness as she got from shaking hands with these old Palmachniks, who were now gazing at her appraisingly. As she met the eyes of each of them she saw that they paid her the ordinary basic compliment of acknowledging her femininity. Not in any predatory way. They were not going to try to get off with her. But they will kiss me when we say goodbye today, she thought. And they'll also invite me – each one of them, I know it – to visit them in their homes, to meet the wives and families they adore, and that is part of their way of communicating with me as an attractive woman. It will be like saying to me, 'You appeal to me as a woman, so I'll show you and share with you my love life and its products. This will be all the explanation you will need of why I can't make approaches to you, as I might very well do if we were both free, because you find charm in my eyes.'

Someone bent over her and put a cold drink into her hand. She looked up swiftly – it was Eli, tall and grey as a heron, and as remote and shy. Yet he touched her arm as he gave her the drink, and smiled a direct message of warmth and welcome at her before withdrawing into his usual quiet corner, out of the mêlée of talk. Ann felt moved, as always, by this silent man, and especially by the way he reached out from his introvert's fortress with a smile or a touch, making an exception of her.

The lively talk Ann had interrupted with her arrival had swelled up again and now closed over her head. She had little hope that any of it would be usable for her book, though this had been Ruth's original idea – to bring her together with some old fighters and let her get their stories. But Ann knew from experience that, politely as they had all changed to English for her benefit, this would wear off when the conversation hotted up. On past form of such gatherings this should, she reckoned, occur in between three and five minutes' time. Another reason was that when five Israelis – six if you counted Eli – got together and began reminiscing about past wars, or talking upon any subject whatever, the resulting overlap or simultaneity of dialogue would render any form of recording, mechanical, manual or mental, out of the question.

Still, she took out her notebook. She had not yet fixed in her mind the structure her book would take. It might be long interviews or it might be excerpts under different headings – sitting with Shula this morning, one possible heading had come to her: the Traumas of War. Amnon's story about the sweet papers could come under the Trivia of War. She let her mind wander alliteratively . . . trials, truths, tragedies . . . No. Affected and self-conscious, also almost certainly unworkable. And the last category would be overloaded. Though to judge by present company, one would have to include 'Triumphs and Treasures' as well! They were all fairly revelling in the more positive memories of their individual wars . . . She quietly opened her notebook.

No traumas here. No tragedies. Just little nuggets of memories, the stories they had told over and over again, 'with advantages', until they had become part of each man's personal legend. Was it any wonder wars went on being fought? There was always this element of delight, of mischief, of thrill in them . . . She had noticed it from the beginning of the assignment; it was as easy as pressing a button. 'Tell me about the war . . .' It never failed. Even Peter, who claimed to hate war and to have loathed every moment of his service with a deep, gut-loathing, could be induced without difficulty to dust off the old desert-rat tales in the right company . . . So far only Shula had exuded disgust for the whole business, and even she had not refused to talk. The profound need to talk was still there, thirty, forty years later – it would die only with the participants. Perhaps not even then . . . Old soldiers often die, but their memoirs linger on. It must mean something.

The talk lapsed into rapid Hebrew. Ann scribbled: 'What does it all come down to? Why *another* book? What am I catering to, isn't it a kind of pandering to something we'd do better to suppress? Who wants to read all these war books (all those mail-orders Peter gets, from young and old, all over the world!). Why? Why do kids play war? What is important in it? Is it possible that war does people good – that it's an essential element of human equilibrium? Which means that women need it too – Christ – ' She stopped writing.

What, she asked herself, do people really want? Is it peace – contentment – a civilised veneer? Tolerance? Leisure? A quiet life? Kindness and decency, sound institutions, a knowledge that it will all be there tomorrow? Of course. Of course that is what people want. Every sane person would agree to that without even considering the alternative . . .

But even while one looks at this image of human aspiration and human exchange, a mental picture comes. A mythical country in a cliff-walled valley, where there is no word for 'war' or 'hate' or any of the negative, despicable, destructive things; and up those cliffs, like a fly, a little figure clambering, desperate to escape . . . Candide, who, despite the horrors he had experienced in his young life before finding himself in this emotionally immaculate haven, got his surfeit of its perfections and then found it unendurable.

All Ann had ever heard or read about war pointed ineluctably to the fact that participants enjoy at least parts of it, that their loudly declared revulsion from it afterwards was to some extent a self-deceptive pose. Even Englishmen, so civilised, moderate and – somehow – domesticated, were not different in this respect from the men here; or war films would have no audiences, re-union dinners no attendants, proud parades to cenotaphs would wither and die – and Peter's war book business would cease to make money. Eagerness as war approached, lifelong nostalgia as it receded – that was the almost universal pattern, even among those who swore they detested everything about it.

And where do women fit into the picture? The matronly harpies of the First World War, pressing white feathers into the hands of total strangers, might seem very far off, but there had been no Lysistratas lately either.

Was part of the attraction of all these men – and Peter – for her, the fact that they had *not* been conscientious objectors, that they had had guts enough, and masculinity enough, to fight when they

66

had to, and kill when they had to? If England were attacked, and young men in large numbers turned pacifist and refused to defend their freedom, what stood between it and the tyrant except a Cruise missile?

She sat musing. Ruth crept up to her, crouched by her chair and squeezed her hand. 'Do you like them?'

'Yes, they're lovely. They're like Menachem . . .'

'You still think of him. After all this time.'

'Only sometimes. When I'm here, mostly. It's like coming back to his planet from mine. You haven't been back to the kibbutz?' She always asked that.

'No. I told you. I don't believe in going back, anywhere, ever. And you shouldn't, either.'

Why are you so anxious to stop me from going back? Ann wondered. What is it you don't want me to see or find out?

'Tell me about these men,' she said, to change the subject.

'Ephraim – that one – ' Ruth pointed with her eyes. 'I haven't seen for years until a month ago. It's sad you weren't here for our reunion . . . We go every April to Kiryat Anavim, where the Palmach cemetery is, for a remembrance ceremony. You know, I was standing by the roadside, in my white shirt that we always wear to remind us of those days, and a car drove up, and there was Ephraim. He knew by my shirt where I was going, but he'd forgotten me. I said, "Why have you come this time? You never come." It must be twenty years I didn't see him at the reunion. And he said, "This year I felt like apologising to our dead." ' Two hairpins slid from her bun, though her head was held still, and she fumbled for them on the tiles, still looking at Ann to see if she had understood.

Ann was staring at Ephraim. He seemed full of life and good cheer at the moment. How extraordinary, when he was capable of the despair behind that story, that remark!

'Where does he live?'

'Tel Aviv.'

'He left his kibbutz, then.'

'Yes . . . Like so many of us . . . But it stays in you somewhere. You may be much happier, more fulfilled in town. But there is always that, in the background . . .'

'And guilt? For leaving?'

'Yes, that too. We all have that. Even you.'

Why *even* me? Because I'm not a Jew?

'Ruth – '

'Yes?'

'Have you ever heard of a man called Boaz Shachterman?'

'Who?'

'Boaz Shachterman,' Ann repeated, a little louder above the hubbub of voices. The man sitting nearest to her turned his head.

'No,' said Ruth. 'Was he in the Palmach?'

'No.'

'In *Khish*, then? Where did he fight?'

'He wasn't in the '48 War, he'd have been too young.'

'So why are you asking about him? I thought you were only interested in fighters from the '48 War.'

'It doesn't matter. He's just someone I met a couple of times.'

I'll bet Shula knows him. She knows everyone. Ruth specialises in the Palmach. I should have asked Shula.

CHAPTER 6

Due to the heat, nobody had much appetite for the picnic – a splendid array of refreshing dairy foods, appropriate for *Shavu'oth*, which Ruth produced from the fridge at teatime. This was sad because she'd clearly been to a lot of trouble, and, Ann guessed, spent too much for her family's narrow purse.

At the first clink of plates, the children awoke from their naps and came tumbling, bleary-eyed, into the room. Doron, blond as a Dane and thus known sardonically to his parents as King Olaf, aged seven, was their own child, born to Ruth in her forty-second year. Tamar, aged three, had been picked up by Ruth's mother, who did part-time welfare work at a state-run children's home, and subsequently adopted by the Gilboas. She was as 'black' as Doron was blond, the one-too-many of an overburdened Moroccan mother, who had produced her and then disappeared from the hospital, leaving her to her fate.

Ann watched the faces of the old campaigners light up as she was passed from hand to hand, being fed, petted and admired by the entire company. It was impossible not to compare this child-centred scene with what would be likely to happen in a middle-class English living-room if two little children in their underwear, one with wet pants, had burst thus into a serious-minded adult gathering. Here, the small intruders, simply by their arrival, became equal participants in everything that was going on. They were not appendages to the grown-up world; they were its kernel.

Having made the rounds and received their due from everyone present, Doron took a dish of salt-sticks and went out onto the small balcony overlooking the Valley to play. This involved the opening of the shutters and french windows and the inrush of hot air from outside; but nobody objected.

Meanwhile wet-bottomed Tamar selected Ann's knee to sit on. Ruth handed her a clean pair of pants, saying, with the air of one conferring a favour, 'You can change her, she won't mind.' Ann accomplished this with Tamar's co-operation while the men looked on, smiling benignly as if at some engaging form of entertainment which touched their hearts. Then, with one accord, they stopped talking about the war and began talking about their children and grandchildren.

Ann dropped the wet pants behind her chair and settled Tamar on her lap. The hot little body made her hotter, if possible; the impulse to put her own comfort first was shamingly strong, and grew stronger when Eli brought a tub of *shemenet* for Tamar to eat. This proved a messy process for both of them. As the cream transferred itself first to Tamar's face and next to Ann's dress, Ann's hands tightened on Tamar's waist, preparatory to lifting her onto the floor.

But suddenly the man sitting nearest to her (Shimshon, it was) leaned to her and said, 'One can see you have kids. How many? Have you photos?' It was an accolade, however undeserved, that Ann found so irresistible in the present atmosphere that her self-centredness gave way. The pushing-off grip yielded to a cuddle.

'I haven't a photo here,' she hedged.

'Tell me about them.'

Ann hesitated. To tell the truth would be to set herself apart from these people whom she felt so strong a need to identify with. Yet it went against the grain to lie to a man like this, with his open face, his 'kibbutz look' which had, the whole afternoon, stood Menachem at her very shoulder.

'I have a step-son,' she said. Then, as Shimshon smiled encouragingly and waited, she went on slowly, her eyes on Tamar's blue-black hair, 'He's grown-up now, he's twenty-five. My husband was a divorcé. William – that's my step-son – was fifteen when I married. And I was thirty-nine,' she added, flashing the last, unspoken sentence into Shimshon's eyes so that she wouldn't have to explain – 'and that's why I had none of my own.'

But it didn't work.

'My wife was thirty-nine when she had our last one,' he said, with pride verging on smugness. 'A beautiful daughter she gave me – the cream of the crop. Late children are often the best.'

He was getting out a wallet of snaps, and Ann, after wiping her sticky fingers, dutifully took and looked at them one by one. But she was not listening to the verbal captions. She was recalling her struggles with William.

It would be nice if now, ten years later, she were able to console herself with the thought that at least she had been good with her husband's child; but it would be the worst of self-deceptions to claim it. She had been awful with William, and he had been awful right back. Or maybe (to be as just to herself as her memories and honesty allowed) it had been the other way round.

He was never an easy child. His mother's early decampment

70

and Peter's natural reserve had seen to that. He had spent seven years in a boys' boarding-school before he fell to Ann's lot; but as soon as she agreed to marry Peter, William was brought home. 'Now he can have a real family life, poor little devil,' Peter had said, sighing with paternal relief. 'I only hope it's not too late . . .'

But it was. William was at once introverted and aggressive, insecure and arrogant, and withal a sexist of the first order, having had no acquaintance with the female sex beyond a hated matron or two, several remote masters' wives, and (Ann subsequently discovered) a wide-ranging assortment of hard pornography. It would have taken a step-mother with the patience of an angel and the selfless devotion of a Yiddishe mama to have won him over to anything like a co-operative, or even tolerant attitude to her or to womankind in general.

The truth, which she had faced up to long ago (though she had never confessed it to anyone but herself) was that, after an initial period of hard trying, she'd settled for simmering mutual antagonism. There had been breaks in the simmering – eruptions – which still had power to turn her hot and cold. Once, when his dislike of her had goaded him past mere silent contempt and rudeness into open verbal aggression, some deep streak of violence in her nature, usually firmly suppressed, had broken out and she had attacked him physically. A terrible, scalding memory, for he had fought back, glad of the excuse to hurt her. And he had defeated her, of course – how should he not, a strapping sixteen-year-old against a forty-year-old woman?

And she had had to nurse her shame and her bruises in silence, for *this* she could never have told Peter. Her rage, her uncontrollable desire to strike out on that dreadful occasion had taught her something about herself that she would far rather not have known. William's decision to leave home at seventeen had been an unspoken relief of the first magnitude to all of them, and now their mercifully rare family gatherings at least had a veneer of good manners over them, for which Ann was grateful. But she gave herself no credit. The credit belonged to the training William had since received for the Diplomatic Service; it had nothing to do with any softening warmth she had blessed him with during her brief tenure of step-motherhood, nor to any natural sweetness buried in William's own character; it was based on civilised hypocrisy.

Naught for her comfort there, as she sat among proud and loving parents and fell back upon claiming a surrogate son. But

71

William owed her *something* for trying – and repayment in this form cost him nothing! Let him be my stand-in child, she thought, to protect me from their pity for my childless state which I could not bear. It's bad enough that I share so little with them, that I stand so far on the outside of their world which I long to be part of . . . Children are so basic in that world . . . they're the other side of the war coin, she realised suddenly. That's why the conversation flipped over so smoothly. Children are the other thing they all have in common, the deepest core of fear at the heart of war, the thing-to-be-preserved – and the thing that, grown to manhood, will preserve them. A poem of Amichai's, which many readings had fixed in her mind, recited itself to her:

> My father fought their war for four years
> And he didn't hate his enemies or love them.
> But I know, that even there
> He formed me daily out of his little calms
> So rare; he gathered them out of the bombs
> And the smoke,
> And he put them in his frayed knapsack
> With the last bits of his mother's hardening cake.
>
> And with his eyes he gathered name-less dead,
> He gathered many dead on my behalf,
> So that I will know them in his look and love them.
>
> And not die, like them, in horror . . .
>
> And he filled his eyes with them in vain:
>
> I go out to all my wars.

'How well do you know Boaz Shachterman?'

Ann started. Shimshon had thrown it in quite casually, his eyes still on the photos he was remorselessly handing her one by one.

'Not very – Oh, this is a charming one! Isn't she adorable . . . Why, do you know him?'

'I've heard him lecture.'

'Lecture? On what?'

'The West Bank – the Palestinians.'

'Who does he lecture to?'

'Army units . . . anyone who'll invite him. He is full with things he wants to say.'

'How did you hear him?'

'I'm an officer in the reserves. Unfortunately not very high up. I

72

have no authority to choose lecturers – or stop them from being chosen.'

Ann stared at him.

'Would you stop them inviting Boaz Shachterman?'

'I would, yes. Or perhaps not. I mean, censorship is undemocratic, we should not stifle opinions, but . . . I can't pretend I enjoy seeing impressionable youngsters being encouraged, under official – what do you say? – patronage, to believe that the West Bank is strategically vital to Israel, meaning we can never give it up, and that the Arabs who live in it neither want, nor really deserve any kind of real autonomy – '

'Is that what he says?'

'Yes. Why do you think they invite him? There's a lot of uneasiness in the ranks these days. There are boys sitting in prison now – not many, but enough to worry the Government – for refusing to serve in the Occupied Territories. The "Peace Now" people may be a little quiet at the moment, but they had their effect. They aroused a few sleeping consciences, filled up a few areas of ignorance with some of the facts of history . . . Men like Shachterman are needed by the Establishment to restore things to what they were before, to reassure young soldiers that they are on good ground when they patrol the streets of Nablus or take supplies to the Gush settlements . . . It would be awkward if too many of them woke up to what it all really means and what it will surely lead to . . .'

He stood up without excusing himself and went to fetch another bottle of grapefruit juice. Before he came back, another of the men, Ephraim, had got up from the sofa and occupied Shimshon's chair.

'So you are writing a book about the first of our wars,' he said. 'No doubt you believe, from the way we were all talking, that we all had quite a good time in those days.'

'Well . . . it evidently had its moments.'

'Some of it was good. Though you know – '

'What?'

'I don't know. Sometimes I feel badly after such conversations. Most of us do it, we can't help it – talking about it, remembering the comradeship, the good times. I'll tell you an incident. Incidents are the important things, you can see more in an incident remembered for thirty-two years than in whole books about tactics and strategies. Once we were loading shells onto a lorry before a battle. Little shells, you know, we had nothing big at that time, passing them along a chain of us in boxes, stacking them . . . And we were laughing and joking, we were enjoying ourselves. And I thought *then* – really, *at that time*, not later – I thought, we are stacking up death and wounds, and grief, and we are making jokes. Are we human beings? I still ask myself. I'm afraid the answer is, yes. We are. Because that is how human beings behave.'

'I asked my husband once how he coped with having killed people. He said they were a bunch of bloody Huns, he had a healthy hatred for them and he never gave them a thought, then or later.'

'Yes,' said Ephraim slowly, 'It was different, fighting the Germans and fighting the Arabs. I did both . . . I mean, I didn't actually kill Germans because in the British Army I never managed to get into a fighting unit – they saw to that! Anyway, I wouldn't have minded killing Germans, I don't think so. But I never hated the Arabs enough not to mind. Even when we heard the stories . . . You know, mutilating our dead, that sort of thing. Even when I saw it. It is a very horrible thing when you see it for the first time, but my father, who knew Arabs well, he explained it to me – it is not so much a custom, it is their way of carrying on the fight, and in any case only certain tribes do it, they have to be educated to do it. It is not a natural thing with them.'

'A man I spoke to yesterday went on and on about it. He said that sort of behaviour proves that they are almost a different species from the Jews because Jews never do that sort of thing.'

'Was he from Lehi? – the Stern gang?'

'Yes – how did you know?'

Ephraim laughed. 'That's how they all talk. That is *their* education, that's how they justify the things they did. I know a man – he was wounded later and he drinks a lot, for the pain – who told me he used to collect ears. Not in our war – later – but we should not say we are so pure. And one should remember the time, not long ago, when those terrorists were killed in Beit Shean and the Jewish residents burned their bodies and celebrated the flames . . . Shamelessly, enjoying their revenge. They were primitive Jews from North Africa. Yes, and everyone else was shocked. Why? Because this incident forced us to see that such an after-death vengeance is *not* only an Arab speciality, it is, as I said, a matter of cultural background, of education. In the countries those Beit Shean Jews came from, such things were done.'

'Arab countries,' Ann reminded him.

Ephraim smiled. 'You're a woman of mystery,' he said. 'Ruth said you are not Jewish. You are not Israeli. Why you bother yourself at all with such a mess as we are in now, is a puzzle to start with. But I see that you are in worse *shtukh* even than that. You want to find excuses for us. If you want to be reassured that the Jews have special rights that the Arabs don't have, because we are different and better, I am happy to refer you to your friend Shachterman. He is a chauvinist. He will make you feel very comfortable.'

Ann sat in silence for a while. Ephraim watched her with an expression combining rue and sympathy. Finally she said, 'I'm not afraid of the truth, and I prefer active consciences. I feel very uncomfortable with people who are free of doubts, because I've come to believe that doubt is the mark of the intellectual . . .'

Ephraim threw back his head and laughed loudly. 'You are decidedly not one, if you make such a simple definition! Is every kibbutznik an intellectual? Is half of Israel? We are all poisoned by doubt, but many of us are quite stupid as well! Don't you smell doubt in the air like a toxic gas? We have gained a sort of immunity, but I don't know how an outsider like you can breathe it.'

'Don't call me an outsider,' said Ann quietly. 'Even though it's eternally true, I don't like it being said to me.'

'Oh! I apologise. If you can breathe our poisoned air and live, in any case you must be one of us.'

It was six o'clock before the troops reluctantly concluded it was no use waiting any longer for the *sharav* to break, and began heaving themselves to their feet and girding up their loins for the weary drive back to their scattered houses.

Ann received from each the kiss and the invitation that she had anticipated. Ephraim's embrace was particularly warm, and after it he led her out into the narrow street. The sun was getting ready for its abrupt drop below the horizon, and was struggling to press upon the Old City walls across the Valley its golden handshake of light, but it was hindered by the clogging layers of sand and dust raised by the *sharav*. The heat was still intense; somehow the body, conditioned to expect some relief at evening and finding none, resented it more. Ephraim stared balefully at the dust-charged sky.

'Will you come to us, then?'

'If I can. I'd like to. But I'm working. It couldn't be just a social visit. I'd have to interview you properly.'

'I was nothing special in the war. You want people whose rôle was really crucial – people like our Deputy Prime Minister. He was very much of a *mensch* in those days . . . Now he is like El Cid. He is just stuck to that Minister's chair and he has died there and no one has noticed, because he hardly moved or spoke since he got into it . . .'

Ann didn't laugh. She looked at him as he stood there with his hands in his pockets staring bleakly at the bleak sky, and became conscious of a physical ache in her heart, for him and his like, which had been intermittently nagging her, as painful as indigestion, since her arrival in the country.

'If I did interview you, would you tell me why you said that to Ruth, about apologising to the dead?'

His attention snapped back to her. 'At the Reunion? She told you that?'

'Yes.'

He jingled his car keys in his pocket, measuring her.

'Don't you understand it?'

'I think so. But my book is for people who might not.'

'Perhaps you noticed,' he said, 'that we Palmachniks thought well of ourselves. We believed we were – not just the best fighters, but . . . It sounds better in Hebrew, but I will say it: the most pure-hearted. But the truth is, if we were like that, the survivors were just milk, not cream, after all. In our kind of army, where the finest lead the way, it's the finest who don't come back. The rest of us got our lives given to us as a present. *They* would not have let happen what has happened. They would have found a way to stop the rot. I am *sure*, when I think about them, what they were, that they could have stopped it. And if those who lie in Kiryat Anavim could talk, they'd say to us, "We won the war. Did you win the peace?" Well, we didn't, and what is more, if they came back they would look round and ask us what they died for. For *that* I went there to apologise. But even while I stood there among the graves, I thought that I shouldn't have come. It was too – cheap, too easy. I should have been elsewhere, doing something that counted. Like your suffragettes, perhaps – chaining myself to Polombo's Gate, outside the Knesset. But then I thought, what's the use? Even if I set fire to myself on their steps, it would change nothing. And my wife had said, don't be late for supper, or I shall worry . . . There. Now I have saved you a journey.'

He suddenly cleared his throat and straightened himself.

'I must go, it's late. Goodbye.'

He put out his hand to shake hands with her, an odd formality in the midst of their verbal intimacy, as if he had said too much and must push her to a safe distance. But even as they shook hands he changed his grip, so that his fingers curled round the base of her thumb, and she instinctively did the same. Their eyes met again and the years rolled back and it was Menachem, outside that sordid little dockside café, when, after one shared meal and one hour's talk, she already knew she would love him. He had altered his grasp of her hand in just this way, like a Masonic sign.

She squeezed in to the house again, past the crowd still jamming the doorway, to make notes of what he had said. The goodbyes went on for a further ten minutes, while the *khamsin* filled the little house beyond the possibility of subsequent exclusion; but there were so many last things to say. Doron appeared, and then Tamar, necessitating more kisses, handshakes and farewells. At last they were gone, and Ruth was able to close the door and fall full-length onto the divan.

Ann said, 'Shall I wash up?'

'Please,' said Ruth with her eyes shut. 'I am finished, completely.'

Ann and Eli gathered the empty plates and coffee-cups and ashtrays and carried them through to the kitchen, a small annex off the main room. Even here there were evidences of artistry. Eli had carved all the cupboard fronts and made shelves in thick pine which held small abstract sculptures. One was a piece of driftwood, a miniature jewel-tree hung with Hebron beads and twists of metal and coins and 'hands of Fatma' in brass.

'How are things, Eli?'

'Things? What things?' Eli's voice (which, so far as she recalled, she hadn't heard all afternoon) was gruff and strongly accented.

'Your work.'

'Ah. My work!' He shrugged his stooped shoulders, looking more than ever like a heron, hunching its grey wings. 'Well. Sometime I sell a little. Once in a long time I sell a big. Just now I don't sell because May is a bad month. Not many tourists come. But is one good hope.'

'Oh? What?'

'Bronstein.'

'Who's he?'

'You don't hear of Bronstein? The millionaire from Miami?'

'Millionaries are thick on the ground in Miami. What's so special about this one?'

'What is special is he like my work. Very much he like. He

come with his wife every day to my studio. He don't know nothing about pictures, not nothing. But his wife, she know a lot. She tell him all the time how good is my work, she tell him to buy this one and that one. I think maybe, not just they buy for themself, they buy to give to some institute here. He talk about it. He don't want to give more money. He say he don't always like what they do with his money. So now he buy present. A big work which will have his name on it.'

'I trust it will have your name on it too,' said Ann. She was washing while Eli put away. Drying was unnecessary.

Eli smiled slowly at her joke. 'I see that he don't put his name on top of mine,' he said.

'Is it definite that they'll buy?'

'Ann, you don't know rich Americans. They are like big cats with small mice, they play games before they buy and before they give. That is what they do with their life. Another way, for them their money don't give them no fun. So they play with me a long time. They also play with the *irya* – how do you say?'

'The Municipality. How do they play with them?'

'The Bronsteins are guests of the City. They stay in the King David and the Municipality pay.'

'Why? – If they're so stinking rich?'

'*Because* they are stink from rich. It is little fish to catch a big fish. And every day the Bronsteins are sitting at dinner with this man or that one who try to find out what will they give this time, what they want to support. Will they give to build a building or make a park or give scholarship at the University? But I know a secret the *irya* don't know yet. Bronstein don't do nothing of all that. He buy from Elihu Gilboa a picture or sculpture and give it to our Mayor and say him what to do with it.'

Ann could not repress a shriek of laughter. 'And when will His Worship be given this delightful instruction?'

'In one week, they leave, the Bronsteins – they go home to Miami. Before that, will happen what will happen. And *if* it will happen, then we invite you to eat with us at the restaurant of Mishkenot Sha'ananim.'

'Don't go crazy! That'll cost half of what he pays you.'

'You don't know what he pay me. I don't sell my work cheap. I rather not sell than sell cheap.'

Ann knew this already. She had craved one of his oils ever since Ruth had brought him to London twelve years ago to try (unsuccessfully) to arrange an exhibition for him there. Instead Ann had bought a number of his watercolours, which hung in her study.

The reason they hung in her study, and not in some more prominent room in the London flat or indeed in the cottage in Suffolk which was her real home, was because Peter didn't like them. Peter's taste in paintings ran to Constable and Turner and, in more modern vein, Ruskin Spear. But that was not the only reason he didn't like Eli's work. He didn't like Eli.

Doron and Tamar saw to it that Ruth did not actually get any rest. Before the washing-up was finished, she came staggering into the kitchen to get them drinks. Doron had been out in the heat too long and was whingeing. Tamar, totally immune to the *sharav* which the grown-ups now agreed would quite shortly be the death of all of them, demanded a frog-hunt. *'Tsvardaya! Tsvardaya!'* she kept insisting, dragging remorselessly on their arms. It was quite useless to insist that there would be no frogs, that it was not their season, or that they had all gone to bed. She had seen a beautiful speckled frog at her kindergarten, she knew where it had come from and she wanted one in her bath. Eventually Eli, with a martyred sigh, agreed to walk with her towards the Valley in the forlorn hope of locating a frog which had not yet shrivelled to a lump of dried leather.

'Why don't we all go?' suggested Ann innocently. 'It is a bit cooler, surely.'

Ruth eyed her narrowly. 'What is this strange interest you have in frogs all of a sudden?'

'I only thought – '

'I know what you thought. The frogs, if any, are in the Valley, and beyond the Valley is the Jaffa Gate, and through the Jaffa Gate is the *shuk*. But *mottik*, we are not going to the *shuk*, and not just because it is too hot but because I will not go any more into the Old City and you will not persuade me to go.'

Ann heaved a sigh in her turn. She loved the Arab market passionately and she hadn't had a moment this trip to so much as poke her nose through the Gate. 'I don't see why not,' she said mulishly.

'I have explained.'

'Explain again. I don't get it.'

'I will explain while we frog-hunt. Eli, you stay here with Doron.' Eli's martyred look vanished instantly and his beaky face broke into a grin of reprieve. The two women each took a little brown hand in theirs and left the house.

'But no swinging!' Ruth informed Tamar firmly.

At the end of the little street, flights of wide stone steps led up towards the Windmill, and down towards the Valley. Down they went, needless to say swinging Tamar between them down ever-increasing numbers of the shallow steps. At the bottom they turned left and wandered along the Valley's lip, stopping every few yards at olive trees rising, like billowing ash-green sails, from little boat-like structures of stone, while Tamar combed the grass for her frog.

Below, the floor of the Valley was also grassed for most of its length. It was a beautiful sight, a credit to the Municipality, which had turned a hideous no-man's-land into an unspoilt garden. Beyond, up the stony slope, rose the walls built by Suleiman the Great, with David's Citadel as their matchless crown.

'Did you know Ben Gurion wanted to pull those walls down?' Ann asked. Ruth stopped and stared at her.

'He didn't!'

'Yes, after the Six-Day War he was all for pulling them down. To unite the City more effectively.'

Ruth walked on, looking incredulously at the City's chief glory. 'Well. He was very old by then. And even great men have their moments of madness. But he was great. A great leader. My God, Ann,' she burst out suddenly, 'I wish he would come back now, or someone of his quality! I would pull that beautiful wall down myself, stone by stone, if that were the price of a little real leadership! We need it so badly.'

'Israel depends too much on leadership.'

'You think?' Ruth sounded surprised.

'Yes. In a democracy it's supposed to be public opinion that guides the Government, but here it's the other way round. The Government does what it likes, or what it can get away with, and the people may grumble and march and write to the papers, but they put up with it, and in the end Government policy shapes public opinion. Look at the situation now! The polls all tell us the Government is madly unpopular and *everyone*, even former supporters, are dying for it to fall, but it doesn't. Why the hell doesn't it?'

'Because the Prime Minister has been very clever and given important posts to his coalition partners so they won't vote him out of power.'

'That's only a symptom. In a real democracy, the people who voted those so-called coalition partners into the Knesset, with no idea of their propping up a right-wing government, would lean on them so damned hard they'd be forced to give up their perks and bring the Government down. But under this system, they're not answerable to the electorate at all. You should all be kicking up hell about what's going on.'

'That's not how we do things here,' said Ruth tightly, and Ann saw she was hurt, that some subtle barrier of acceptable comment had been crossed. They walked on in silence, and then Ruth thawed a bit and said, 'Anyway, we can't. You don't know how tired we are, how hard it is just to live from day to day in Israel. I don't want to jerk your tears, but really! It takes all my energy just to manage with the children and do my knitting . . . And fear, you know, that takes energy too. Not just fear of war and so on. Every time I go to the shops I have to sit on my fear, because of the prices. They go up every month, Ann, sometimes more often. Where will it end? Sometimes I come home, with my shopping bag never so full as last time, and I leave it on the table and put away just the dairy stuff so it won't go bad, and in one minute I am at my machine, knitting like a mad woman to make more money. Because *we* have no salary going up all the time to keep up with inflation, we just have to work harder. Eli has to lick rich Americans' *tochuses* harder, and American *tochuses* don't taste good to him or help him to do good work. He was not made for that. He's not a businessman, to fight in the rat race – and painting is a rat race here, they must all push themselves and try to push out the other artists to get whatever little bits of sales there are. Whatever little bits of millionaires. All that is tiring, too. And you ask us to march to Knesset and pull down governments! I can hardly march up those steps some days, I am so exhausted with all of it.'

Ann walked with her remorse, swallowing and digesting it. She loved Ruth. But deep down some fierce stubborn voice in her said, If people like you are passive, all that you fear will only get worse. But who am I – childless, English, inflation at a mere twenty per cent – to dare to tell you so?

Ruth stopped, looking round. 'Tamar! *Bo-i, Bubele, ayn sham shum tsvardaya!* Really, it's like waiting at every tree for a dog to do its peepee.' Tamar came running on her little fat legs and they strolled on through the dwindling light. 'It'll be dark soon. She'll have to give up and then we can turn back.'

Ann didn't want to turn back. For all the talk of the day, she was not yet satiated. 'Why won't you go to the Old City?'

'I've told you. I won't go because I don't like to be where I am

81

not wanted.'

'What makes you think you're not wanted? Times are hard. Surely they want buyers.'

'Even when they take my money I can feel their hate.'

'I don't feel it, at least I didn't last year.'

'You are not Jewish.'

'They don't know that.'

'They know you are not Israeli.'

'How? I bet any Israeli who can speak English speaks to them in English and not Hebrew, so how could they know?'

Ruth was silent for a while, her eyes on the Jaffa Gate, lit up at the end of the Valley like the entrance to Shangri-La.

'It's not *what* you speak to them. It's how.'

'What do you mean?'

'I remember when we were there together last April, and you wanted that table with the brass top, you remember? And that merchant was asking a price from you that was ridiculous. And instead of laughing at his *chutzpah* and walking away and letting him call you back, what did you do? You told him it was absolutely a fair price for such a beautiful thing and that you would not dream of asking him to take less but that it was much more than you could pay, and in the end he was begging you to take less. The more you praised his table and his honesty the more he lowered his price until you got it for half. No Israeli praises an Arab's goods or refuses to doubt his honesty in business the way you did.'

'But that's just my way of bargaining. I learnt it buying jewellery from the worst rogue in the antique business – a Persian Jew.'

'You didn't learn it from him. You learnt it from something inside yourself which is English, English, English, and not Jewish, and not Middle Eastern, and certainly not Israeli. You may say it's just your way of getting the price down but it is a way that comes out of your deep wish not to insult people or hurt their feelings. For that to work, you must have no hidden hostility. *I* don't wish to insult the Arabs either. Our being here at all is insult enough to them. But I cannot flatter them because deep down I *know* they are trying to cheat me, I know they would cut my neck if they could. I fear them and that is another good reason for not going through that gate, because one day there will be a sniper or a bomb or just a stone . . .'

She didn't complete the sentence. She turned round in her tracks and set off for home and Ann followed her.

'You did agree to go last year,' Ann reminded her.

'Last year was last year and this year is this year. This year we have settlements all over Samaria and Judea and they hate us worse than they ever did before, they hate us so that their wish to sell us things is not so strong to hide their hate, like it did even only one year ago. I see it in their faces, I feel it against my back as I walk past. Do you think I don't love the Old City? Listen, even when all my neighbours told me I would get ill from eating their fruit and vegetables – my mother washed everything I brought home from there in detergent – even their meat I bought sometimes, though I never told Eli where it came from. I shopped there *not* just because it was so exciting. It was because I thought, that's the way to make it work between us and them, to mix with them, trade with them, not to keep separate. I thought, if we are using them to build our buildings and do our dirty jobs, if they are good enough to work for us, they are good enough to buy from and to smile while you buy. So I tried to feel at home in the Old City, and I smiled, and when they smiled back I thought, You see, it's possible, we depend on each other, we're neighbours and we can live together if we try. But I was stupid. They were just waiting.'

'For what?'

'For us to get a government like this one that will push them to have more anger. So they can get up their courage to come out in the open with the hate they feel. Now we give it to them. With more land grabs, with more blowing up houses, more arrests, shooting them when they demonstrate in the villages. With those religious hooligans in Hebron. And now what – we send their leaders across the border, to make propaganda against us abroad . . . With all this we put a fuse to the bomb that has been thirteen years in their bellies, and soon it will blow up.' She turned back suddenly and pointed with a tense, straight arm at David's Tower. 'Now you see it,' she said loudly. 'Boom! Now you don't.'

Ann took her arm as it dropped, and felt it tremble. She tugged gently and Ruth let herself be drawn on. It was dark now. Tamar trotted ahead. Suddenly she gave a cry and darted aside, into the grass and wilting weeds by the roadway.

'What, *mottik*, what is it?' Ruth asked.

'*Tsvardaya!*' she cried in triumph – and held up the most beautiful frog Ann had ever seen: cream and olive green, with golden eyes, badly in need of a bath.

CHAPTER 7

Ann didn't stay to supper. She felt they needed to be on their own.

'I'll be over when I can,' she said. 'Thank you for a wonderful afternoon.'

'On the hills at Kastel, it would have been better,' Ruth said stubbornly.

'You know what, Ruth? I'm not that sorry we couldn't go to Kastel. I'd like to go there, but not for a picnic. The ground . . .'

'There's hardly any ground here that has not drunk blood, if that's what you're thinking. Perhaps picnics heal its wounds.'

'Family picnics maybe. I don't know about old soldiers' picnics.'

'Where you go now?' asked Eli as she gathered up her things.

'To the theatre, I think.'

'You don't need a shower?'

'I do need a shower, I need two showers, but Tamar and her frog are in residence.'

'You should have said – '

'Children and frogs first. Never mind, I'll survive . . .' She stood on tiptoe to kiss him. 'Good luck with Bronstein. Let me know.'

He gave her his enigmatic grin and hunched his wings.

Outside the street lights stuck their necks out from corners of the little houses, the bold floodlights blazed from across the Valley. The sky lowered overhead, thick with sand-motes. Ann walked up to the road, her hold-all heavy in her hand. Something was worrying her. She must try to get some Arabs. It was so hard to achieve anything like balance, standing where she did . . . She didn't want to perpetuate the myth that only the Jews had fought, only the Jews had defended their homes and land, only the Jews had right on their side . . . But why should they speak to her, a known Zionist, why should they trust her impulse to be fair?

She found Boaz Shachterman in her mind again, waiting, offering her a way in to the West Bank, to Arab notables. Notables? She wasn't sure she wanted 'notables'. She had seen for herself how they hid behind rhetoric and dogma, how they contradicted even themselves, confused and unmanned by their impossible positions as 'leaders' without jurisdiction, without real authority, ultimately at the mercy of the two grindstones between which they were constantly being pressed – the Israeli Military occupiers, who threatened their freedom and their positions if they spoke out openly against the occupation or appeared to be preaching revolution among their followers, and the P L O, which menaced their lives if they dared to raise their heads as independent Palestinian leaders or neglected to pay the terrorist organisation lip service.

Shachterman, that day on the West Bank, had said as they drove homeward, 'Of course, they don't really support the P L O, they just see them as their best chance to get rid of us. What they can't be made to see – because they're too frightened of Arafat and Habash – is that, until they *are* willing to divorce themselves from the P L O, we couldn't hand over autonomy to them even if we wanted to.'

'But if they dared try to negotiate with the Israelis, they'd be shot.'

'But *until* they do, there is nothing to talk about and nobody to talk to, and all the half-baked ideas of you and your idiot peace-niks are just a bad joke.'

'How can they be expected to stand up as moderates, at the risk of their lives?'

Schachterman had suddenly scared the wits out of her by opening his mouth and roaring at the top of his lungs: '*Why the fuck not?* Where has there ever been an occupied people who have not risked their lives? Algeria? Cuba? Indonesia? If they really wanted their freedom – and I mean their freedom to be independent of the P L O murderers as well as of us – they would fight for it! Do you know where I would be now if I were a Palestinian living under occupation? I would be *there* – ' he pointed – 'there, behind that rock, with a stolen hand-grenade or a molotov cock-tail, getting ready to blow up this car with its Israeli number-plate! That's how the Jews fought against the British. But then, the Jews *really* wanted independence. "At the risk of their lives" – yes! That's how all fighting is done!'

'Would you really like a full-blown underground insurrection-ist movement here with all that that would involve?'

He had looked at her as if she had lost her wits. 'It's not a question of what *I*'d like, but of what *they* want!' he shouted. '*I* don't care a shit for them. I care for Israel, and Israel needs this area, and we must hang on to it. Of course it's better for us if they are passive. But we would have to do what was necessary, *what-ever* was necessary. We had better be oppressors, as bad as you like – not as we've been till now, but real oppressors – than give

85

up these highly strategic hills. It's better to be a villain than a dead man.'

'You're serious? Wouldn't it be preferable, for Israel, to try a Palestinian state, than to become – tyrants?'

'A Palestinian state!' he had roared. 'Never! It would be absolute insanity, we might as well give up our country and jump into the sea like so many lemmings!'

He had taken a curve far too fast as he spoke, throwing her against the door of his old car. It had come open, giving her the worst moment of physical fear of her life; the car was hurtling round a bend on a hillside with a deep drop below. For a split second she had hung above it, the centrifugal pressure sucking her out irresistibly. But then his hard right hand had caught her, yanking her back; his foot slammed on the brake at the same moment, and she had ended up across his chest with her ribs bruised by the steering-wheel and her head by the far door-frame. The afterwave of panic was still drowning her as if in a bath of fire, and his angry, trembling hands were gripping more bruises on to her. It was not a moment to forget easily.

A year later, the fear, and the relief, flushed over her again, causing her to stumble. It disturbed her to think she had only to pick up a phone and dial to hear his dark voice growling at her . . .

No. He was dangerous. What she'd heard today had confirmed it.

The buses had begun to run again when the Feast officially ended at sunset, but they were still few and far between. She couldn't walk any more, however; she was footsore. She stood at the bus stop near the King David and waited for a number 18 to carry her to the Jaffa Road, or for a taxi. They were a long time coming. Fortunately there was a bench. She fell asleep on it, leaning against one of the thick metal pipes that held up the aged shelter; it felt cool against her temple.

She woke with a jump to a fearful outburst of noise. A little old lady was standing almost on her feet, gripping a dark youth by the arm and screeching at him: 'Thief! Thief!' The boy was looking desperately about him, pulling to get away, but she was clinging to his arm with all her strength and kicking his shins. As Ann jumped to her feet, she saw him, *in extremis*, raise his free hand to the old lady, whereupon she let out a scream louder than any previously.

'Would you hit an old woman? You don't have any limits? First you rob, then you strike? Be ashamed, be ashamed!' Then, seeing

Ann awake and potentially her ally, she screeched: 'Help me hold the young thief, it was you he was stealing from! Stop him, hold him, call the police! They're never where they're wanted!'

Too late. As Ann, still in a daze, moved indecisively to help, the boy broke free and fled across the park, clearing the lumps of decorative stone with ungainly leaps, and vanished over the brow of the hill. The old lady stood panting and raging, trembling like a leaf, tears running down her cheeks.

'Call themselves Jews!' she cried, and spat on the pavement. 'They are *dreck*! Filth! Animals! Like him it's a pity we didn't leave in their caves! They are spoiling everything. Once we need not lock our doors, now we are not safe in the streets!'

Ann put her arm round her and made her sit on the bench. 'But what was he doing?' she asked in her stilted Hebrew.

'I saw him! I saw him! He was putting his hand in your bag. He was going to steal from you. But I stopped him! I gave him a good fright, anyway!' She was getting calmer. Ann dried her tears with her own much-abused headscarf.

'It was very brave of you. He might have hurt you.'

The old lady made a gesture of contempt, blowing through her lips. Then she picked up Ann's hold-all and began rummaging in it. 'You have something valuable in here?'

'Yes. My tape recorder and my camera. And my wallet.'

The old lady looked up, beaming.

'You see? What I saved for you! I chased him off! He won't try that again in a hurry!'

'I bet he won't. Pity there aren't more like you.'

'I get so furious. I don't stop to think. One day I'll get into real trouble,' she said proudly. 'My sons keep telling me, "Ima, don't interfere. Mind your own business. You think everything that happens in the country is your business – it's not. Things have gone too far, and you're old now, you can't fight everybody." Of course I take no notice of them. How can I change at my age? I've always interfered, I've always been a fighter. I can't bear to see the things that go on. If I see something wrong, whether it's small or big, I can't just pass by, I have to do something. Even if it's dangerous. That's my nature. I tell my sons, I can't change. If your generation would fight like mine, things would not have got so bad. There wouldn't be young men who should be working to build the country, stealing from women in the streets. How could anyone pass by and not do anything?'

'I'm very glad and grateful that you didn't.'

'Well,' she said, handing back the hold-all, 'at least you appreciate the risk I took. My sons don't. When I'm carried home in an ambulance one day, they won't appreciate it, they'll just say, "You see, Ima? What did we tell you? That's what comes of butting in!" That's all the thanks I get.' She sniffed deeply.

'How old are your sons?'

'Michael is thirty-eight and Dov is forty. What do they know? They are too young to know anything that matters. I should have had them a few years earlier. You know that nobody under forty-five, forty-six knows the things that matter.'

'What things? What do you mean?'

The old woman looked at her speculatively.

'How old are you?' she asked, using the Hebrew phrase which literally means, 'A daughter of how much are you?' For the first time Ann heard it as meaning, 'How much of a woman are you? By your years shall you be measured.'

'I'm forty-nine.'

'Ah well. That's all right. You are on the right side of the border. You remember how things were before.'

'Before?'

'Before we had a state. There, under the Germans. Here, under the British. My sons don't know what it means to be pushed around by the *goyim*. They take independence for granted. All *they* have as a goal is to make Israel like America. They want to be rich and to travel and to buy lots of junk to fill their big flats with. The jobs they do! The things they discuss! The rubbish in their heads! And their wives! Well, you can't blame my boys for choosing such silly girls, where are any other kind these days? Women's liberation! They don't know what it means, even. They never fired a gun. They never bandaged a wound. They never buried a dead person who'd been lying three days in the sun. They leave that to the men. They think wars are fought just to save their lives! Even so, they are not prepared to bloody their hands.'

'Did you fight, in '48?'

The old lady – who was actually not all that old, about sixty-five, but with snowy hair and many wrinkles, and the camp number on the underside of her forearm – gave Ann the same measuring look she had received from Ephraim.

'In that time,' she said, 'women used to be part of *everything*. That was what we wanted. We were prepared to take part in the hatred and the bloodshed and the sweating with fear as well, why shouldn't we? Weren't we Jews? Why should our men do it all?

Why should they earn our country alone? We understood in those days, we had *seen*, we had *lived* what it meant not to have a place, to be *untermenschen*. We were willing to jump into it all up to our necks because we knew what the war was for. We couldn't stand aside – any more than I could, just now. It was more than a matter of values, it was a matter of instinct. We weren't just fighting to save our skins. We were fighting to save our souls.'

'But they didn't let you, did they? – the men.'

'They did. At first. But after a while, a new kind of man came into our army. It was not just young socialist idealists any more, our comrades – it was men from the towns, from the camps in Cyprus, in Europe. They couldn't get used to seeing women fighting. They wouldn't stand for them as officers. They wouldn't take their orders from a woman, however good she was. So they stood us down. That was the beginning.'

'Of what?'

'Of what has ended up with my daughters-in-law. Women who have nothing in their heads or their lives but shiny furniture and cream *tortes*.'

'And their children.'

The old woman shrugged.

'I had my boys already by '48. I gave them to my mother and I volunteered. Golda said it. There are moments when even one's children take second place.' She sat still for a moment, gazing into the dark street, watching the cars go by. 'My mother once asked me. "Which is more important to you, your country or your children?" I tried to get out of it. "The one is for the other," I said. But she insisted. "Which comes first with you?" I never answered her. But she knew. She didn't agree with me, but perhaps she understood. She had survived the camps too. One can have more children. But for what, if they have no place, no upright life, nothing to dedicate themselves to or fight for? Lives are precious, but they are not – ultimate things. Irreplaceable values. Eretz Israel is. At least,' she added, 'so it seemed to me then.' A long silence followed, and at last she broke it with a profound sigh. 'Here comes your bus at last,' she said. 'And I have talked too much.'

She stood up. Ann couldn't think of a thing to say to her. She couldn't even look at her, somehow. She muttered thanks as the bus drew up and then, as the doors hissed shut between them, she looked back and down. The old lady under the bus shelter nodded and lifted her hand, and the bus drew away along King George.

The theatre was awkward to get at. There was no direct bus route from the New City to that part of the Arab sector. The best way was to get to the Damascus Gate and then take a taxi. One of the reasons the local Arabs had come to welcome the theatre in their midst was the improvement to business – taxis, restaurants and even the late-opening shops all benefited.

Ann treated herself to a taxi from the Central Post Office and was soon driving through shabby, dimly lit streets. How abruptly it changed, the whole atmosphere! It was like jumping into a previous century, almost into a different country. Things brightened up briefly round about the American Colony hotel, which, together with adjacent Christian sites such as the Garden Tomb and St George's Cathedral, had created its own little extension of the tourist beat. But beyond lay Arab territory. Even the street-names had not been Hebraised here. Ibn Batuta, Al Hariri . . . the taxi moved slowly and cautiously along the narrow roads, as if the Jewish driver were nervous, edging uneasily past parked trucks and giving way to oncoming traffic in a fashion highly uncharacteristic of Israeli drivers.

Every time Ann came to the theatre she marvelled anew at Amnon's stubborn courage in what must have seemed to racial pessimists a foredoomed enterprise. The atmosphere tonight was almost tangibly hostile . . . But surely it hadn't been like that last year? Then, she remembered walking up to the theatre with Amnon after a meal at the City Restaurant, his favourite Arab eating-place, just inside Herod's Gate, and though the streets were just as dark and dingy then, she had not felt the slightest alarm. Now, infected perhaps by the driver's obvious unease, she was annoyed to find herself leaning back in her seat instead of adopting her usual position, one arm along the open window and her chin resting on it to get as close to the passing scene as possible. She didn't really like taking taxis, not only because she thought it an extravagance, but because it held her aloof from the city, swept her past without allowing her to participate in its tactile, sensuous life.

They reached the theatre, and Ann became aware that although it was lit up, there seemed to be very little activity in the entrance. She looked at her watch. Nearly eight o'clock. Where were the customers?

She hurried in through the arched entrance. The small foyer, lined with the current art display, was sparsely populated by a handful of people standing about uneasily, as theatre-goers do when they become aware that they are the first, and last, of the few. The box office, which had once been the pay-desk of the restaurant, was occupied by Amatsia himself, in place of the usual girl – an Arab, as it happened – who was his secretary by day and manned the box office at night. Ann approached the conspicuously queueless window.

'Hallo, Amatsia.'

'Ah! Shalom! You liked it so much last time?' said Amatsia in his faintly American-accented voice.

'Well . . . I thought I'd drop by. Can I buy a ticket?'

Amatsia tore one off and presented it to her with an ironic flourish.

'Be our guest. No, no – put away your purse. We may not play, anyway. There is hardly anyone in the house. You can see for yourself.'

'How many?'

'About twenty.'

'Not so terrible. Surely you'll play.'

'The company isn't too happy. They're used to rowdy street crowds. Empty theatres spook them.'

They spook me too, thought Ann, and Amatsia didn't look precisely unspooked himself. He was a big, slightly portly man still not quite out of his thirties, with a handsome head of dark curls and a ravishing beard of which he was justly proud. He reminded Ann of a well-fed version of one of the younger prophets, a resemblance increased by his delight in holding forth. Sometimes when Ann watched him growing heated in a political discussion, flourishing his strong stubby forefinger didactically and employing his splendid speaking voice to full histrionic advantage, she thought he was rather wasted as an impresario. He was actually a born politician, with an actor's gift of oratory, and Ann would wonder sometimes whether the Mayor didn't regret his decision to rid himself of Amatsia's flamboyant services on the City council.

Just now, however, his natural buoyancy seemed a little deflated. The grin that gleamed through the glossy black whiskers shone with a weaker radiance than usual.

'There was a good enough house the other night,' Ann said. 'What's happened?'

'Happened? A three-day *khamsin*'s happened, what else? Who

wants to swelter in a theatre on a night like this?'

'Oh well, if that's all – '

Someone tapped her on the shoulder and she turned. A familiar rotund figure stood behind her, rocking on his heels.

'Hallo, Neville! Nice to see you.'

'And you, luv. Going in? What about a drink first?'

'If there's time.'

'There's time,' said Amatsia a trifle grimly.

Neville Baum was the Jerusalem correspondent of the London *Gazette*. He was a short, bald, stubby Liverpudlian, an unprepossessing figure; but he was a brilliant newsman, who could be very kind to friends who were not his rivals. He had helped Ann with contacts and background information several times. He also had a very sociable wife.

'Where's Jacqui?' Ann asked.

'Copped out.'

'Too hot for her?'

'You could say that. In more senses than one. You won't catch my little woman in the Arab sector on dark and windy nights. She prefers our salubrious nest on French Hill.'

Ann frowned. They walked through into the 'bar', so-called, though like all such places in Israel it served only soft drinks and coffee.

'My God!' said Neville. 'Couldn't I just do with a Scotch! Oh, well. What'll it be – will you settle for coffee, or go a bust on the grapefruit juice?'

'Oh, *mitz* for me. I can't get enough to drink in this weather.'

'I can't get enough to drink in this *country*,' said Neville gloomily, 'and if I add, "especially in the present climate", I'm not referring to the *khamsin*, believe me.'

He brought her grapefruit juice in a plastic cup. It was after eight but there had been no bells yet.

'They must be waiting on the off-chance of latecomers,' said Ann.

'They'll be lucky.'

They strolled out into the courtyard at the back. The olive trees were in minute blossom but one had to put one's nose right into the low-hanging sprays to get the scent; like every other, of any delicacy, it was drowned out by the all-pervading smell of dust. Neville seemed nervy. He was wearing a loose open-necked shirt outside his trousers but it seemed to be catching him round the neck and armpits.

'How I hate this bleeding weather!' he said irritably.

'Why did you come out in it? I wouldn't have thought this sort of show was your cup of tea.'

Neville didn't answer at once. He stared round the yard, which they had to themselves. Maybe it was the mind-bending effect of the *khamsin*, but for a moment Ann could see it again as it had been, full of tables and chairs crowded with Arab men in their rusty black robes and turned-back white headdresses, their fingers active on their worry beads or backgammon pieces or tiny coffee cups while their faces (Ann had watched them in other places) remained, for the most part, enigmatically blank . . .

'It's a beach head,' Neville said. 'This place. One can come here legitimately and suss out the atmosphere in the Arab area. I had the futile hope that I might see a few of the locals here and . . . Not that they'd talk to me, as things are . . .'

'Have you any Arab friends?' Ann asked curiously.

'Friends? No. Acquaintances.'

'You couldn't introduce me to any of them?'

'I could have done, a month ago. Now I wouldn't advise it.'

'You mean because of Hebron.'

'I mean because of the whole lousy situation. Culminating, for the time being only, in Hebron. Next week or the week after, no doubt it will have culminated again, and in something worse.'

'What, for instance?'

'I'm a reporter, luv, I'm not a futurologist. But they won't take the expulsion of their mayors and their *kadi* lying down, not now they won't. Why should they? They've got the whole bloody world on their side.' He drained his coffee cup abruptly, as if it had been the whisky he said he needed, and took her arm. 'Come on then, let's go in and join the festivities.'

As they turned they came face to face with Amnon. He looked somewhat spooked, too, Ann thought.

'You are an angel to come. Two angels,' he added, for Neville's benefit. '*Nu?*' Did they phone?'

'Who?' asked Ann.

'*Who?* The Circus, of course! I've been nearly going round the wall all day from worry.'

'He means "up the bend" ' put in Neville, but Amnon ignored him.

'If they really made it to Massada they must have melted right into the rock. I am only hoping they – well, did they phone?'

'I haven't been home all day, I'm afraid.'

'What! I was counting on you to take calls!'

'Sorry – '

'Oy, God!' he exclaimed, and ran both hands over his gingery hair. 'They've probably been sending out calls for rescue for hours! Well, come on then, if you are coming. We need every *tochus*.'

It was true enough. Sitting, reluctantly, close to the stage so that the unfortunate actors would get as much support as possible, Ann counted the house. Twenty was an overstatement; there were precisely fifteen people, including two staff members. They sat in silence, dotted about the bench-seats in ones and twos, looking less like the great eager many-headed animal that an audience is supposed to be, than an outpatients' department on a slack day.

'Christ, I wish I hadn't come!' Neville whispered. 'This is awful! I don't even want to see them again. Have *you* seen them?'

'Yes.'

'Dead crude, if you ask me.'

'They're not meant to be sophisticated.'

'I can get all the knockabout comics I want in a Liverpool working-men's club, thanks.'

'Oh, don't be crass, Neville! Their show is a political act.'

'Stop talking like a bloody Marxist, it doesn't suit you. Anyone can see you're middle-class to your backbone. I bet you voted for the Iron Lady.'

Ann found herself getting annoyed. She got on well with Neville, but he could be exasperating. Five years 'on the beat' in Israel had not scratched the surface of his particular brand of north country Jewish Englishness. The fact was he didn't really like Israel, nor had he ever felt at home with Israelis. He found this hard to admit, because one firm tenet he clung to through thick and thin was that the Jews were one people and could never be basically alien to each other, however much the varied cultures of their countries of dispersion might have diversified them; this cherished illusion, however, didn't help him to fit in here. He took his perennial unease and irritation out on the classic drawbacks of Israeli life – the climate, the political vagaries, the bureaucracy, the bad driving, and most of all, the lamentable neglect of what he called 'the ordinary decencies of life'; pubs, orderly queueing, unsmelly public conveniences, quick transactions at banks, padded seats and limited standing in buses, and a sensible amount of mild pornography in one's everyday surroundings. About all these things he felt free to maintain a constant flow of complaint, while piously professing a deep underlying affinity for the place and its people; but this didn't fool Ann. She had seen enough of the disorientation and disillusion caused in visiting Jews by the basic clash between minority and majority cultures to recognise its symptoms in Neville. In any case, his wife Jacqui felt the same way and was much franker about it. This dichotomy between parents and *locus vivendi* was currently exacerbating the natural traumas of adolescence for Eric and Wendy, their teenage children.

'Neville,' said Ann, in an effort to divert him from his scratchiness and herself from her irritation with him. 'What do you honestly think about the Hebron business?'

Although they were sitting alone, at several seats' radius from the next lonely members of the audience, she at once sensed that her whisper had taken advantage of the splendid natural acoustics of the vaulted auditorium. A sudden alertness behind her made her spine prickle.

Neville, all oblivious, scarcely even troubled to lower his voice.

'Well, the first thing to note is that it's divided Israel. You'll have noticed that, of course. It's put the Minister of Defence on a nasty spot – he let those harpies squat there in the first place, and then he failed to protect them. My money's on him resigning pretty soon, which will make everything worse, because he's the only half-way moderate voice in the Cabinet. If he goes, it won't bring down the Government. It'll just make the Arabs think they haven't got a prayer – they'll know chauvinists like Sharon are in charge, going ahead all-out with their settlement plans with no one to say them nay. They'll get more desperate and do worse things. From my own point of view, the sickening thing was the tear-jerking line we were all fed by the Government press spokesmen – unarmed civilians walking home from prayer, innocents shot in the back, etc., etc. Codswallop. First of all, they weren't unarmed. One of the men who copped it was carrying a sten. They're nutters but not that nutty, they never step outside their township without an armed guard. As for getting shot in the back, what did they expect? Since when are ambushes mounted from the front? That's not cowardice, it's plain common sense.'

There was a movement from behind, and the next moment somebody was breathing down their necks. They turned to find a woman, who had evidently scrambled over the four intervening benches with the speed of a hurdler, to arrive at their undefended rear before Neville had finished speaking. She was not exactly built, or dressed, for hurdling.

'How is it *possible!*' she cried in a strong American accent. 'Who *are* you, anyway? How can you talk like that about the cold-blooded, cowardly massacre of our people? Didn't we lose enough already? Can we afford more losses? Six million wasn't enough for you, you have to sit there and make excuses for our enemies? I told my husband – didn't I, Sam?' she cried up the slope to a man, sitting with averted eyes and hands clutched between his fat thighs like a child caught short. ' – Not another dime are we giving to the Joint, not another cent! It's all going straight into the funds of the Gush. They're the only ones who are prepared to sacrifice for the complete Land of Israel, that we were promised in the Bible!'

'Do you live here?' asked Neville innocently.

'No we don't. But I don't accept that as a reason for not being allowed an opinion. My husband and I have donated literally thousands of dollars – '

'Tell her to shut up about her dollars,' came a voice in Hebrew from the other side of the stage. The woman looked up sharply.

'What did he say?'

Neville translated faithfully. The woman flushed darkly and became, for the moment, speechless.

'Tell her,' the voice went on, 'that we don't want her Greater Israel. We want what we fought for in '48. That was enough. If she wants to give money for settlements, let her give it to settle the Negev and the *Galil*, so that my son, the one I have left, can stop what he's doing and come home where he belongs, before he turns into something I can't recognise. Tell her,' he went on, still in the same unemotional voice, 'to go back where she came from and put her dollars into her "little pocket", if there's room there.'

Neville, with infinite courtesy, was translating in his flat Liverpool voice exactly what the man had said. When he reached the final injunction, the woman's husband finally roused himself in her defence.

'That is disgusting!' he exclaimed in shaky outrage. 'My God! How can anyone speak to a woman that way? That is – it's – it's *disgusting*!'

'Don't shoot the interpreter,' said Neville, winking at Ann.

'How can one Jew speak that way to another?' wailed the woman, on the verge of tears. 'After all we've done, we have to come to Israel to be insulted!'

'You asked for it, lady,' called a woman who was leaning across the catwalk listening.

The American woman forgot Neville. She edged between the benches to get closer to her new antagonist, and they began arguing, like belligerent housewives over a garden wall, across the raised catwalk. When Amatsia walked down it to get to the stage, he had practically to step over them.

A top light came on to illuminate him, and the noise died down.

'Ladies and gentleman,' he said in Hebrew. 'I'm sorry to announce that there will be no performance tonight due to illness.'

'A nechtige tog,' murmured Neville. 'Illness my Aunt Fanny, they don't want to play to this mini-madhouse and who can blame 'em? The whole country's a madhouse if you want my opinion.' He rose heavily to his feet. 'Come on, let's go and find a drink.'

CHAPTER 8

Ann looked for Amnon on the way out, but all she saw, as they walked by what passed for a greenroom, was the four members of the Gesher troupe – two Jews, two Arabs – engaged in a noisy and animated dispute.

'Contentious buggers,' grunted Neville. 'Very ill, I'm sure!'

They wandered out into the stifling darkness of the ill-lit street, and suddenly found themselves hurrying.

'I hope the car's all right,' muttered Neville.

'Why shouldn't it be?'

It was, and they got into it, and Neville at once zoomed away.

'Shall we go for a meal?'

'Okay,' said Ann, though what her body craved was a shower and bed. Even on such a night, after such a day, she found herself loath to forge another conversation, another meal, another hour of experience – the possibility of more encounters, squeezed in during time when she would normally be sleeping. 'What about the City Restaurant?'

'Not tonight.'

'Why not?'

'I think they're all on strike anyway.'

'Who are?'

'Everything in the Moslem Quarter of the Old City was shut up yesterday, and the day before. Protest about the hoofing out of the loud-mouthed mayors . . . Let's go to Fink's.'

'What's wrong with the American Colony Hotel?' suggested Ann, who far preferred Arab food to Jewish.

Neville hitched his shoulders uneasily. 'Must we? That's in the Arab sector as well. Oh, they'll be open all right, but . . . the waiters have a way of letting you know when there's a bad atmosphere. Let's go where the bright lights are.'

So they went to Fink's off King George. It was like entering an oven, and there weren't many people there either, but at least it felt friendly.

'What'll you have?'

'I don't care – chicken.'

'Me too.'

They sat in unaccountable, and for both of them highly uncharacteristic, silence, waiting. Neville really did seem to be in a

98

gloomy mood. Ann felt sorry she'd been annoyed with him before, though she didn't think she'd shown it.

'Is anything wrong, Neville? You seem very down.'

He glanced up at her and his mouth and nose gave a rabbit-like twitch. 'This place is beginning to get to me,' he said.

'Fink's? or Israel?'

'All of it. It's getting Jacqui down too. The plain fact is, we're homesick.'

'For *Liverpool*?' Ann couldn't help saying incredulously.

'Nice stable place, Liverpool. Hardly any wars. You know where you are. You know where your *kids* are,' he added meaningly.

'I would have thought it would be easier to keep tabs on them here – somehow.' Ann was remembering the horrors of William, the sitting-up half the night, the frantic phonings round, the ghastly rows when he rolled home at last from grotty discoes with grotty friends, seeing no reason why he should ever account for his movements or his manners or anything else, even while expecting to be cared about and waited on hand and foot . . . Suffolk, where the cottage was, seemed to provide only marginally fewer opportunities and locations for adolescent debauchery and parental anxiety than London, so why shouldn't Liverpool excel them both, with its dockland and its sleaziness and its unemployment problem? But Neville was emphatic.

'I don't mean where they *are*,' he said impatiently. 'I mean where they're *at*. If you see what I mean . . .'

'No.'

'Well, look . . . When I was first posted here, Wendy was ten and Eric was twelve. We figured they'd take to it like ducks to water, the sun, the free-and-easy life, the sports and all that . . . Ha bloody ha. I want to tell you, Ann, it was *absolute murder*. For the first – oh, well over a year, they never stopped moaning. Eric was quite impossible. The number of times we talked about sending him home to boarding school – and not only to satisfy his obsessive passion to get back to England but to get him out of our hair. He acted as if we'd dragged him into some mediaeval torture-chamber and were driving him to desperation for the fun of it. At the end of a year I was ready to pack it in, but my editor wouldn't hear of it – liked my stuff and said I was just getting the hang of things, getting contacts, that sort of thing – he was right of course, it would have been a waste of that awful year if we'd gone back then. Besides, you don't like to be beat. This was supposed to be our bloody country in a way, we'd been Zionist from way back. That's why we'd pitched the kids in at the deep end. No Anglican school for us, with English curriculum and all that – we'd sent 'em to the local school. Hoping they'd get integrated. There was this bit of me, y'see, wanted to see if my kids couldn't grow up to be the other kind of Jew.'

'The what?'

'Oh, come on, you know what I mean! You've been around us *yidden* for long enough, there *and* here. You must have noticed the difference. Jews at home hug their psychoses. Cherish them even. On one level there they are, bravely struggling to maintain their separate identity in a sea of *goyim*. On a deeper level, they're doing their damnedest to sink into it without trace. Go on and on about the persecutions of the past – trade on them, thrive on them. You heard that woman tonight. I've done it myself, if anyone attacks us. But we use 'em for more than that. I used to run a Jewish social club in Calderstones, that invited guest speakers. I soon learnt what went down and what didn't. Ask someone in to talk about the positive aspects of Israel – agriculture, the arts, you name it – and you get a turn-out like tonight. But have a speaker who's going to rave on about the Holocaust – it's a sell-out. They love it. It makes them feel their Jewishness again – it's about the only thing that does in England now, where most of 'em are getting more English every day. In the most bourgeois way of course! Nothing too flamboyant or too intellectual, the English frown on anything like that, and the English have been so kind to us . . . Well, I was raised that way; I'm stuck with it. I don't always admire it, but by God I understand it. I call it the Low Profile Syndrome. You know how the most outstanding thing in a profile is a big nose?

'So when we came here, I wanted Eric and Wendy to begin sticking their profiles out a bit. Why should they inherit all our hang-ups? When I thought it wasn't going to take, though, at heart I was relieved. Because I'll tell you straight, Ann, I don't understand these buggers here at all. If being a "whole Jew" means acting like a lot of 'em here, well – I don't know, maybe it's better for them, but it's nothing *I* can identify with. I'm more at home behind the net curtains and ding-dong door chimes in Calderstones, even if it *is* bloody dull most of the time. I get all the excitement I can be doing with, at work. When I get home, I *like* it dull.'

He lit his fourth cigarette and brooded gloomily with his chin in his stubby hand.

'What was I saying?'

'About the children.'

'Oh, yes. Well. So I thought to myself, I thought, *I* can't change, I'm Liverpool-Jewish to my gut linings, but I'm not saying it's the highest aspiration a man could have for his children. So I pressed on. I made 'em stick it out. Force-fed 'em on Israeli culture. Total immersion. Do you know I wouldn't even take 'em home with us when we went on our annual leave? Put 'em into these oh-be-joyful summer camps they specialise in here. And that was probably my undoing.'

The chicken had arrived and they were picking at it desultorily. The heat was now all but intolerable, and why they had ordered hot, heavy food, Ann couldn't imagine. Her brain was gently giving way under the burden of the day and its various trials and impacts, and she was scarcely listening to Neville's monologue. Her mind was wandering. She feared it might wander right off to sleep if she wasn't careful.

'All of a sudden,' Neville went on, 'about three years ago, the moaning stopped. First Wendy, then Eric. And boom, boom, just like that, they weren't English any more. They took off into Israeli teenage life and before we knew it, they were strangers. Oh, they kindly agreed to speak English to us if pressed, or if they wanted something. But you have no idea what it feels like to sit at your own dinner-table while your kids have a good old sniggle about you in a foreign language. Typical *sabra*! I never felt such a right tata in my life.'

'I bet. But it was what you'd wanted.'

'Don't remind me! And from then on, *they* were part of the majority culture, while *we* were still in the *gola*. In our own house. All right, you'll say, fair enough, we'd bought it. And they were happy. But I never thought they'd carry it this far.'

'Why, what's happened?'

'I'll tell you what's happened. Eric finishes high school next month. And guess what?'

Ann woke up and guessed at once. 'He wants to join the army.'

'Right. *And*, if you don't mind, he fancies himself as a commando. No less!'

'I should have thought there must be an element of pride in your reaction to that.'

'Pride? I've no energy left to feel any pride. I'm using it all in arguments. Jacqui's going spare. D'you know what they get those

101

commandos doing? Diving under ships pinning on limpet mines. Crossing into Lebanon, blowing up aircraft – '

'Oh, nonsense, Neville! That was years ago.'

'I daresay they've found even more exciting jobs for them now. You know, when I look at him, I hardly recognise him. He's beautiful. Don't laugh. Stroppy as hell, independent, casual, but stunning to look at – stunning, Ann. Tops me by a good yard, and looks like a bloody film star. They say it's all genes but I swear if he'd've grown up in Liverpool he'd've never looked like that. Jacqui can't believe he's ours. Two little fat yids like us turning out a thing like that, it's not natural. But when we look at him and think of something happening to him, think of him maybe getting hurt or . . . well, I've been covering wars and that for more years than I care to remember, I've seen a thing or two in my time and I've heard of worse. You know what they did to 'em here-abouts – on the Golan Heights, for instance, in '73, they could only recognise 'em by the marks on their underwear. I talked to a chap who found his own nephew like that, he never got over it. Well, hell, I'm not about to let Eric . . . Oh. And that's another thing. You know what else he wants?'

'What?'

'To change his name. Eric's not good enough for him, he says it's a stupid name. Wants to call himself Eppi. Eppi! I ask you! Talk about bloody silly names – '

'Short for Ephraim, I suppose. I met an Ephraim today.'

'Well, you'll meet another one, soon's you get out to our place. What can I do? That's a minor battleground of course, next to the other, but it's heartbreaking just the same – chucking out a perfectly good English name in favour of one that sounds like something out of – out of – '

'The Bible?' Ann suggested helpfully.

'I was going to say, out of *Seven Brides for Seven Brothers*, but I suppose it's the same thing in the end. Now ask about Wendy.'

'No, I'll guess. Are there any Hebrew names beginning with W? No. Next best thing . . . V. Varda?'

'Vered.'

'Oh dear!'

'Don't you dare laugh!'

'I'm not, Neville. Honestly. But there is a certain irony to your objections to all this – all except the commando business, I quite see your point about that. And Jacqui's.'

'Jacqui's point goes well beyond objections. She's getting down the suitcases and advertising the car, passport to passport.'

'Are you serious?'

'The question is, is she? I reckon yes. The look in her eye, I reckon she'd rather us jobless in our old semi in Calderstones, in the pouring rain, than our place in the sun on French Hill talking about "our son the commando".'

'The *Gazette* wouldn't chuck you, would they? – just for wanting a home posting?'

'Listen, it's a bad time to cop out. Things are really beginning to fizz. The Hebron business, the Mayors – they're swarming all over Europe giving press conferences, did you know that? – and they're booked for the States next, maddest thing even this mad Government ever did, letting that lot out on the loose to blacken Israel's name still further . . . There's a new twist every day, and bigger stuff coming, if I don't miss my guess. Workwise, I'm the right man in the right place, and no journalist worth his chip-butty would want to be anywhere else.'

'Must be odd for you, in a way. A Jew, a Zionist – of sorts – all that must mean you're as worried about the situation as I am, on a human level. But from a professional point of view, the worse things get, the better.'

'Nothing like a good train wreck on a slack day, my old news editor used to say . . . It's true. A bit of me rejoices at any news story, even today's . . .'

'What was that?'

'Haven't you heard? They found an arms cache on the roof of a religious school in Kiryat Arba. All good army issue . . . You know what that means.'

'No I don't,' said Ann blankly. 'Some terrorists hid it there, to blow up the *yeshiva*?'

'Yep, that's right. Some terrorists. Only not the Palestinian variety. And not to blow up the *yeshiva*. I gather they may have had one of the bigger mosques in mind.'

'I don't get it.'

'Don't you? Well, never mind. It's all grist to the mill of a good impartial reporter; who cares who's the baddy and who's the goody? The story, that's the thing.' He stubbed out his cigarette and tipped back the last of his beer. 'I can't choke down any more nosh, can you? Come on. I'll drive you home.'

Ann sat in his car in subdued silence. Not the Palestinian variety . . . what could it mean? A recrudescence of *Jewish* terrorism? Terror against terror, as in the old days of David of the flower shop and his Stern gang pals? She shuddered.

'Neville, do you know a man called Shachterman?'

'The one that was hurt in that grenade incident in Ramallah?'

She turned to stare at him in the passing lamplight. Her brain seemed to stumble.

'What do you mean?'

'Is it the Shachterman who lives in the Arab sector? The one we all think is some sort of spy?'

She swallowed. 'Spy? For whom? What are you talking about?'

'What's his first name?'

'Boaz.'

'Yeah, that's the one. Big fellow, bit of a mystery man. Spent a couple of months in hospital in the winter. I tried to get a line on it when it came over the grapevine, but it was hushed up.'

'Neville, please. This is all – it's all news to me, I know nothing about it. Tell me.'

He glanced at her through the smoke of a new cigarette. 'D'you know him then?'

'On and off.'

'When did you last see him?'

'Last spring, when I came for the Book Fair.'

'How'd you meet him? He's not exactly one of your *Mafiosi* of the Left.'

'Not what?'

'That's the right wingers' answer to being called fascists. They call the peaceniks the left-wing Mafia.'

'The Government Press Office put me on to him years ago. After '73 when I came to get material for a novel about the Yom Kippur War.'

'I never read that one.'

'I never actually wrote it. It – the reality didn't tally with the fiction.' Cravenly, she was glad of the digression. She knew she would have to hear, but she fended it off.

'What fiction?'

'Oh . . . it was rather silly really. I had the impression that the Arabs – 'our' Arabs, I mean, the Israeli Arabs – had been rather . . . well, almost supportive during that war, compared to '67. I'd heard they'd given blood, stood guard, come to work, donated money for war-bonds and so on . . . It seemed important. You remember how they holed up in their villages in the Six-Day War and were generally pretty scared and hostile. I thought there'd been a significant change, I thought I could make a plot out of the

104

relationship between a kibbutz and a neighbouring Arab village, with the war as its catalyst . . . The Government press people loved the idea, they were very keen.'

'I bet they were.'

'They gave me a car, I traipsed all over the place meeting Archbishops and communist Members of Knesset and Nazareth big-shots and God knows what . . . Shachterman was my guide.'

'Interesting. He wears a lot of different hats.'

'What do you *mean*, Neville? What are you getting at?'

Neville was silent for a moment. 'I oughtn't to say too much. I don't know anything positive about him, really. He's a pretty enigmatic figure. No one really knows what he does or who he represents. Officially he does research for some local equivalent of a quango. And he does the guiding and lecturing on the side. But there are rumours he's on the payroll of the Ministry of Defence.'

'For doing what?'

'Well, you work it out. Could be Shin Bet.'

'The Secret Service? In what capacity?'

'The obvious one. Keeping tabs on what goes on on the West Bank.'

'That's not feasible,' Ann said slowly.

'Why not?'

'He . . . I've seen how he moves among the Arabs there. They accept him. They trust him. I've been into their homes with him. They welcome him as a friend.'

'They welcome anyone. It's their custom. That doesn't imply trust. And it wouldn't stop them from taking a pot-shot at him as he goes out their front door, if they thought they could get away with it.'

'But they don't.'

'But they do. They did!'

'When? How?'

'Well, it wasn't a shot in the back, it was a hand grenade in through his car window, but the effect was much the same. It nearly blew his arm off.'

She felt the clutch of nausea and bile rose into her throat.

'Is he . . .?'

'Oh, he's all right now. They saved his arm, I heard. Can't have done it any good, of course. Here you are, out you get. I won't come in, I'm knackered and Jacqui'll be worried. Listen, gi' us a ring and come over. You can go all the way nearly, on a number

4 bus. Give Amnon my regards. I hope all this pissing about doesn't put people off coming to his little theatre, that'd be a right pity.' He leant over and planted a damp kiss on her cheek. 'Tara, well. See you.' As she crossed the narrow pavement to the door of the building, he called after her, 'Oh, by the way! What did you find out, in '73, about our Arabs supporting the Jewish war effort?'

'That, on the whole, they didn't.'

'Fancy that! Surprise, surprise. Still an' all, you met a lot of interesting Arabs.'

And one very interesting Jew, Ann thought.

There was an ominous silence as she mounted the steps to the front door. If the Circus was back, safe and sound, would there not be cheerful and festive noises coming through even closed doors and windows? When there was a gathering at Amnon's you could usually hear it half a block away, even with the wind behind you.

She let herself in. The flat was in darkness. She groped for the light switch and went into the kitchen. On the table was the remains of a hastily devoured snack and a scribbled note:

'No sign of them. Disaster obviously. Phoned hospitals. Phoned police. Phoned army. Gone to look for them along road to Massada, no doubt broken down, why does nobody listen to me. Where have *you* been? Stay by phone. A.'

Ann sat down, cursing herself. When Neville had asked her to eat with him, why hadn't she remembered Amnon's anxiety – now shown to be entirely justified and not just one of his worries for the sake of worrying – and hurried home to lend moral support? She re-read the note. Gone to look for them? All the way to Massada? Insanity! It was on a main road, somebody would have found them long ago if they really had broken down . . . But in that case, where were they?

The door bell rang.

She started with sudden fright, and then rushed to open it. It must be them! But it wasn't. Two young men stood outside in the dusty darkness.

'Amnon Segev *yeshno*?'

In her confusion, her Hebrew deserted her. 'No, he's not here.'

They looked at each other, and one said to the other in Hebrew, 'Your English is better than mine.' The second one said, 'We are from *Zahal*. Army. Amnon is call up.'

'*Tonight*?'

He handed her a sheet of flimsy paper.

'He come soon? You give to him this. He know what to do. Call up these names. Before morning. Okay? You tell him? Not to forget?'

She took the paper and looked at it. About a dozen names, ranks and addresses were written on it.

'Do you mean he has to go round to all these people tonight, and notify them that they're called up?'

'*Ze'u.*' They grinned at her matily and turned to go down the steps.

'Wait!' They turned. 'He's gone to Massada and God knows when he'll be back, maybe not till morning.'

They exchanged looks again.

'If he come back, you give him the list, okay? If not . . .' They shrugged and continued down the steps.

'But how important is it?' she called after them.

The English-speaking one turned at the bottom. '*Zahal* always important!' he called up, half laughing, and they went out, letting the metal door to the street clang behind them.

She retreated into the flat, flummoxed. She stared at the list. Ten names. Addresses all over Jerusalem. What on earth could she do now to help Amnon? Could she possibly go herself? Without a car . . . impossible. And probably the men on the list would refuse to accept her as their call-up officer, anyway.

The situation was not entirely unfamiliar to her. She remembered a similar visitation once before. Three a.m., and a vigorous banging on the screen door of the room-and-a-half she'd shared with Menachem, bangs which eventually and with difficulty dragged them from their love-drugged sleep. Menachem, stark naked, staggering to the door. A burst of ribald laughter and a lot of male backchat, and then his return, still chuckling. 'Who is it, what's going on?' 'Just the army.' He was pulling on his underwear, then the army fatigues he kept in the cupboard with the heavy winter quilt. His gun stood at the back of the wardrobe, its butt rising domestically from among the shoes. He fished it out while she lay propped on her elbow, tousle-headed, benumbed, gazing at him. 'You've got to go *now*? What's wrong? Is it a war?' 'A *war*?' he'd said, as if such an eventuality were beyond the bounds of possibility. 'Of course not, don't be silly! It's just routine, a practice. Go to sleep.' 'But when will you come back?' 'Probably tomorrow.' He had taken her head in his free hand, holding it firmly so he could kiss her lips and her eyes. She could relive that moment precisely, the strong scent of night-flowering shrubs under their window; the moonlight coming in over the pines at the back of their building, gleaming on the barrel of the *uzi*, and the icy feel as it accidentally touched her bare arm. And Menachem's eyes close to hers, smiling that smile that stopped her breath . . . 'I think we did it tonight,' he whispered. 'I shot extra hard tonight, did you feel it go right in, deep, deep . . .? Don't get up to see me off. Lie still and don't let my seed run away . . . It's a pity the womb cannot suck.' One more kiss, his tongue diving into her mouth, so that she lay back instinctively, luring him, wanting to keep him with her, to ram that beautiful male seed back if it should be creeping out with its task undone. But she knew he couldn't stay. The gun barrel pressing her arm told her, a chill reminder. He drew his hand out from behind her head, over the top, and down gently over her face, closing her eyes and lying there for a second, strong, warm and comforting. She pressed both her own hands over it and licked its salty palm and tried to bite it. How she had loved him, how she had wanted to make every part of him a part of her! She used to imagine, as he made love to her, that her body lost solidity and his sank into it altogether, till she possessed him and enclosed him, his shell. For their love, all the laws of physics should be suspendible . . . But no. Not even little laws like going into the army when they called you might be gainsaid. Not for any passion in the world.

Ann wandered into Amnon's bathroom. She washed her face in cold water before looking in the mirror. She stared at herself. Fancy crying about it after all these years. The seed had crept away uselessly, that night and all the other nights . . . Had he had better luck with some other woman, after she had left him? The better part of her hoped so. He had wanted children so badly! Perhaps – this was not the first time this had occurred to her, of course; she had agonised over it often in the lonely years before her marriage – that was the true, deep reason why he had not struggled harder to hold her. Six years of nights and mornings and long, shuttered Sabbath afternoons; love in every mood, in every position . . . Towards the end he had favoured one above others, what he'd jokingly called the 'Hemming Way', with her buttocks on a pillow. But there was nothing jocular about his thrusts and his strained, upturned face, like the face of a man desperately praying . . . Oh yes! She hoped it had happened. Of course she hoped that some other woman had succeeded where she had failed. Of course! Except that, if so, she never wanted to find out about it, because it would be unendurable.

She sighed profoundly, undressed and had another shower.

She turned her mind again to Amnon. She was terribly worried about the call-up paper. She didn't know what to do. Was it really important or wasn't it? Who did she know whom she could phone up so late, and consult? . . . Neville? Of course not, he wouldn't know. Amatsia?

There were scores of Mizrahis in the Jerusalem phone book. She dared not risk waking the wrong families at this hour. The soldiers, after all, had laughed – surely the situation wasn't really urgent? It was probably just routine. Although, with all the tension . . . Maybe Amnon would get into real trouble if she couldn't find him. Even if he did come in, dead-beat probably, what a bombshell! Having to go traipsing out in the middle of the night, flogging round to all those different addresses . . . She didn't look forward to giving him the news, whatever sort of mood he returned in.

She put the phone book back in its place on the fridge. Maybe Amnon had Amatsia's home number in a book of his own somewhere. She went into his bedroom and searched through the heaps of discarded clothes, piles of theatre programmes, empty cigarette packets, scraps of paper and endless other rubbish that cluttered his bedside table and the other surfaces of the room. She even ventured to look into the drawers, but the total chaos they contained disheartened her before she began.

Maybe one of the other rooms? She didn't have much hope, but she remembered that the one occupied last night by the Circus couple and their stilt-walking offspring contained a desk. She went in there, switched on a light and made for the big mahogany piece in the corner.

'Is my Mom home yet?'

If the doorbell had startled Ann, the sound of the little voice from the double bed nearly gave her heart failure. Sticking out from the rumpled quilt like an orange chrysanthemum protruding from a snowbank was Pickle, red hair on end, androgynous torso gleaming with night sweat. The cheeks, if she was not mistaken, gleamed with smeared tears.

'You nearly made me jump out of my skin! How long have you been here?'

'I don't know. Hours. I was asleep but it's so hot under this crappy old thing.'

'I should just think it would be! Why don't you kick it off?'

'Mommy said I shouldn't in case it got cool in the night.'

'Well, it doesn't look as if it's going to. I'll give you a light blanket instead, shall I? Would you like a cold drink?'

'Mommy said I shouldn't when I'm hot. It's bad for the stomach.'

'Have you got trouble with your stomach?'

The flower head shook to and fro. 'No. But I *could* have. If I drink iced drinks when I'm hot. You can *die*.'

They stared at each other, while Ann thought what this apparition signified.

'Where are your parents, Pickle?'

'They went out. Don't call me Pickle. My name's Dill.'

'And Sue-Ella? And Mary?'

'Yeah. They all went out on the razzle.'

'On the razzle, eh?'

The flower nodded solemnly on its fragile stem. Ann moved to the bed and dragged off the quilt which, being made of solid cotton wool, weighed half a ton. She glanced at the thin hot little body, clad only in purple Y-fronts. Well, anyway, that told her one thing she wanted to know.

'I suggest you come into the kitchen and have a drink, and then maybe a cool shower,' she said.

'Mommy said I shouldn't – '

And maybe Mommy shouldn't go out on the razzle complete with second and third strings, leaving you all on your own.

'Not a very cold one,' she said. 'Just a cool one. And a cool drink, not from the fridge. You know, you need to drink lots in this weather.'

Dill slid out of bed and padded after her into the kitchen. 'Sure was awful hot today on that mountain,' he agreed.

'Oh! You got there?'

'Yeah. And we wished we hadn't. Lucky they got that cable-car and we didn't have to walk up that path! When we got to the top it was like being fried. We only stayed about half an hour. Then we came down and went to a better place.'

Ann poured him water from the tap and added some raspberry syrup. He put it to his lips and gulped and gulped and gulped.

'Jeez, that's good!' he said, emerging with a pink moustache.

'What place?'

'A place. By the Dead Sea. Where you could swim in little cold pools. Only Mommy said I shouldn't.'

'But you did?'

110

'Yeah. Daddy said I *should*.'

Bloody good for Daddy.

'Did you go into the Dead Sea?'

'Yeah, a bit. It stung. There was an old, old lady there from New York. I thought she was a black lady, but turned out she was all covered with some yukky mud. She was smearing it all over herself – I watched her – she just loved that gunk, I thought she was gonna eat it. When she saw me looking at her, she kinda shrieked at me, "I don't call this the Dead Sea, I call it the Live Sea! It's just so good for you, it keeps me young!" She was about ninety. I didn't like to say anything.'

Ann was rummaging in the fridge for fruit for him. Her hand, groping in the vegetable drawer, fell upon something soft and cold. She drew it out. It was something white wrapped in a plastic bag.

'What on earth is this?' she asked rhetorically, but he promptly replied, 'Oh, that's Sue-Ella's pants.'

'I beg your pardon?'

'She put 'em in there tonight, to be cool for the morning.'

Ann took them out and felt them, and imagined the bliss of putting them on.

'What a marvellous idea.'

'Are you gonna do it with yours?'

'No. But I would if it was my fridge.'

'You better put 'em back. She doesn't like it when you fool around with her gear.'

Ann obediently rolled them up again and replaced the bag. She brought out something more edible – half a watermelon. Amnon had bought it after all, though he'd only put it in recently and it hadn't got fully cold. They ate huge slices of it just the same.

'Jeez, this is fun,' said Dill appreciatively.

'Did your parents say *where* they were going – on the razzle?'

He shook his head.

'Weren't they very tired when they got back?'

'Yeah, we all were. We got home early, though, and they all flopped for an hour or two. Then they got cleaned up and had something to drink and made a few phone calls. Then Mary put me to bed and they went.'

'What time was that?'

'I dunno. Eight o'clock, maybe.'

'They didn't write a note, or leave a message for Amnon?'

'Don't ask me. Can I have a peanut butter sandwich?'

111

He could, and did.

'How old are you?' Ann asked curiously.

'Nine. Don't tell 'em I told you.'

'Nine! Amnon told me seven.'

'I'm small for my age, and Mom pretends I'm younger because it looks good in the act. When I was really seven, they said I was five. Everyone thought I was some kinda genius because I could walk on stilts. Jeez. Any gook can walk on stilts.'

The phone rang. Ann grabbed it.

'Hallo – Amnon?'

'Hi there – Amnon?' said a voice at the same moment.

Ann's heart sank, and hardened, all at the same time. 'Amnon's out. Is that Bob?'

'Yeah! Say, who's that?'

'It's Ann Randall, the one who cooked the eggs. Where are you?'

'Yeah, well, that's the thing, you see. I'm not sure! We can't find where we left the car.'

Ann set her teeth.

'Tell me the whole story.'

They'd gone out for a meal, and then they'd gone for a drive. They'd parked the car somewhere and started wandering round some 'village'. (Village? What kind of village? An Arab village?) They'd had a 'fantastic' walk through the dark but when they tried to find their way back to the car they found they were lost.

Ann suddenly realised that she was so tired that in another minute she might fall into unconsciousness. She felt a fairly powerful rage in herself somewhere, but exhaustion was keeping it at a distance, and she was able to say, calmly but wearily, at the end of this idiotic recital, 'Look, Bob. You shouldn't be wandering about late at night when you don't know your way. Where are you phoning from? A kiosk?'

'Yeah.'

'Well, go out of it and walk about until you see some kind of landmark or sign, like a street sign.'

While he was gone she groped in her hold-all and found her street map of Jerusalem. She sent Dill into the bathroom for a shower, while she spread the map open on the table before her. Her weariness was overwhelming her like a creeping black wave; she lusted for her bed, and cursed Bob soundly. A voice on the other end of the phone brought her fury dangerously close to the surface by chirping brightly, 'Isn't this just too exciting for

112

words?'

'Oh, for God's sake,' Ann muttered. Then Bob was back.

'We seem to be on the edge of some wilderness,' he reported. 'But there's a kind of a big building off to one side, and some houses . . .'

'That's a fat lot of help. Can you see the Old City walls?'

'All lit up?'

'Yes!'

'No . . .'

'You mean, it's dark where you are?'

'Yeah, kind of. It's a bit spooky, to tell the truth.'

She had one more try.

'Are there *any* cars going past?'

'About one every ten minutes.'

'So stop the next one and – '

'Hell, I couldn't do *that*!'

Abruptly and unexpectedly, the anger surfaced. She slammed her hand down on the map she was hopelessly poring over and shouted down the line, 'Do you realise Amnon has gone belting off to Massada hunting for you? Why on earth couldn't you phone him at the theatre, or leave a message here? And how could you leave your son here all alone, poor little boy, roasting to death under a quilt that'd do for Santa Claus's sleigh? Haven't you got the slightest idea where you left your stupid car?'

There was a deathly silence which seemed to stretch interminably. Then Bob, in a very meek voice, said faintly, 'I remember it was somewhere near a big red sculpture.'

'A big red – You don't mean the Stabile? Like an arrangement of rusty girders?'

'Yeah! That's it!'

'Why the hell didn't you say so before? Everyone knows that thing! You must have walked down to Ein Karem. You said there were houses near you. Go to the first one still showing a light, knock on the door, and say, *Efo Hapessel ha'adom!* Can you say that?' He said it, several times. 'It means, where's the red sculpture? They'll tell you. Walk to it and drive home quickly.'

'The girls sure are tired. I guess you couldn't come get us – ?'

'No, I couldn't, and even if I could – ' Ann bit back her words. 'You'll have to make it on your own. And I just hope Amnon's home before you.'

113

CHAPTER 9

She bedded Dill down, laying a sheet over him in the teeth of Mommy's putative disapproval, and watched him till he dropped off to sleep. Then she began to prowl the flat, struggling to keep herself awake.

She could, of course, leave the fatal list pinned to an explanatory note on the kitchen table, and take herself to her longed-for rest. But she felt that would be a kind of treachery. She must break it to Amnon personally and be around to absorb his reaction, make him coffee or whatever, and perhaps even accompany him on his lonely night errand if he wanted her to. Also, there was the secondary worry about the Circus. If only she had not been too mean to hire a car of her own, she could have gone to the rescue . . . Not that they deserved it . . . but for Amnon's sake. If only he would phone her! At least she could set his mind at rest about their safety. Of course it was partly his own silly fault for not searching the flat thoroughly enough to uncover Dill under the mountain of smothering quilt, before rushing off into the night on his fool's errand.

At last, at about one o'clock, she could keep her feet no longer. Instead of going to her own room, from which she could hear neither the phone nor the doorbell, she lay down on Amnon's bed, first clearing it of its scattered burden of pyjamas, newspapers, files, crumpled shirts and three enormous Japanese sandals, as if he were Jake the Peg. She drew up the sheet, turned over the pillow, and lay full-length, meaning to rest for a few moments. She fell instantly asleep.

Some time later she woke again slowly. She was still dead tired. Her body was as heavy as a stone figure on a crusader's tomb – she felt she would never be able to get up again. She turned her head slowly and looked at the radio-clock, which said, in ghostly green figures, 02.35. This galvanised her, at least as far as a sitting position. Where the hell *was* everybody?

And what, in their continuing absence, had wakened her? Not a noise. There was some change in the air. She dragged her legs over the edge of the bed and levered herself upright. The room had a pair of double doors with metal shutters, which opened onto a balcony at the back of the house. With some difficulty she forced them open. The moment she did so, she knew that the *sharav* had broken.

The first breath of air from outside proved it. Cool, clean, it flowed into the room like water down a parched throat. The dust was already blowing away, though the balcony-tiles were still gritty under her bare soles. Late as it was, one or two other people, perhaps wakened as she had been, were coming out into the open, gazing up almost incredulously at a sky from which some unseen, pressurising lid had been abruptly lifted. The fir trees and eucalyptus broke out of their dusty lethargy and began to dance energetically, scattering mixed scents, rustling to a vigorous wind-tune. Ann, leaning against the iron shutter, sucked in the new air greedily. Her very skin seemed to inhale it. Not only her tired body, but her heart responded to it, drinking in fresh strength. She felt her energies renewed, and some dichotomy in her personality cohering.

Suddenly she stood straight. Leaving the balcony window wide, she walked through to the kitchen and took her own small red address book out of her hold-all. She looked up a number and without hesitation, dialled.

It rang four times. Then a deep, sleepy voice answered.

'Shachterman.'

'Hallo, Boaz.'

Silence for only a moment. Then he said ironically, 'What a long time it took you to get up your courage to phone.'

'I've only been here a few days,' she said, defensive at once.

'Why do you lie to me? I know to the day when you came.'

'How?'

'It's a small town, and I hear what I need to hear.'

'You have a most efficient network.'

'It's not bad.' There was a pause, and then he said, in an altered voice. 'The *sharav*'s broken.'

'Yes.'

'Now I know where the courage came from.'

'It's nothing to do with courage, Boaz, I assure you.'

'I won't challenge you tonight,' he said, his harsh voice softening a little. 'You're exhausted.' Not, as another man might have said, 'You sound exhausted,' or 'Are you tired?' Just a statement. She was aware of a strange vulnerability that she had felt with him before, as if he knew too much about her.

'Boaz, I rang because I've got a problem. I'm sorry if I woke you.'

'Never mind, I'm a light sleeper.'

'I'm staying at Amnon Segev's – '

'That shit! Why do you compromise yourself by staying with that *debil*? Why don't you come to me, if you need a place to stay? Or aren't I naive and infantile enough for you?'

Ann met the abrasiveness in his voice with a defensive silence. After a moment he said more quietly, 'All right. Go on.'

Subdued, she told him about the visitation. 'How important is it?'

'He should go. You can never know if it's important. But it's not general mobilisation. Probably just a routine exercise to make sure everyone is on his toes.'

'I'm afraid Amnon's gone south looking for his actors – who've got mislaid in Jerusalem meanwhile – and he may stay away overnight.'

'He must phone you.'

'Maybe he'll think I'm in bed. I wish to God I were. I'm tired to death.'

'You should rest on days like this. You're not a child or an American, to run about in the heat.'

'I didn't want to waste a day.'

'So go to your kibbutz and watch them prancing about doing Shavu'oth dances with pretty flowers in their hair, pretending they are still pioneers and breakers of the land. Eat their once-a-year butter and cream – only not too much, I don't like fat women – and sing the old songs, and visit with your old lover.'

Ann said, controlling her gasp, 'What old lover, what are you talking about?' For a moment she was appalled at herself – could she possibly have spoken to him about Menachem, and not remembered such a betrayal?

'Oh, you have never mentioned him to me, thank God, I would be so bored if you did. But self-evidently there was a lover. Why else would you stay in a kibbutz for six years? You see, I don't always need my "network" as you call it, I can make educated guesses.'

'Boaz, could we talk about my current problem?'

'Why not? So what can I do to help you?'

She swallowed, trying to think about what she was doing, and why, and, simultaneously, trying not to.

'Well – Boaz – I was wondering – whatever you may think of Amnon, he's a good friend of mine.'

'*Not* a lover.'

'Not a lover. A friend. It can happen.'

'Certainly. I just wanted to be sure, before you continue,

116

because I have guessed what is coming.'

'No doubt a really educated guesser like you could see it a mile off.' She heard him chuckle, a rather rare sound, as she recalled, and not infectious. 'I was going to ask whether, if you aren't too tired, and if your wife would spare you for a couple of hours, you could do Amnon's rounds for him.'

The chuckle had been rather disconcertingly going on as a sort of contrapuntal background to her speech. Now it burst out into a full-bellied laugh which went on for quite a while before he silenced it and said:

'Very good! I like it. Most jokes these days are bad jokes, but this is a good one. I am to get Amnon Segev off the hook. Amnon Segev! The well-known advocate of a Palestinian state, the man born without a sense of national self-preservation. The man who, to my face, in my own house, called me a fascist. I am to do his army duty while he hunts for lost actors in the desert. If my wife can spare me, of course . . .' There was a pause. 'Wait while I light a cigarette and then I will decide if I will take part in this excellent joke.'

After a moment, Ann heard him blowing out smoke, tensely, as Shula had done that morning.

'Now. You want me to get dressed and get in my car and drive to the cosy nest of Amnon Segev the Arab-lover, and collect his *reshima*, and spend the rest of the night knocking on doors and waking poor bastards up or interrupting their fucks to get them to sign against their names. Is that it?'

'Yes, Boaz, if – '

'Ann.'

'Yes?'

'Ann.'

'What?'

'Does it send a shiver through your loins when I say your name?'

'Your English is very good,' she said after a breath-stopped moment. ' "Loins" is very good.'

'Yes. And I know other words too, for that place in you that I want to send shivers through, as a preliminary.'

'Boaz,' she said carefully, 'I think, after all – '

'Ah. Now you "think after all". Well, don't think after all, because I have decided the joke is too good to resist, and I am coming. Make some very black coffee because you have to come with me, despite how tired you are. I'm sorry for that, but really,

117

without your presence in my car again, the joke would not be quite good enough to bring me out of my house tonight. With or without my wife's permission.'

'Boaz, wait a minute!'

'Well?'

'Are you sure it matters that much?'

'To have you in my car?'

'*No*. To do the list tonight. If it's just an exercise – if they just want to see how well it works – then perhaps it defeats the whole purpose of the thing if somebody does somebody else's duty.'

'That's almost certainly the fact. So what?'

'Is that how it works? One particular man has to go round to the homes of his particular people?'

'Yes.'

'So mightn't it confuse everybody if the wrong man shows up?'

'On the other hand, what if it were a real emergency?'

'Then you'd know about it by now, everyone would know. There'd be planes buzzing the city, all the radios would be on – we wouldn't be sitting here calmly talking about it, and the men who came wouldn't have been so joky.'

'If you realise all this,' he said, 'why did you phone me?'

Why, indeed! 'I really wanted you just to tell me it wasn't important and that there was nothing to worry about, that I could go to bed with an easy mind.'

'For my part I would think it a disgrace for a woman like you ever to go to bed with an easy mind, as if there were nothing better for you to take there . . . Besides, that's not what you said. Not at all. Your suggestion was that I come and do Amnon Segev's military task.'

'But now I think about it properly – '

' – You would prefer me not to come. You're afraid to let me come, because now you have remembered.'

She found she was taking deep breaths, opposing a weight that seemed to be pressing against her breast bone.

'Listen, Boaz – '

'If you really don't want me now to come, you'd better stop saying "Boaz" to me in that incredibly erotic English voice.'

She contrived a feeble laugh. 'Don't tell me *your* loins are a-quiver at the sound of your own name!' some demon of self-destruction made her say, as if this man were no more dangerous than another Amnon who might be flirted with and teased with impunity.

'I would not speak of loins in my case. My cock is standing up like a ripe cucumber. The long, English kind.'

Good God! she thought, torn between hysterical laughter and something very like panic. What am I doing? I must be as mad as he is! Stop this. Stop it now.

'Enough. Don't come.'

'But I want to. I want to see you. I've been waiting. I haven't seen you for over a whole year. The *sharav* has just broken and it's the middle of the night, always a good time to be with a woman one is attached to.'

'I hope you don't think I phoned you with any – '

'Beware. Beware of lies, English, maidenly lies.'

'I'm no "maiden", Boaz! I'm – '

'A married woman. Yes, you told me so. And now, please start the coffee, because I am coming.'

As she hung up slowly on the dead line, she felt herself descending into turmoil. The first question to ask, of course, was one flavoured with self-rebuke. How she could have allowed herself to invite this threatening situation? But the question that seemed to have priority was, how was it possible to get into such a state of sexual arousal over the phone? Quivers in the loins weren't the half of it. She felt as if her pelvis and its entire contents were on fire.

It was not a sensation that she was any longer accustomed to, and she was thrown into further confusion trying to remember when she had last felt it. Not so far back as Menachem, no. It was rather more recent than that. Almost exactly a year ago, as a matter of honesty-faced fact . . . standing in Boaz Shachterman's garden, the night Amnon came to fetch her, the night the two men had argued politics and their mutual antipathy had been born . . . Earlier that same evening, while Boaz' wife (a strange, dark, withdrawn woman who had left little imprint on Ann's memory) was making them some coffee after their trip to the West Bank, Boaz had led Ann out through the back of his house in an Arab suburb of East Jerusalem to look at his small plantation of citrus, fig and pomegranate; and while they had stood there chatting and sampling late clementines, he had, without warning, in full view of the windows of his house, put his hand up her skirt and left the hard imprint of his fingers, wet with fruit juice, on the inside of her thigh. It had been almost the first time, in their spasmodic six year acquaintance, that he had ever touched her.

119

She had been too astonished (outraged? No, alas, not outraged, just astonished) to move, or look at him, or say a word of protest. He had stood there pressing her thigh for a timeless moment, his voice halted in the middle of whatever impersonal remark he had been making, and then he'd muttered hoarsely in Hebrew: '*Ani rotseh otakh*. I want you.' Then he dropped his hand; her dress fell back; and he went on eating his clementine and telling her about his problems with his Arab landlord.

Because of this extraordinary, and in her experience totally unprecedented incident, the rest of that evening had passed in a haze of confusion, mental and physical. The prolonged discussion between Amnon and Boaz, blending into argument, climaxing in outright brawling, which accompanied the coffee, passed over her head. She had sat in a wicker rocking-chair, as she remembered, looking from one man to the other as if at a tennis match, but actually exclusively absorbed in her own residual physical sensations. Throughout, Boaz' wife – a shadowy figure in a long dress with a headscarf covering all her hair, like a religious woman – moved in and out with a copper *finjan*, replenishing the cups, taking as little part in the conversation as Ann. And never looking at her once. (Had she seen? It didn't bear thinking of.)

On the way home, Amnon had fulminated: 'How can you associate with a crude chauvinist bastard like that? A woman's friends are always carbon copies of herself. I read it somewhere. I hope that fellow's stinking Revisionist views are not at all copies of yours, or I shall have to throw you from my house!'

But Ann had not been thinking about opinions. She had been thinking (if that is the word) of the stickiness between her thighs, not all caused by the juice of the sweet, overripe fruit . . .

She thought about it again now, and thought about why until ten minutes ago she'd stifled the memory of it so successfully that, in her 'hour of need' she had, in the teeth of all her instinctive, self-protective resolutions, been able to pick up the phone and ring his number. Crude, Amnon had said. Who could deny it? Crude in speech, crude in action. How had he dared, that day! How he dared to speak to her *now*, as he had, was obvious – because she had submitted to his outrageous caress and then (as it must seem to him and now seemed fairly obvious to herself as well) come back for more at the first opportunity. She had liked it. More than he knew, for she remembered now very clearly that she had lived on it, sexually, like a hungry man with a well-

120

gnawed crust, for weeks afterwards, after her return to Suffolk, to Peter . . .

She put her head down on the kitchen table, hard, striking her forehead on the backs of her hands. *Disloyal bitch!* One might suppose Peter were impotent, or effeminate, or enfeebled by age. How glad he had been to see her, how enthusiastically he had listened to her doings, how well he had hidden his underlying antipathy to them! And when bed-time came, how warmly he'd embraced her, how well he had made love to her! And it was making love – decently, irreproachably, complete with foreplay and afterplay and loving tender words – as civilised men make love, to the satisfaction of civilised women.

The only trouble was, she had not wanted to be loved in a civilised manner by Peter. She had wanted an altogether rougher kind of wooing at the hands of Boaz Shachterman.

Be that as it might, she had no intention of embarking on an affair with him, tonight or at all. Her actions might belie this determination but what mattered was, not what she had done or not done till now or what interpretation he had chosen to place on these commissions or omissions, but what she did from now on.

He had as good as said there was no need to go out to make the army calls, so they would not do so. When he arrived she would invite him in – this would be perfectly safe because at any moment, probably before he came, the Circus would invade in force. How much longer could it possibly take to find the Red Statue, their car, and the road home? She would give every-body coffee, she and Boaz would exchange a word or two, she would apologise as profusely as seemed dignified and then he would have to go home. He would have gambled, and lost, some exorbitantly expensive petrol; she would have learned a rather searing lesson in decent behaviour; and then all she would have to do would be to see the Circus safely to their beds and mattresses and fall into a simple slough of anxiety about where Amnon had got to.

Unless of course Amnon arrived home in the meantime, in which case Boaz would certainly leave very promptly, and she could go to bed and sleep whatever remained of the night in chaste and self-respecting peace.

At least she would have seen him. She did, most painfully and undeniably, want to see him.

She began to hurry. First, from the kitchen to Amnon's bedroom, where she closed the shutters, straightened the bed, and picked up her sandals from the mat. Then back to the kitchen, where she put on a kettle. Then to the bathroom, where, in what she trusted would be her final shower of the day, she washed away the last traces of the *khamsin*, brushed out her tousled hair and pinned it up afresh, and did something – the minimum, she refused to permit herself more – to her face. She then hurried to her own room, and from her small supply of clothes selected an Indian cotton dress with a high neck and long, billowing sleeves, for its unprovocativeness. It also happened to be the most feminine garment she possessed.

The kettle was whistling. She ran back to the kitchen, turned the gas down, unhooked six mugs, put into them six spoonfuls of Nescafé, and turned the gas low. Then she sat at the table and made a strong effort to calm herself.

But she couldn't. She felt almost frantic with apprehension. If only it weren't the middle of the night! One felt so vulnerable then, one's head was light, one was not in a normal state of mind or body. She should have felt half-dead or at the least, half-asleep, but instead the change in the weather had rendered her restless, vigorous, full of sap. This, on the other hand, had its advantages. The more vigorous and sappy, the stronger and more resistant.

She forced herself to relax. That was the key: she must regard Boaz as a challenge. A challenge to her maturity, to her selfhood – to her marriage. What was loyalty, what was self-sufficiency, what was womanhood or its prides and decent, conditioned restraints, if they were never tested? Good God, she was nearly fifty. She had had affairs; she had had a *love* affair; she had been married for ten years to a man who trusted her and to whom she was devoted. What possible threat was a man like Boaz, alien to all her *moeurs* and values, a foreigner in every sense of the word? He had not even the charm of an Ephraim or a Shimshon, whose minds she felt kin to.

Amnon had been right! If a woman's friends must be reasonable facsimiles of herself, surely, surely her lovers must be her spiritual twins? Boaz Shachterman challenged her upon one ground only, the rough, animal playground of sex, and she had been there, she knew it for what it was: without love it was a snare and a delusion. She could not be caught that way. Let him fix her with his yellow lion's eyes, let him use raw words to inflict illicit thrills, let him frighten her or fill her with lust – he could not get to where she really was. Because she lived up here, in her

122

head, not between her legs, and with words she could keep him away. Crude he might be, and lusty, and perhaps (though she was not sure of this) ruthless and even unprincipled, but he was not a savage. He would not – she searched for the word. He might *accost* her, but he would not *molest* her.

She laughed aloud. Trusty, old-fashioned language! Anglo-Saxon for him, Shakespearean for her! It suited. And Shakespeare, as the more civilised, must win! She made her own coffee, drank it, and felt suddenly on top of the world.

She heard the clang of the iron door, and her heart all but stopped, but then came the chatter and the shrieks of American mirth. There – it was the Circus. Good. Just as she had planned. Now she could invite Boaz in without the slightest fear of anything, from misinterpretation to molestation! She hurried to open the front door and met them as they tottered, more dead than alive, up the last steps.

'Oh my God! Folks – we made it! We got home! I can't believe it – '

'Out of the way, I'm gonna fall flat on my face – '

'I dare not look at my legs. I just know they're worn right up to the knees – I never walked that far in my god-damn life – '

They shambled past her, a parody procession of exhaustion, and streamed into the 'seraglio room' where the four of them dissolved into boneless heaps among the embroidered cushions. Ann, following, turned the top light on and regarded them. Mary and Sue-Ella had both been walking with their shoes off. Their bare feet – the soles of Sue-Ella's actually blacker than Mary's – were extended along their respective mattresses towards Ann, giving them a foreshortened, cartoon-like appearance. Bob was still managing to remain sitting, though slumped with his head between his knees, while his lanky wife had fallen into some kind of yoga position, or perhaps she was praying for strength – she was kneeling on a rug with her thin flanks, in crumpled, dust-stained trousers, in the air and her face on the floor between her arms. It reminded Ann of a posture she'd been advised to adopt in adolescence to alleviate curse pains.

'Who's for coffee?'

There was silence for a moment, and then Bob groaned hollowly, 'To hell with coffee. I'm for a glass of best bourbon.'

With that he scrambled to his feet and shuffled across to the glass-fronted cabinet in which Amnon stored the cartoned bottles of duty-free drink that his casts were wont to bring him, and which he himself seldom touched. Though Ann well knew that, if he were here, he would offer his liquor generously, she was not amused to see Bob making free with it when he wasn't.

'Did Amnon tell you you could help yourself?' she asked with a slight edge, as Bob poured four man-sized glasses from a previously unbreached bottle of Old Kentucky.

'Shit, lady, he won't mind. This is an emergency.'

'You don't understand, honey,' said Sue-Ella, sitting up enough to accept her glass, 'the ordeal we've been through. We have been *lost* – lost is just not the word for what we've been!'

'I did like you told me,' said Bob. 'I went to the nearest house, and I said, *Efo hapessel ha'adom*? Some old lady screamed and slammed the door and next thing I know, there's a Dobermann pinscher or something, baying after me up the hill like the Hound of the Baskervilles. And that happened three times. What's the matter with these people, what do they take me for? Do Jewish burglars come knocking politely at the front door?'

'No,' Ann said, 'but Arab terrorists occasionally do.'

Bob did a bug-eyed double-take.

'Terrorists! Jesus! What are you saying, that we might have met some Ay-rabs in that wilderness-area?'

'That's all we needed,' said his wife in muffled tones from the carpet pile.

'Drink your drink, Chloe,' Bob said shortly.

Now Mary sat up. 'And when we finally found the car,' she drawled, 'what do you think? Good news time. It had been broken into. We lost our cameras, our binoculars – '

'Not your passports and travellers' cheques? Don't tell me you left those!' Ann exclaimed, appalled at the bureaucratic problems such a loss would entail for Amnon.

Mary looked at her and curled her damson lips in scorn.

'You must think we're dumb,' she said, lying flat again.

'Where'd you say Amnon went to?' Bob now had the grace to ask somewhat uneasily. He pronounced it 'Amnone'.

'To Massada. He thought, when you didn't show up, that you might have got stuck somewhere.'

'Aw, Jesus Christ! We should've left a note. But we thought he'd come back from the theatre same time as us.'

'There was no show tonight, he came back early.'

'No show!' exclaimed Chloe, springing upright on her knees like a released willow wand and swaying there. 'Why no show? No show is bad news! No show is – '

124

'Drink your drink now, Chloe,' said Bob.

'I don't want a drink,' she said. 'Bob. Where is it? I gave it to you.'

'I gave it to Mary,' said Bob.

Mary reached into her shoulder-bag and fished out a plastic packet with a sigh. 'Lucky those thieves didn't get their cotton-pickin' hands on *this*,' she said, tossing it to Chloe.

Ann watched in fascination as Chloe got out a filter-tip cigarette and began digging out its contents into a big copper ashtray which she set on the floor between her knees. Then she got some brown crumbly stuff out of the packet and mixed it in with the tobacco.

'Is that going to be a "joint"?' asked Ann, intrigued.

'Don't tell me you never made one!'

'I've never even seen the stuff before.'

Four faces blank with amazement were turned to her.

'Gee, you British sure are living in a different world,' said Sue-Ella. 'How do you get by? How do you get *high*?'

'I don't often need to. When I do, I generally have a drink.'

'This is better,' said Chloe firmly, now stuffing the mixture expertly back into the paper tube. 'No hangover. No problems.'

'Other than the law. It's rather strict in these parts, I believe.'

They all smiled tolerantly, and Mary even sniggered. But when the bell suddenly pealed out they all froze, and the smirks dropped off their faces. Chloe instinctively thrust the packet under the nearest mattress and the 'joint' into her cleavage.

'Who in hell's *that*?' asked Sue-Ella, pansy eyes wide.

'Must be a terrorist! And me without my Dobermann!' said Bob, in mock alarm.

'It's all right,' said Ann, amazed by the steadiness of her voice and needing only one deep breath to calm her heartbeat. 'I'm expecting someone.' She turned to leave, but Chloe stopped her.

'Did you look in on Dill Boy?'

'Yes. He's all right, but I took that heavy quilt off him. He was melting.'

Chloe glared at her. 'And now it's turned cool, just as I said it would,' she said severely. 'That child only has to be *breathed* on – you'll see, he'll be streaming with cold by tomorrow. He can't do hand-stands with a runny nose, you know.'

Ann went out, leaving doors wide open all the way to the hall, but she didn't turn the light on there. She was suddenly aware that it was late, that she was, even if she'd lost the awareness of it,

125

very tired, and that she was a year older than she'd been a year ago. That was, of course, another advantage she had in this coming encounter – she was three years the elder. And she would remember that, and use it. Still, there was no need to flood the place with light straight away. The merciless kitchen neon would betray her years soon enough.

She opened the door. He stood there, in silhouette against the swaying trees and the deflected glow of the street-lamp. She'd forgotten how big he was – a huge man, broadly-built and heavy, with stiff curly hair, unmoved by the cool wind . . . But this was not the first thing she noticed and remembered. It was the impact, something like the pressure-wave from a blast, that she felt as soon as she stood before him.

'Come on,' he said at once in his voice of gravel.

'What – ? Not this minute! Come in – '

'No.'

'What do you mean, why not?'

'I'm not coming in. Let's go if we're going.'

'But the coffee – '

'The coffee was for you. I've had. Have you got the list?'

'It's in the kitchen.'

'Get it. And bring a coat or something, it's cool now.'

'Boaz, I've been thinking – '

'So have I. We both think far too much. Hurry up, I don't want to be all night over this.'

For a second she stood still. What was going on in her mind hardly justified the term 'debate'. It was more a hopeless glance round her at the ruins of her defence system, or her plan of campaign. Then she walked silently back into the flat, leaving him outside.

She told Bob she was going out. She scratched a note to Amnon – ('Troops home, I'm out, all well, explain in the morning.'). She picked up her hold-all, lifted Amnon's velour zip-up jacket off its hook in place of the only coat she possessed, which was too heavy, and returned to the dark hall.

She felt benumbed. He had not greeted her, or touched her. His manner had been terse, irritable, as if this excursion were an imposition which he resented. If that was how, on reflection, he now saw it, then she had nothing to worry about. They would make the rounds and come home and she would have nothing worse to face than his ill temper and taciturnity, of which she had had several tastes at previous meetings. After their row in the car,

126

he had scarcely spoken a word to her for the hour it took them to get home, even when they had stopped in Jericho for a cold drink and a *felafel* . . . He had not been merely unamorous but positively uncongenial. He was disquieting in this mood – he gave off emanations of violence – but she could cope with that with equanimity, compared to the other.

She could still refuse to go. That was what she'd intended. She turned to face the open doorway and opened her mouth to speak to the brooding giant silhouette; but a sudden jerk of impatience which turned his head into profile stopped her. He had not had a beard last year, and now he had one, stiff and wiry like his hair. She stood in the dark, poised to deliver her refusal. He reached his right hand into his jacket pocket and took out cigarettes and a lighter. As it flared she saw that the beard was full of grey, and that his left arm was no use . . . A strong impulse with nothing sexual about it pushed her towards him.

'Okay,' he said curtly. 'Let's go.'

CHAPTER 10

The old two-door Volkswagen, which she very well remembered, was parked under a street lamp just outside the house. He had been careful to lock it up, though the night was silent and empty of malefactors. Ann, who was by nature so trusting that she left her car open windowed and unlocked even in London, regarded this as a sign of paranoia. The car showed signs of advanced age and considerable wear and tear, but not of having been subjected to the effects of a hand grenade. Perhaps he had been driving a government car at the time.

He got in at his side and leaned across to open the passenger door for her. As she got in she saw that the car had been adapted for an invalid driver, with a foot-gear and a gadget on the steering wheel. His left arm lay half on his lap, but with the hand just resting on the bottom curve of the wheel. She glanced at it and instinctively averted her eyes. There was something terribly wrong with it. In the light from the street lamp it looked as if half the fingers were gone.

She realised now that she hadn't allowed herself to take in what Neville had told her. It had affected her, of course; probably it had pushed her, subconsciously, into making that phone call. But she hadn't envisaged him crippled. Though she knew him, in fact, so little, she intuitively knew that any sort of physical incapacity, however come by, would be psychologically hard for him to bear. For her part, her one horrified glimpse of that ruined hand had had a really alarming effect on her heart, which began to thump all but audibly and very distressingly.

Boaz took a torch out of the glove-compartment and switched it on.

'Give me the thing,' he said.

She gave the list to him. He pinned it to the wheel with what was left of the fingers on his left hand and shone the light on it, studying the first address. Then he shoved it in his pocket, grunted and started the car. He still drove as recklessly as ever. The bad hand helped only marginally on the wheel. With his right, he spun and wrestled with it as if it were trying to get the better of him.

She stared ahead, concentrating on calming her heart rate, which the speed of the car, even in empty streets, was not helping. She longed to look at him. How had his ordeal, and the last year in general, changed him? She wanted to look at the beard. The grey in it somehow strengthened his attraction for her. He had always seemed so much younger than herself, before; now that he was grey and she was not, that moderating factor was diminished. She admitted this to herself in order to avoid suppressing it. The half-dead arm, the broken-off fingers, moved her so powerfully that she could not deny it to herself.

But she didn't want him to feel she was looking at him, so she observed him through his driving. He was evidently in a different mood altogether from the one on the phone. He seemed to be tense and furious about something. She could feel it in his silence, in the angry way his body moved, bullying the wheel and the car, forcing it to do as much for him as it had done when he was whole . . . At this thought, Ann turned right away, automatically adopting her habitual position, her chin on her arm along the window-sill. The wind blew her hair back and made her eyes sting: there was still some residual dust in it.

The first address was in Katamon. They were there in five or six minutes. Boaz stood on the brakes, opened his door by reaching his right hand across and through his window (the inside handle must be broken), got out, slamming it after him, and strode away up the flagged path and into the shadows under the stilt-raised building. She stayed where she was, watching the landing lights go on, and saw him mount to the third floor. Then there was a pause of several minutes. The lights went off by themselves. She waited for them to go on again, but he came out before they did – he must have come downstairs in the dark.

He got into the car, again slamming the door. She winced, thinking of the many sleepers within earshot in this densely inhabited district. Without a word he took out his torch and looked at the second name on the list. Ann looked too, sideways. There was no signature beside the first.

'Didn't he sign it?' she ventured to ask. It was the first word spoken since they'd started.

'No.'

'Was he there?'

'Sure he was there. He refused to sign because he didn't know me.'

'Was he angry?'

'Yes. And so was I.'

He threw the car into gear again and performed a screeching

129

U-turn, twisting his body till his back was towards her in order to put a hard lock on the wheel. He accelerated sharply and they drove back the way they had come.

'Might they all be like that?'

'It's possible.'

'So what's the point? Let's forget it.'

He didn't answer. They drove through the darkness. It was strange to see the city so empty. The car formed a little moving, noise-making, lighted entity in the midst of silence and lifelessness. She felt a strong desire to move closer to him. She could feel the warmth of his body near her and yet not near enough. She shivered, and for the first time he glanced at her – not a tender glance.

'I told you to bring a coat.'

'I brought this jacket of Amnon's.'

'So you wear his clothes? What an intimacy. I see it just fits you. Or is it a little too small?'

'Do you allow yourself to despise him for his size?'

'I give myself full permission to despise him for being an idiot who talks nothing but bullshit.'

'He likes you, too,' she couldn't resist saying.

He gave a grunt that might have been half-humorous had he not been in such a bad mood. 'Did he cry to you, after that meeting at my house?' he asked.

'It was more of a snarl, really.'

'I might give him a point for that, if he were an opponent I could at all respect.'

She was opening her mouth to ask a question when they screeched once more to a stop. The second address was not far from the first – probably all the people on Amnon's list lived reasonably close to him, for the sake of efficiency and speed of call-up in an emergency. The process was repeated – only that this time, the flat was on the ground floor, at the front, and she could hear the altercation. This man signed all right, but with bad grace and after a good deal of noisy argument and complaint. The slam of the car door this time nearly shook it from its hinges, and caused several lights to go on in nearby dwellings.

'Boaz, please calm down. Your driving always scared me, even when you weren't in a rage.'

'Even when I had two good arms?'

'Yes, if you want to put it that way.'

'I should have warned you on the phone,' he said after a moment. 'Perhaps I wanted to shock you. Or had you heard?'

'Yes.'

'Who from? Not your little friend Segev?'

'No. A newspaperman.'

'Baum.'

'Yes, as a matter of fact.'

'I heard he was nosing around at the time.'

'He said it was hushed up.'

'Not that I know of,' Boaz said. 'I simply told the doctors not to let anyone in. Except my wife, of course.'

'How is she?' Ann asked, her English politeness compelling her.

Now he threw her a curious look.

'Didn't Baum tell you about that too?'

'About what?'

'About my wife. Did he, for instance, tell you she was in the car with me when it happened?'

After a shocked moment, Ann turned fully towards him. 'My God, Boaz! Did anything happen to her?'

He smiled. 'How you English specialise in the well-turned euphemism! You mean, was she killed, was she blown out onto the road, did she lose a leg or have her head blown off?' He glanced at her. 'H'm? Why don't you ask that?'

'Just tell me, will you? What happened?'

They were driving now through the fringes of Talbiyeh. He was going more slowly, looking out for the street-names, printed in ridiculously small letters and often concealed by trees.

'Nothing,' he said after a bit. 'She was on the side away from the window where the grenade entered the car.'

'But if it exploded inside the car – '

'You won't be satisfied without all the details, will you? We were stopped at the time. We'd had a meal in Ramallah, at that café I took you to once, on our way back from the North. We'd just got into the car and I was going to start when I saw a man dash across the street and throw something. I knew at once what it was. If I'd been outside the car I could have caught it like a ball and lobbed it back. It came in and landed first on my leg, then as I grabbed at it, it rolled onto the floor just by my left foot. I snatched it up and flung it out. It exploded just then, just as it left my hand. I was lucky. A second earlier and I wouldn't even have this much left.' He took his right hand off the wheel for long enough to lift the other up by the wrist for her to see.

131

Now she saw the extent of the damage. The forefinger was gone; the next two were still misshaped stumps, not yet quite fully healed. The little finger was intact, but the thumb had only its first joint. After a second or two, he grabbed the wheel as the car swerved and the crippled hand dropped out of sight.

'Does it disgust you?' he asked, his harsh voice suddenly muted.

'Yes, deeply. But not in the way you mean.'

'Could you touch that wreck of a thing? Doesn't it make you want to spew?'

'You evidently know very little about women.'

He gave a brief, surprised laugh.

'I said nothing about your experience in the field. I said you know very little about women if you imagine that I or any of us could be repelled, in that sense, by that kind of wound.'

He drove in silence for a moment, and then said, 'It's you who don't understand your own sex. My wife came to see me dutifully each day until the dressings came off. Of course it looked much worse then – swollen, pussy, deformed – it was a terrible sight, as a matter of fact. Even I couldn't look at it for a day or two. But she demanded to see it. And when she did, she vomited on the hospital floor.'

After a moment, Ann managed to say, 'That wasn't revulsion, Boaz. It was empathy.'

'Was it? So why did she leave me the week after I got home?'

They had reached the next address. He stopped more circumspectly this time, and they sat in silence for a while. Ann was wrestling with conflicting feelings. There was nothing she felt safe in saying. After a minute or two, Boaz once again got out of the car, closing the door, but instead of stamping away, he leaned in and asked, curiously and without aggressiveness this time: 'Why did she do that? I'm asking you to tell me.'

'Didn't she tell you?'

'She was bad at talking. Of course she said it was not because of *this*. You are right in one thing, no woman would confess to such a negative reaction to her injured husband. She spoke about other things. The house we lived in. The district. She asked me to move into the Jewish sector of the city. I couldn't even consider it of course, because of my work, my contacts . . . everything. And now also because – '

He stood upright and she lost sight of his head and shoulders.

'Because it would look like an admission of fear, after the

attack on you?'

'Of defeat.' His voice came faintly through the open window. 'I couldn't. Anyway it would be stupid. You can't ever let them see you are running. The sight of an enemy's back is enough to bring out in them the ultimate savagery – the savagery of triumph. Of course, your little friend would call me a fascist for saying so.'

'No, Boaz.'

'You think not. You don't know how his pissy little peacenik's mind works.'

With that he left. He was gone a full ten minutes this time. She sat alone in the dark (he had parked between street lamps) and did battle with a compassion that threatened to spill over into a sort of *bogus* sensuality. She was aware of an overriding need to keep sentimentality out of it, to whittle down her emotions to something real and genuine. It was quite hard enough to cope with that core.

He returned and climbed into the car stiffly, as if the vigour generated by his anger was leaving him and he was tired. No irritated lights snapped on for the door slam this time. He took out the cigarette packet, and now she noticed his awkwardness, how his mouth had to help with the business, his lips groping . . .

'You're not right-handed,' she said suddenly.

'I am now,' he grimly replied.

'Oh God! What abominable luck – '

'It was good luck. The grenade fell on my left side – I told you. Even with my training, at a moment like that I'm not sure I could have picked it up and thrown it if it had been not on my good side.'

'Why do you think it was done?'

'Why does a snake strike? They hate us and they're killers.'

'But why pick on you?'

He gave her a swift look, as if suspecting that something lay behind the question. Perhaps it did. Neville's words were coming back to her – 'On the payroll of the Ministry of Defence'. He said, 'I don't think they picked on me. Someone had stolen a grenade. I was there. That's how it normally happens – at random. They don't plan.'

'They planned Hebron.'

'Yes,' he said slowly. 'They planned Hebron.' He smoked in silence for a while. She was aware that the atmosphere between them had subtly altered. She had gone on to the offensive. It seemed as good a method of defence as any. She followed it up.

133

'Perhaps it wasn't just an accident. Perhaps they owed you something.'

'What makes you say that? You've seen how I move among them. Do I do anything to arouse their homicidal anger?'

'I've never been clear exactly what your business with them is.'

He sat round to face her, the cigarette glow coming and going as he drew on it, showing his powerful jutting nose, slanting eyebrows and a strange expression – half humorous, half embittered.

'You know,' he said, 'I like a hard challenge from a woman, a tough fight. I mean, of course, a mental one. Physically I don't welcome resistance. If a woman wants me, I can't be bothered with a lot of coy pretences, and if she doesn't, let her say so and finish. I don't like coquettes and I don't like little girls . . .' He smoked and watched her and she forced herself to look back at him in the dark. 'I haven't changed,' he said quietly, 'since last year, and the years before. Oh, I have changed – I don't recognise myself in many things – but not about you. These attachments go very deep with me. And they're rare, now.'

She said nothing. She was fighting all right, but it was against some strengthening compulsion within herself, not against him. Don't touch me, she thought, don't come an inch nearer – I can't stand up to it. How could I have lived thirty years of womanhood and never had to stand up to anything like this before?

'Don't go to sleep.'

'I'm not.'

'Why have you closed your eyes? Are you afraid of me?'

'Yes. And you're glad of it,' she said in a low, tense voice. 'The savagery of triumph . . .'

He let out a single sudden, astonished laugh, and turned to start the car. 'Is that your way of fighting? To throw my words back at me, completely out of context? In any case, there's no triumph yet. And there'll be no savagery, or not more than you want. I fuck with passion, not brutality.'

For some reason the word 'fuck' always made her want to laugh – some residual embarrassment, perhaps, shared by many of her generation who had never managed to overcome early conditioning, despite those with the advantage Ann had had, of a step-son who regarded it as a word for all seasons. The desire to giggle at Boaz' rather portentous, Lawrentian use of the word restored to her now some sense of proportion and she was able to smile a bit and say, 'Thank you, Boaz. There's no actual need for you to give yourself the hard sell in that department.'

'I admire your English,' he said. 'I model myself on you. 'Hard sell' could not be more appropriate. Did you mean it to be?'

The fiery knots of lust loosened themselves for the moment. She leant back in her seat and took a few slow, deep breaths and blew them out in jerks.

'Why are you laughing?' he demanded.

'Oh, Boaz! If you want me to take you seriously, you'd better mend your choice of words. Model your English on mine, indeed! I'm not flattered. You talk like a navvy, or a young boy showing off. My step-son used to pepper his dinner-table conversation with your kind of English in an effort to shock his father and me.'

'I don't do it to shock anyone, but because I like those words, for their directness. I've no time to waste in . . . Come on, give me a good word now – '

'How about "circumlocutions"?'

'Nice. Very nice. I've nothing *against* words of more than four letters.'

And now, the first touch – light and fleeting, on the knee. On one level, she hardly felt it. On another – a knife cut could not have been more poignant. She curbed a gasp and sought escape.

'Boaz, did the last one sign?'

'No.'

'Don't you think we ought to give up and go home? It must be nearly four o'clock. Do you have to work tomorrow?'

'I have a report to write, but it can wait till I've slept.'

(A report . . .? For whom? On what?)

'Well, I have an interview at 10 a.m. with a professor of history. He's a busy and important man and he's agreed to see me at his home. I shall be too tired to ask him any intelligent questions if I don't get some sleep.'

'Need I remind you this was your idea?'

'No. Need I remind you that I conceded in advance that it was a bad one?'

'It was a very good one. It was a wonderful excuse for ringing me up. It gives us now an occasion to spend some hours alone together.'

'Then why did you arrive in such a filthy temper?'

He pulled up by the side of the road. She expected him to go through the routine of consulting the list and getting out of the car, but he didn't. He threw away his cigarette end and stared through the windscreen, frowning.

'Why are you living with him?'

135

'Who? Amnon?' Ann was startled. 'I'm not "living with" him, Boaz, I'm just staying there.'

'Why?'

'Why? Because it's very convenient. Three bus routes pass the door. There are shops within two minutes' walk. I'm free to use the phone, make myself meals, entertain people, come and go exactly as I please – in a word, make myself completely at home.'

'You could do all that with me.'

'No, Boaz!'

'Why?'

'Isn't it perfectly obvious?'

'It would have been, if you had known that I am living alone. But you thought my wife was still with me. No danger to your precious "reputation", if that is what your English conventionalness worried about. I mean, if you had considered it.'

'I didn't consider it, Boaz. Not for a moment. For one thing I always stay with Amnon when I come. I like him – '

'That's incredible to me.'

She turned to face him. 'After that meeting between you, he said the same to me about you. He said he hoped my political opinions were nothing like yours or I would hardly be welcome in his house any more.'

'If I didn't know he is a fucker of any woman he can lay hands on, I would say that is the remark of a homosexual. Petty. Stupid. Weak. Would I deny you my house because your ideas are full of *shit*?' he asked, raising his voice on a sudden impulse of rage. 'Do I demand political credentials from my friends? Only you so-called liberals are that illiberal! And the women are the worst – that's why I say Segev's remark was effeminate. Friends that we had for years have drawn back from us because of my views, which seem to turn their delicate pink stomachs. Only a few are secure enough in their utopianism to stand up to reality. There is one editor of a certain leftish magazine who comes to my house and uses me to test out his half-cocked reconciliation theories. We shout back and forth for three hours, then we shake hands and he goes away and writes a lot of rubbish about the wickedness of us hard-liners who would not for any price have a Palestinian state on our flank, who would go to any lengths to keep those hills in our hands and who don't wish to play into the hands of the Russians in this region . . . It is endlessly astonishing to me that someone like you, with some pretensions to intelligence, can play the Kremlin's game like any blinkered Communist – '

Ann felt heat of an entirely asexual nature rising in her.

'Don't call me a Communist, please. I know what Communism is. I hate it.'

'Then why do you ally yourself with these simpletons and traitors who want Palestinian sovereignty in Samaria and Judea? Don't you know the Russians would be in there the week after, that this is all they are waiting for? You and your kind – ' he was shouting again – 'are as good for the Soviet Union's plan for a new Dark Age under their domination as any Red agitators they could plant and pay to do their work for them!'

'And would you have called yourself a Red henchman in 1948, when they took a pro-Zionist stand in the UN and helped lead world opinion in favour of a Jewish state? One simply can't orientate oneself politically on the basis of what the Russians want or don't want, or are for or against at any given moment! As a matter of fact you're wrong, even about now. Their basic interest is in unrest in the Middle East. If there were ever peace in the region, they'd lose all their clout. Anything, such as the Egyptian peace treaty, that looks as if it might militate against unrest, they oppose. If Israel were to stop building settlements and dispossessing Palestinians on the West Bank – which I notice you call Samaria and Judea like any religious fanatic – and help the indigenous population towards the self-determination they need as much as the Jews ever did, the Russians would be furious, because they'd see it as a step in the defusing of this hideously dangerous situation.'

Her voice was now almost as loud as his. This had happened before. It was an old battleground, and she was enjoying herself. It excited her to quarrel with him. At the same time it reassured her, because if that excitement had a sexual element, she was active enough mentally to keep it in the background. 'Intellectual passion casts out sensuality.'

'I take back my very rare compliment about your intelligence,' he was saying. 'You are actually quite stupid, I find. You can see and admit that the situation is dangerous and yet you fail to understand the logical consequence of us stripping ourselves naked. We stripped ourselves naked in Sinai. Not enough for you? We yielded everything – strategic mountain passes, airfields, military installations costing millions, *oil* – our own oil fields that we developed, that never have we needed so desperately as we need them now. Even settlements will have to be abandoned – do you have any idea what that means for us? And we got for all of it, nothing – not a bloody thing except bits of paper and empty words.'

'Oh, come! We got all we've ever asked for,' interrupted Ann hotly, falling unconsciously into an ambivalent use of the first person pronoun. 'We got recognition. We got a peace treaty. We got a formal acknowledgement of our right to exist, from our strongest enemy – '

'So they acknowledged our right to exist! Very kind of them, to grant us what the world gave us thirty-two years ago and what we have fought and died proving ever since! All that is nothing but a bad joke. They can take it all back at any time. There is now a hitch in the autonomy talks, and you'll see how fast Sadat will threaten to take it all back when we don't put our head straight on the block to save his face! Can *we* take back our dismantled installations? Can we repair, in a year or so from now, the fatal damage we shall have done to the Negev, the most beautiful and purest part of our heritage, by forcing it to replace the Sinai as our military area? Can we recover our oil wells as easily as the Egyptians can withdraw their ambassador and suspend the treaty? I suppose you think you can trust Sadat – '

'Yes, I do think so.'

'We are lucky you're not our Minister of Defence! Though you're no worse than a lot of our so-called politicians who would give the Arabs our whole country on a plate. See what our present so-called hawkish Prime Minister gave, like a puppet on Carter's fingers – his own devoted followers, of which I was never one, are calling him a traitor. But of course, no one gives us any credit for this idiotic sacrifice, and they never will, because the world is just one big oil-hungry anti-semite who would rather grovel to murderers than pay another half-dollar a litre for *benzine*. If they knew what sort of people they are dealing with – if they had to live with them . . . But it would make no difference. The Jews are alone as they've always been. The difference is that now we have our own ground under us and our own army. If we show them a face they can stamp on again, they'll stamp on it fast enough – Europe, America, Russia – who has not stamped on the Jewish face, or at best, stood by watching while it was done? And don't say "the Muslims". It is a myth that we lived with them for centuries in peace, they have eaten us with a spoon as greedily as any other people . . . What we have to show them, all of them, is a face that if they stamp on it, it will blow up under their feet. We have to show them that we will fight, not just like a tiger – a nice clean handsome tiger that the world can admire before they lay its hide on their polished floors – but like wolves, like rats, like mad dogs, like whatever will frighten them into leaving us alone. The image of *Shelli*, the peace party – that will frighten them? The image of the held-out hand, the humane brotherly conciliating smile? The image of the intellectual, the civilised internationalist? We've been all those things. Look where it got us. Nobel prizes for the few and the gas chambers for the millions, and the deepest shame it's possible for a people to feel, those who lived and those who died. Now the only shame we need ever feel, ever again, is if we are *fools* enough to put ourselves back in their power. Stupidity is the greatest danger, stupidity like yours.'

She sat beside him in silence. The windscreen was spattered with little flecks of his saliva.

'Boaz, there's something I want to ask you.'

'Go on.'

'How much of your life – just as a matter of interest – would you mind me knowing about?'

'Ninety per cent,' he answered instantly.

'What! Why so much?'

'Because I don't share my life with anyone, or my past, which is the same thing. Even with the people I care for. Especially them. I'm not like these old warriors who pour out their war stories when you press a button, as if they were Catholics easing their consciences with confessions, as if telling the tales again and again could rid them of the burden. I could tell you things that would make most men's war stories sound like a lullaby. And perhaps it would help me in the cheap and easy way it helps them, not to think of these things any more, except selectively, the good brave parts that keep the ego afloat in a sea of – '

He stopped. (What word had he stopped himself from saying?)

'But I won't do it,' he went on. 'Those things *must* be thought about. They *must* be lived with. Silently, inwardly. Telling them is like crying out with pain, or groaning with pleasure in sex. It's all the same, the animal noises of letting out emotions which should be held in to do their natural work. People judge a man weak if he weeps. I don't despise a man for weeping, I wept myself when I saw my hand, when my wife left me. But I wept silently. I judge a man if he talks too much, if he can't bear his memories alone.'

'Memories can eat the soul like acid.'

'So what? They're meant to.'

'No, Boaz! Communication is the name of the human game. It's a greater healer than time.'

'Who's talking about healing?' he said. 'I don't want to be healed.'

They fell into a lull. He lit another cigarette and drove on to the next address, and the next, while she sat motionless and silent, her brain and her emotions meeting on a rising pinnacle. Boaz. Boaz. What is happening? What are you doing? What is it you're making me want? It's not just sex with you any more. I think I could endure wanting that; to find I could hold this much desire in control would add to my self-respect, and besides – sexual tension is creatively potent. Who knows, it might be the making of a good novel, if I could resist you. And I think I could have stood against the demands I feel clamouring, though I've never felt them so sharply, no, never, not even with Menachem because with him they were never frustrated. What is growing harder to endure with every word you speak is the dawning realisation of what you mean to me, what you represent. In some almost metaphysical way, *you are Israel* . . . I'll think about that later. Now I am here with you, and about what's going to happen between us – what I've already, before any real struggle has begun, acknowledged is bound to happen – there's nothing metaphysical. Or is there? Yes, there is now. You've given the whole thing an added dimension.

Why did I want you from the moment I saw you? As an antidote to some guilt? What guilt could be so great that its serum would need to be someone like you? Perhaps the ultimate human sin – shallowness of spirit, self-righteousness in judgement, failure of empathy and participation. If you take hold of me you will open me wide and dig me deep – sexual imagery, yes, but spiritual as well. Because I am spoilt. I am naive. I live free from the taint of violence which is a fundamental part of life on this planet, and, as I learnt from my step-son, also of me. I live in security and in a kind of moral blindness while soldiers and spies, policemen, jailors, politicians and simple butchers do my dirty work for me. In every sense imaginable, I eat meat and turn my face from the slaughter. Is that living?

I love this country. I love its intensity, its closeness to the wellsprings of life and its intimacy with death and tragedy. I pretend to love only its so-called finest elements, its intellec-tuals, its pioneers and idealists, its courageous soldiers, its poets and artists. But all of them float on the sea of – what was the word you stopped at? Could it have been blood, blood-guiltiness? Isn't that what you have been talking about?

I am coming perilously close to the secret of the dark tress, of the rank water into which it's dipped at night to rid it of its clean, sunlit fairness, to impregnate it with the blackness of that part of humanity's business which is violence and not love, war and destruction and not peace and creativeness. You're trying so hard not to give me a glimpse into the depths. You know instinctively that it's safer for both of us if I see only my own face reflected on the surface – ageing but still callow with lack of suffering and of the blood-guiltiness which you and others I've talked to have to bear, each in his own way, to make my pleasant, guilt-free life possible. But you *shall* show me what lies under the surface. I am asking to be shown. I am sitting here in self-invited peril, and tomorrow I will not be the same, because you will have taken possession of me. Not only my body. It's not that side of it – not the violence that you are bound to wreak on me and which part of me passionately wants – that I am concerned with now. It's not even my honour, around which I won't put quote marks because Peter wouldn't, that I'm thinking about. It is that after we have made love, or fucked, or whatever you please to call it – tomorrow, when I am changed for ever – I shall leave no stone unturned to find out what it is that you are hiding from me. I shan't rest till I've discovered the truth. Not because I want to break into your private world, Boaz, but because I demand to be part of it, to share it in the only way I can. That old woman at the bus stop was right! Why should women escape, when they claim their share of the spoils? I *want* to lose my innocence. Innocence is for the young and for the non-participants and I am neither. It's not an innocent world I live in and I am not a member of an innocent species. I don't want to live any longer on the surface of that sea you would not name, which is really the dark pool, in my cosy little boat. I want to swim with you and with the rest who probe life at profound levels hardly known to the likes of me. And if I have to drown as payment for my temerity, then down I shall go, blind and choking, with or without your arms round me. But at least I shall not spend the rest of my life floating on the surface or paddling in the shallows, with my skirts held clean and dry.

A woman in a play once said, 'I can't bear it. I can't take part in all this suffering.' I want to be able to say: *I can*.

CHAPTER 11

They went to all the addresses. Only about half of the men on the list were at home, and agreed to sign. But Boaz wouldn't give up. Talking little, smoking a lot, he drove doggedly through the night streets until dawn came and the traffic of the day reasserted its sovereignty.

And at last it was done. He drove her back to Amnon's flat and pulled up outside the iron door. It was already light, and the market trucks and early workers' buses were roaring down between the stone walls, their racket buffetting the ears, as the sun came up out of a clean, dust-free sky over the golden city.

'Okay. We've finished.'

'What time is it?' She'd forgotten to wind her watch.

'Five past five.'

They sat for a few more moments in silence. Then he took the list out of his pocket. It was crumpled now. There were six hard-won signatures scribbled on it.

'Here. Give it to him. Tell him who did it for him. Listen to the laugh he gives when you say it. He will tell you it wasn't important, that a phone call this morning to his officer would fix it, that you shouldn't have called me.'

She took the list, waiting.

'I've bought you from him.'

Startled, she looked at him. His face in the cool, lucid dawn light was drawn.

'Go in, leave a note for him, say what you like about it, or nothing. Take your things, what you need. Not everything. I don't expect you to move in with me, you can decide that later. Just take what you need at once. Live with me till 9 a.m. In four hours you will know where you belong. And so will I.'

He didn't touch her or try to seduce or persuade her. The need of a man without a wife that might have been employed to grapple her to him was not in evidence. She took the list and her hold-all and got out of the car without a word and went through the door and up the steps and let herself into the flat.

Everything was quiet. She went straight to the kitchen. Her note was still there – Amnon had not returned. She tore it up, and replaced it with another, which she pinned to the list: 'This was delivered late last night. In your absence, I contacted Boaz Shach-

142

terman and we got as many signatures as we could. Hope I did the right thing. I've gone to – '

She stopped. It was nobody's business but hers and it was very private and she didn't want Amnon, who was an inveterate gossip, to know anything. It was most unlikely he would be home before eight, and it was not unheard-of for her to have an interview at that time. She continued:

' – an interview. See you later. As you'll see, Circus all present and correct. Hope you didn't have a ghastly night.' She signed it, from habit, 'love, A.' She did love him, she thought. She would continue to love him. Boaz might change much, but he would not change her affection for Amnon and Ruth and Eli and all those she had loved before him. She felt, nonetheless, as if she were being pulled away from her life, leaving everything familiar and safe behind.

Now she stood for a moment, looking round. 'Take what you need,' he had said. What did she need? Before she went to Boaz' bed she needed to be clean. That she could perhaps arrange. But she also needed to be twenty years younger, a stone lighter, and very, very beautiful. She needed to be many things that she was not, including as womanly as Mother Earth and as wise as all the sages. Only then, she felt, could she steal him from his darker self, conquer his evil djinn and compel it back into its scaly bottle, subdue that angry fighting spirit, which kept glaring rawly out at her like a jungle animal, for the pleasure of watching it sink down behind his eyes – not crushed because he didn't want it crushed, and neither did she, but quelled for the time. She needed the skills to make him groan with pleasure and not be ashamed of it or consider it a weakness, to make him laugh as the primitives do as they make love, from however temporary an innocence and a longer-lasting joy, impossible to him now, surrounded and filled as he was with all that angry anguish.

But her needs did not really include a toothbrush or a nightgown. However, she went to the lavatory. Even at that moment, her severely practical side asserted itself.

And now came the point of no return. If she walked out of the flat and down the steps, the iron door at the bottom was the last frontier. As surely as she passed through it, she would become an unfaithful wife and the mistress of a man she hardly knew, and had good reason to fear. She stood by Amnon's kitchen table under the workaday neon and felt her deep tiredness and the utter unwisdom of making such an irrevocable decision now. It was not too late. She could still turn back, be her safe, integrated, moral self for some time longer. No guilt need torment her, no schisms rend her – she could go to her own bed and wake up in a pleasant state of virtue and tranquillity of mind.

Neither of these reliable sustainers of herself until this moment, however, made the least appeal to her any longer.

She laid the list and the note on the table and went out, turning off the light and locking the door behind her, as the prudent Amnon had instructed. Outside on the balcony she hesitated, turned back, unlocked the door again and went into the hall. There she took off Amnon's velour jacket and replaced it on its hook, then unfastened her watch and slipped it in the pocket. It was a perfectly conscious gesture, not unlike Canute's, bidding time to stop.

Boaz was standing beside the car. He stiffened as she appeared through the iron door. She had a good look at his face by daylight for the first time in a year. She could almost have smiled at the irony . . . What price the much-vaunted 'kibbutz look' now? Boaz almost epitomised its antithesis. There was nothing trim or fine-drawn there. The heavy, brooding face matched his big, thickset body; not only did it lack anything to call good looks, it was almost ugly. It was also the most powerful and masculine face she had ever seen. But at least its expression now was untrammelled, almost happy – no triumph, savage or otherwise, but as bland as she had ever seen it, with a sort of relief . . . But there was as much tension in the gesture with which he threw away his cigarette end, as she felt in herself. She stood before him and he put his whole hand up and touched her face.

They got into the car and he drove in silence the longish way to his home. The route took them across the valley bridge below Yemin Moshe, round the base of Mount Zion, past Talpiot, on the Bethlehem Road to the Arab district where he had chosen to live, and his wife had chosen to live no longer. Ann had not felt any kinship for her, but she understood this decision rather better, it seemed, than Boaz did. Because Ann felt as alien here as she had felt last night in the taxi, though it was now broad daylight and everyone she saw was busy in routine, unexceptional ways – opening up shops, standing in queues, going about their business. Arabs . . . Such as the one who had run across a road to kill Boaz. For thirteen years his wife had lived out here, with no Jewish neighbours, sought out by a dwindling number of friends who probably all either thought them mad or suspected them of some

144

ulterior motive. Of necessity (and not occasionally, for pleasure, like Ruth) she had shopped at their shops and ridden on their crowded decaying buses which had not even yet been brought into the official metropolitan transport system; she had worn western clothes and been stared and pointed at; she had been constantly aware of being different in the eyes of those around her, and an outsider, a possibly inimical one at that. There had been incidents before, which Ann had heard hints of – with the landlord, the tradesmen, the neighbours. Boaz had to go away often, and his wife would have been left alone in the house . . . Ann didn't blame her for wanting to move! And then, to crown it all – the grenade. A ghastly shock, a traumatic outcome – and a husband who *still* refused to budge, who *still* would not understand . . .

Why am I thinking of her now? Ann wondered. I have never thought of her. This is a fine moment to begin to empathise with her, just when I am on my way to her bed.

Boaz' house was off the main road, separated from its neighbours, backing onto a wide, hilly expanse of empty uncultivated land. The car drew up on the gravel shoulder and they walked along a path, through a well-kept front garden full of fruit trees. The noise of a rattling chain barely preceded the sudden and startling apparition, round the corner of the house, of an enormous dog, a sinister-looking creature half-way between an Alsatian and a Great Dane. It rushed at Boaz and leapt up on him. He ordered it off peremptorily and made it sit while he fumbled for his key; but its hind quarters hardly grazed the path before it made another bound, this time at Ann.

She was not afraid of dogs, and had already seen that it was scarcely more than a puppy. When Boaz turned quickly to rescue her, he found her fondling its ears as it stood with its huge paws on her shoulders. He watched her for a moment and she thought he smiled; then he ordered the dog to get down.

'I'm sorry if she scared you.'

'She didn't scare me. You didn't have a dog last year.'

'Last year I had a human companion. And last year I wasn't so aware of the need to protect myself.'

He unlocked the door and they went into the porch she remembered – it was where they had sat, the night Amnon came. The rocking-chair was still there, with a jumble of other dusty wicker furniture and a lot of half-dead houseplants. These had obviously been *her* concern, as the orchard was his. She wondered fleetingly if he was deliberately letting them die.

They entered the house. It was dark, of course: all Arab buildings are constructed to keep out the sun, with deep window recesses and low lintels and high, shadowy ceilings. Their feet slid over the flagged floor and she was startled to see that it was surfaced in the same beautiful apricot marble that Amnon had insisted on using for his theatre foyer – there was something sensuous about its warm skin-tones; the polished sheen it achieved was also like young skin. Ann had never seen it anywhere else.

Boaz led her into his small sitting-room which she also remembered. It was a man's room, with a desk piled with books and papers, many artefacts in terracotta and copper, and a divan covered with a thickly-embroidered Bedouin cloth. The colours, blood-red and brown, were somehow suggestive. Her eyes went to it. She had no idea how he would go about the matter in hand. She half expected some sudden move, some roughness, evidence of impatience and hunger. Would it happen here? Would he turn in another second and push her down?

He stood at the window, his back turned to her. His right hand hung where she could see it, a little behind him, the thick, rough fingers (she had recently felt them on her face, abrasive) loosely curled. The bad hand he held out of sight on the far side of his body.

'Is there anything you would like?' he asked her with a strange formality. 'I'll make you coffee, or something to eat, if you want it.' His voice was low and steady, but nevertheless she heard the controlled tremor in it.

'I want a shower,' she said.

He turned, changing hands, so that the right one stayed in sight and the left went behind his back.

'Don't wash away the natural smell of your body. I want that too.'

A deep wave of desire flushed over her, and she clenched her hands.

'I need to feel clean,' she said. 'Please.'

He walked past her to the door again and she followed. They went into a small tiled room containing a wash-basin, lavatory and a shower cubicle without a curtain. There were small but poignant evidences of womanlessness everywhere – a heap of unwashed clothes in one corner, a crumpled towel hung on a hook through a tear, the soap, in the bottom of the basin, smeared

146

with red mud. He had been gardening . . . Ann's eyes went to the few shelves. There was nothing feminine on them, not a bottle, not a jar. His wife had not left on impulse, then – she had taken everything. Or else he had thrown them all away.

'I'll light the *dood* for you,' he said.

She knew all about the *dood* from the kibbutz, and watched with a sense of *déjà vu* as he turned on a minute tap, setting the paraffin dripping into a metal funnel leading through a pipe to the base of the old-fashioned water-heater. After a moment he used his lighter to set the wick burning; it caught with a characteristic *broomph* that she remembered from long ago. It made her feel, oddly, less frightened, as if not *all* this were strange and perilous, as if in some small way she had 'been here before'. . . It was absurd, but it helped her to feel a little more in control. She was so afraid of his noticing how terrified she was – she intended to meet him on equal terms, strongly, as he had wanted, not trembling and nervous as a schoolgirl. She had decided to do it. It was very near now, and there was no use backing away, even in her mind.

'Boaz.'

'*Nu.*'

'Shower with me.'

He turned to her slowly. Suddenly she saw that, although in a different fashion, he was afraid himself. He was breathing deeply, as if she were hunting him and he were running away.

'Boaz, what is it? You look ill!' she cried before she could stop herself.

'I don't want – ' he stopped. She waited, longing to go to him, but it was not yet time. 'I don't want,' he repeated carefully, 'that you'll see me naked.'

'Why not?'

'My arm,' he said with some difficulty. 'It's a disgusting mess. It will make you frightened or sick.'

She opened her mouth to say, 'It won't,' or 'It's part of you,' or 'I want to see it'. But then she thought that perhaps his wife had said one or other of those things before she had thrown up on the hospital floor. So she said, 'That's a chance we'll both have to take. You may be a terrifying sight naked, but you're going to look damn silly keeping one sleeve on.'

His face changed. The ridges on his forehead disappeared and his mouth moved in the depths of his beard. He took the one step the tiny room allowed, and the next second she was in his one-armed embrace.

His first kiss was a white burn on her mouth and on her mind. Then the tie at the back of the soft Indian dress was loosened and it came over her head. She had to help with the rest because it's hard to undress a woman one handed, whereas with three hands it's easy. The same with a man. She slipped off his jacket for him, and unbuttoned his shirt, struggling to steady her hands. He managed the trousers alone and with considerable adroitness – they were off before she had drawn down the concealing left sleeve.

The arm *was* awful. Empathetic pains shot up her own arms as she looked. The exploding grenade shrapnel had quarried away lumps of the flesh and muscle, right to the shoulder. In their depths, the excavated pits were still angry looking, though the scabs were off. He stood there exposed to her eyes, and he trembled all over and sweated as if battling with some phobia, as perhaps he was.

'You see?' he said. 'The rats have been at me. If it puts you off, we won't do anything together. I'll make us coffee and then drive you – '

'Back to Amnon's?' she said, ironically. 'But you've bought me. And though I am sold, not yet enjoyed.' She put her arms round his neck and stood close to him. His cock, already erect, jerked up between her legs, big enough to ride on. She rode it, lightly, and felt his good hand behind her, pressing her closer. They kissed again, a long, slow, exploratory kiss, and she had time in it to notice the deeply exciting, masculine smell of his beard, the rasp of it on her face and the soft tickle of it against her throat which was stretched upward. Like Isaac's, for Abraham's knife, she thought, and then dismissed the violent image, for Boaz had spoken no more than the truth. There was nothing brutal about him; as yet he still managed to remind her of a starving man whose ingrained table manners triumph even over his hunger.

She found he was edging her under the shower-head, and then his hand was gone and warm water was streaming over and between them. It ran into their joined mouths and they broke apart. She was half laughing, but he was still stern-faced. He reached across for the cake of earth-streaked soap and turned it over and over in his hand till he had a mass of lather. Then he began the delicious process of washing her, one-handed, from the neck downwards.

She closed her eyes and put her hands on his massive shoulders to steady herself, as much against the ravages of physical sensa-

148

tion as against the steady pressure of his hand. He washed her all over, carefully, concentratedly, paying no more attention to any one part than to the rest, his fingers seeking out the crannies between her toes as thoroughly as the cleft between her legs. Her own hands moved up and down with his shoulders as he crouched and straightened. Once she opened her eyes when he was squatting on his heels below her, and looked down at his wet, thick hair. She moved one hand and sampled its wiry texture, something she had always wanted to do. She found it harsh and inhospitable to the fingers, as different from Peter's fine, soft thatch as the stony scrub of the Judean hills is different from the silken verdancy of the Sussex downs. Convulsively she locked her hands in its rasping coarse abundancy, as if grasping a mass of thistles.

Suddenly she felt his soapy fingers inside her body. It was shocking and exciting, and yet, curiously, she was detached enough to say, 'That's a funny thing to do. Won't the soap sting?'

'Yes. It will increase your desire, and soon I will wash it out in the best way. But I don't do it because of that.'

'So why?'

'I am washing him out of you. Whoever was the last.'

Peter, tall, slender and frail, with his blue-veined, gentle hands and smooth white body, flashed across her mind and was gone, leaving a graze upon her conscience that would smart soon enough.

'It wasn't Amnon.'

'I believe you. But how could even a eunuch have you in the house with him and keep away? How can he sleep at night, knowing you are in the next room?' He pressed his face abruptly to her belly and said, his voice muffled, 'It has been hard enough for me, knowing you were across the city, not to run there and carry you off.' He was not washing her now but deliberately arousing her; his fingers slipped in and out, the heel of his hand pressed upward. The flowing warm water had washed the soap off his hand and from the outside of her body, but inside the sexual and chemical fires conjoined unendurably.

'Boaz – !' she cried out with sudden urgency.

'Yes. Now.'

He switched off the water and took hold of her wrist. Dripping wet, they walked through into his bedroom. The bed was unmade, stripped back where he had got out of it to answer her summons. They fell on it together and at once he turned her on

149

her face and mounted her like a satyr, pinning both her wrists to the bed above her head with one hard hand. She sensed his head thrown back, his teeth locked. She locked her own and raised her hips to accommodate him. He found his mark without assistance, and drove home in one strong stroke.

No civilised foreplay, no love words, no tender wooing. His 'table manners' were not equal to this, and what he did to her amounted to rape with consent. She marvelled at her own fierce pleasure in it, at the confirmation of some dim suspicion she had always had that this was exactly what she wanted from him. It was not love-making as she understood it at all, it was his raw need meeting her willingness to satisfy him, and her joy in his domineering power was so acute that she nearly cried out. But she remembered what he had said, and tried it his way – at first because it was a challenge he had obliquely thrown to her, and because she thought it was what he wanted of her; but later, because she discovered that self-containment intensified what was already an all-but-unbearable emotional and sensual experience. She lay as still as she could, consciously restraining herself from threshing or twisting under him and under the waves of delight that rolled over her like tides of some beneficent fire, paying the closest attention to the *son et lumière* going on in her body. There was no possibility of thought beyond that, so she was not troubled by doubts, fears or comparisons. In any case, the first ferocious mating was soon over.

Down he came on her back like a felled forest tree, and she took his great weight and rejoiced in it. He released her hands. She laid them at her sides and reached up and stroked his flanks and felt his breath heaving against her neck. After a few moments he raised himself and sat up with his back against the wall, and, with his arm beneath her shoulders, drew her up to lean against him. She felt his heart thundering and knew there was more to come and discovered in herself an almost infinite capacity for more; there were also things she wanted him to do with her that she had never wanted before. There was nothing she had ever heard of that men and women can do together that she didn't want with him.

Then came the realisation that, meanwhile, she might touch him as much as she liked. This was a wonder of its own after all the times when she had had to control herself so rigorously, sitting in cars or small rooms with him, walking through streets at his side; he must have felt the same, and that insane moment in his garden, when he had reached – not for her hand, or to make some quasi-accidental contact as another man might, but for her sex, directly, had been the proof of it.

Now she could make free with every part of his body. He was, like Esau in the Bible, 'an hairy man'. She stroked his legs and his hard-muscled, furry stomach, and turned him as he sat there and gently scratched his matted back till she got her reward – little grunts of pleasure. So that was the way. He was not proof against the lesser delights. She laughed in her throat and laid her face against his spine, putting her arms round him.

'Letting yourself go a bit, aren't you, Shachterman? Little sounds escaping? I'll have you groaning before I've finished with you.'

He took her hand and guided it to its entirely superfluous work. 'And what will you be doing?'

'Weeping, perhaps.'

But he wept first. Next time, he laid her on her back where she could look at him, and as she saw him nearing his climax she took his bad hand in both hers. Earlier, as they sat caressing, she had reached tentatively for it, but he had seized her trespassing fingers and held them off. Now he was beyond stopping her. She held the ruined fingers gently and moved them over her breasts . . . She had not seen a man cry since Menachem had burst into their house sixteen years ago, to tell her a kibbutz boy had been killed on manoeuvres. The news, and Menachem's reaction, had struck her to the heart, and she relived the feeling now of having her heart pierced with sorrow. It was not so very different from joy.

The third time, she cried, too. She always cried at orgasm because it happened so seldom now. On those rare occasions when it did, Peter worried about it, asking if he'd hurt her (as if he would!). He little knew that the cause was not pain, but a kind of grief for the rarity with which she achieved the heights of sensation . . . Boaz made no enquiries. For the first time he bent, and took her tears on his tongue. She drew him down on her. His crippled hand crept, with her help, as far as her face and she kissed it and kissed him and nibbled him through his beard and he suddenly said,

'Why are you smiling?'

'The question is, why aren't you? Don't you smile when you're enjoying yourself?'

'Is that how you call it? With me this goes very far beyond

enjoyment.'

'You're too solemn, dearest. One day I'll make you break down completely and laugh as we make love.'

'No. This is to me the most serious matter in life.'

'But one.'

They stared into one another's eyes.

'But one. Yes.'

But he was startled, somehow. After a few moments he said, 'Dearest . . .' as if trying out the word. 'That means, your most dear . . . Does it mean that?'

'Yes.'

But she didn't want him to press this matter of comparisons and degrees and she covered his mouth. He understood, nodding a little. So she moved her fingers over his face and traced its harsh lines, noticing with some disquiet how different it now looked to her, no longer at all inimical, its former coarseness muted, a phenomenon she had learnt to associate with the madness of being in love . . . She dismissed this thought and touched his beard.

'I grew it because I couldn't shave.'

'I like it so much.'

'Because it hides my face?'

'No, because it makes you look older. I don't like to remember that you're younger than I am.'

'Younger than you? You are a baby beside me.'

'But our bodies . . .'

'Mine is damaged and yours is perfect. You have a most beautiful, womanly body.' He was caressing her rather clumsily, as if he'd forgotten how to be gentle, or perhaps had never learnt. His hand passed over her belly and sank between her thighs.

'Such a cunt should put forth as well as taking in,' he said.

It took a moment to understand him. Then she said quietly, 'I'm barren. So you see, my body is neither perfect nor womanly.'

'Are you sure?' he said after a moment. 'Did you have tests? Perhaps it was not your fault.'

'I lived with one man for six years and another for ten,' she said. 'One of them had a son already. The other . . . Well, what does it matter now? But of course it must have been my fault, as you call it.'

He turned away from her a little, lying on his back with his arm across his face.

'It's a very terrible thing to be childless,' he said.

152

'I've often been assured there are many compensations.'

'Perhaps in England they can say so. For a Jew in Israel there is not even one.'

There were questions she could have asked. He had given her a precedent. But something in his voice warned her of some profoundly private sanctum of pain which she must not breach. After a while he uncovered his face and reached out for her. She turned and lay at right angles to him, her head on his stomach. He sleepily gathered up her long hair which had come loose and spread it over his chest and face.

'Your hair smells like a desert morning,' he said. Then he fell asleep.

She lay awake, her thoughts flooded with unashamed eroticism. They had made a good start, enough to prove what she had already guessed, that he was a man of 'infinite variety' who would not be gainsaid and would take her into landscapes of sensuality that even with Menachem she had never ventured to explore. Albeit late, she would gain from him a fullness of experience that she had always supposed was beyond her capacity.

And what would she do for him? Well, she would teach him to be tender, and to enjoy love less portentously. But physical satisfaction was not all he wanted from her. Their relationship had sustained itself on very little for these seven years – sparse encounters under circumscribed conditions, no intimacies of conversation or contact (except that once); no letters, even. It had gained ground and reached this present point with very little to feed it. This had not been the achievement solely of suppressed lust! He wanted *her*, something else besides her body.

She entertained none of the old, feminine fears, lying now beside this satiated man, that when he woke he would be cold or changed toward her. Whatever their relationship was, a material part of it had been established well before this ecstatic fleshly encounter, which was not the climax, but simply one stage in something she felt certain was going to be long-lasting, vital and infinitely affective upon her life.

But how? Strange the way an opaque door came down between a hotly desired bed and even the immediate future; desire satisfied, the barrier miraculously cleared. She saw all the dim shapes in the background beginning to crowd forward again – husband, home, work, friends, a routine and a set-up, even here in Jerusalem, which could be interrupted and broken only at some cost she had not even begun to work out yet. For example, at ten

153

o'clock she had to be in Rehavia, looking alert, well-groomed and cerebral, to interview an eminent elderly professor of history.

Boaz was snoring. She raised herself and gently pushed his head over to one side. The snoring stopped. She lay back as before, facing his legs. The circumcised 'tool of her delight', shrunken now, was lying all but lost in its damp bower of wiry tendrils. She turned it up towards her, looking at it as it lay defenceless in her hand. Even erect, it had not resembled a ripe cucumber so much as some exotic species of large toadstool, with its silky helmet and thick, tough stalk . . .

Poisonous, perhaps . . . she thought. But she didn't believe it. With her hand cupped gently and protectively over it, she dropped into a child's blissful and untroubled sleep.

CHAPTER 12

She woke some time later, her heart and mind still full of him. She opened her eyes to find him kneeling beside her on the bed. Her somnolent, satisfied body felt, to her, so infinitely rejuvenated, so obviously desirable, that she would not have been surprised to find him feasting his eyes on it as on some ravishing dryad; but he was staring fixedly at her face. His body was so still, his expression so intense, that she thought of a statue – a bearded caryatid perhaps, whose broad-muscled shoulders carried some invisible burden. But statues don't have burning eyes, she thought. Nor hairy chests. She was smiling tenderly as she reached up to touch it, rasping the hairs between finger and thumb; then she slid her hand upward to draw his head down to her lips, closing her eyes langorously.

But the column of his neck was as stiff as a treetrunk.

'Why do you talk as you do?' he asked harshly into her darkness. 'Why do you think as you do?'

Her eyes flew open and her hand dropped.

After a moment of shocked surprise, she recovered. 'Boaz', she said sardonically, 'is it possible that you want to straighten me out politically at this of all moments? How can it matter to you just now?'

'What will matter in an hour, when we are up and dressed, must be important now as well. Do you think, now that I've had you at last, I'm going to soften like wax, wash my hands of you, or stop caring what goes on inside your head?'

She raised herself on her elbows and stared at him incredulously. 'Couldn't we have some coffee before the brainwashing begins?' she asked plaintively.

He ignored this. 'When you are in England,' he said, 'you write about Israel. You once told me you even used to lecture.'

She stretched lazily. This was all such nonsense.

'Yep. I still do, when I'm asked – as I believe you do. Only your lectures to Army units of impressionable young men are obviously far more influential than mine to ladies' lunch clubs, WIZO gatherings and occasional B'nai B'rith lodges . . . Oh, don't worry about it, Boaz! I could talk, or you could for that matter, from here till Christmas without stopping for breath, you on one side of a platform and me on the other, using every ounce of our powers of persuasion, and it wouldn't change the fixed ideas of one English Jew. Either they agree with you, that the Jews are a permanently done-down race and that the only good Arab is a dead one, or they agree with me, that the Jews ought to stop basing all their calculations on their persecution complex and that Israel must find her place in the Middle East in order to survive – '

He looked suddenly murderous. 'Who are you to say what Israel must do to survive? You haven't the shadow of a right, not the faintest shadow!'

She slumped on her back. 'Oh, go on then if you must. Tell me why I'm wrong. But if I go to sleep in the middle from lack of coffee, don't blame me.'

'Don't make jokes now. Don't fall asleep. I need you to be awake. You're not only wrong. You're dangerously wrong. You're even, I would say, sickly and neurotically wrong.' Her eyes opened slowly and she frowned. 'You pretend to love the Jewish people – no, you don't say that, you're not so obvious or sentimental. But someone meeting and talking to you might say, Oh yes, this woman, for some reason, identifies with the whole Jewish race. Perhaps it had some simple cause. Perhaps she was fucked by a Jew at some vulnerable time in her life. Or perhaps she heard, when she was still young, about what they did to them in the camps and elsewhere, making them eat their own shit to keep alive among other degradations too many to mention, and perhaps she felt the horror of it enough to become their champion. But I don't believe that. I might have done. I wanted to, because I want this strange obsession of yours with us to have a cause I can at least understand. And I could understand the fucking or the pity – we Jews are well adapted to be fucked and pitied. But when I see what it is you work for, after your so deeply involved and committed visits here, then my mind begins to draw other conclusions.'

She had scrambled hastily and gracelessly to her knees, and was facing him on the hot, crumpled sheet, shocked and frightened out of her post-ecstatic lethargy. Her eyes were wide and fixed on his and her breath was coming fast. She felt her nakedness suddenly, sensing that she was going to have to defend herself against some onslaught. Could it be that he was seriously going to try to distort and undermine what she felt for this place, for his people – ? He must not get *that* wrong, even in his private assessment of her – she must fight to prevent that. She would have done so in any circumstances, but now her need to have him

156

understand and think well of her was as urgent as her need to uncover the truth about him, and reconcile it, somehow, with what she felt for him.

Which is love, she thought with sudden piercing certainty. God help me! Look at him! Gone the passionate lover sharing his need; returned the furious, bitter antagonist, the man of wrath, the wounded animal. And where are my defences now? All gone, all thrown away. His semen is running down my thighs and I am his, I've crossed to his side, wherever that is, and here he is – throwing me back across the border and preparing to shoot me where I stand. What a moment to find out that I am hopelessly in love with him!

She made one desperate effort to avert what was coming. She felt she couldn't fight now – the sensations and traces of their love-making were still all over her mind and body. 'Not now, Boaz!' she whispered imploringly. 'Please, not now!' And she leaned to him, willing the beast to lie.down in its lair. Instead it rose to full sight in his eyes.

'No,' he said in a voice of stone. 'We won't fuck now. Now we'll use our brains. Because *now* I *must* find out the truth about you.'

She started violently. *I don't live between my legs, I live up here, in my head* . . . Now he was hunting her where she had reckoned she truly was. If he seized her in a mental struggle and worsted her, she would have no refuge left. And what could he mean, 'find out the truth'? Was it possible he had suspicions of her, as she had of him?

'Boaz, what truth? *I've* got no secrets!'

'We all have secrets, often that we keep from ourselves. I keep nothing from myself, and if you do I am going to dig it out and show it to you, so that we'll be equals.'

'If that's what you want, you had better start by telling *me* some of your ninety per cent.'

For a moment the beast drew back as if she'd waved a lighted branch in its face.

'No. I have to be ruthless but I'm not so cruel as that. To make you part of all that would injure you. A woman with your blameless history could never accept mine. Have you ever so much as wrung the neck of a chicken? But motives and beliefs, they're not like actions, if only because they can be changed.'

'What beliefs do you want me to change?'

'Your beliefs about our enemies.'

She put her hands on his upper arms, gripping hard, not noticing what her right hand touched until he winced. 'Boaz. This is absurd – it's crazy! After seven years of fencing with each other we've just put down our swords and – you've ploughed me.' She tried to laugh but his face stayed grim. 'Why are you insisting on a battle now, and with escalating weapons? I've just thrown away my armour.'

'You're hurting my arm.'

'You're hurting my heart.'

'I'm opening it – that has to hurt, as if you were a virgin. I have to do it now. Before, it hasn't mattered so much. Because each time, after you would go back to England, I could always get on with my life and tell myself that you were not really important, not to me and not to us. What you thought and said and wrote were just – petty acts of misguided idiocy. Just a few pin-pricks in the back of Israel which is already so full of knives it couldn't feel any more . . . But for me, the second or third fuck is a mental release as well as physical. When we did it that last time I looked at you, lying there under me, and you looked back at me, and even at the most intense moment I could think clearly about what you are. You are no idiot, Ann! *You* aren't one of these blind idealists, these uninformed wishful-thinkers. You're a clever woman. You read and observe and learn about what interests you. And this region interests you very much. *I've* shown you things, and told you things, more than many *Jews* know or ever get a chance to learn – do you know how few Israelis go into Arab homes or tour the West Bank or talk to them as you have, through me? So I can't absolve you any more. I think now that you understand the situation very well and that you're shutting your eyes to what the Arabs obviously are, and what they obviously want, for a good reason.'

'Just a minute, Boaz! I'm not shutting my eyes! I know the Arabs want to dislodge the Jews from this area – '

'Ah! Very good. You know that. So why do you advocate giving them the West Bank and Gaza as a good head start?'

'Because until they get a place of their own, there isn't a hope of peace.'

'Peace?' he shouted. 'Peace? What is it? Who needs it? What peace are you talking about, all of you? You might as well talk about some heaven in the skies! We'll never have "peace" here, how could we? Peace is for places like England. You can have it there. In England your comedians make funny hats out of your flag and your children put pins through their ears and the men get

158

fat beer-bellies. Your country is finished as a dynamic force. *There* you can sit on clouds playing harps. But it is nothing to do with real life. It's nothing, as a matter of fact, to do with human nature. Here we live as men have to live, on an edge, and every few years we go over it when we have to fight for our survival. That's the first condition of our existence here and it always will be, because we can't get rid of the Arabs and they'll never drive us out. But they won't stop trying, and it is *sheer, bloody, suicidal madness* to talk about giving them anything. Is it possible – while you slept so calmly, I have been looking at you, feeling turmoil, and asking myself this – is it *possible* that you really think that appeasing the Palestinians will somehow change our knife-edge situation for the better? Could they have shown us plainer than they have that what they want is to wipe us out?'

'Boaz, listen to me.'

'Go on. I'm listening. I'm here to listen. Explain it to me. I never wanted to understand anything more than I want to understand you.'

She had her arguments ready. But she lacked the drive, the energy, the will to push forward. She felt languid and full of a renewed desire which she didn't even want to overcome. Her lowered eyes saw that he was in much the same state, but that he was grimly refusing to acknowledge or give way to it. She struggled not to smile. One touch of her hand, she thought, and victory of a sort was hers. Why must she engage in a battle of wills, of his choosing? She would refuse the gauntlet. She reached out toward the toadstool which had sprung up unbidden from the sear grass.

He struck her hand stingingly away.

'Boaz – !'

'I have fucked you three times and that is enough until we have talked! Now we are *talking*. Now you are going to explain why you think you know better than I do what the Arabs are like.'

'On the basis that the outsider sees more of the game.'

'So you admit you are an outsider!'

'Yes. I always do. Before anyone can accuse me of it.'

'So by what right – '

'But I am a committed, concerned, informed and caring out-sider. I am a Zionist. I'm not a blind one either. I've read and studied and opened my mind and I believe from my heart that the Jews have a right to nationhood and a territory of their own. I've campaigned for Israel, I've stood on platforms, I've written books and articles, I've spoken on the radio. I've signed petitions and walked in demos and stood all night outside the Foreign Office when hardly any *Jews* bothered to come. I've lived six years of my life here and would be living here still if – '

'If – ?'

'If the demands of my career and my marriage didn't prevent it.'

'Who forced you to have a career and a marriage at odds with your fundamental commitment?'

' "Fundamental commitment?" That sounds oddly familiar. Where did you get that?'

'I have made it my business to read everything I could find of yours that concerned Israel. You wrote in 1973 that Israel was your fundamental commitment. In a letter to *The Times*.'

'I wrote another of those, just before I left England.'

'Was it published?'

'I don't know. Probably not. It accused the paper of taking a biased stand on the Middle East due to its need for Arab advertising.'

'They won't publish that!'

'They might. Look, Boaz, it's only a trifle – I know that. I know everything I do is trifling compared with what you've done.'

'You know nothing about what I've done.'

'You've lived here all your life – you've fought, you've been wounded – ' She stopped at the look on his face, a look which alarmed and disconcerted her.

'My wounds are my own concern and not yours,' he said. 'Let's get back to the Arabs. Tell me what you've learned about them.'

'Chiefly that they're much like the Jews.'

'Oh, are they! Like the Jews? Even your Churchill knew better than that. He said the Jews are fighters – the Arabs are killers. They are killers, Ann. It's their nature.'

'Now, Boaz, please. Don't stoop to that.'

'When they can't get at us, they kill each other. They kill their own sisters and daughters – not in some remote backward corner of the Middle East, but right here in Israel, they cut off their heads or push them down wells for the sake of their honour. Did none of your old Palmachniks tell you how, if they had to leave their wounded behind, they gave them a grenade or a pistol so they needn't fall alive into the enemy's hands? And killing's not the end of it with them. Have you ever seen a man with his cock cut off and stuffed in his mouth?'

Nausea attacked her but she set her teeth.

'You won't convince me this way. All these extreme things, which are by no means universal or characteristic, don't make them somehow unworthy to have what you have, what every national group has a right to.'

'Which is?'

'A place of their own.'

'Oh, don't talk that piss to me! They've got a place of their own. They've got Jordan. Half the population of Jordan is Palestinian! Jordan is Palestine. Any Palestinian who wants to should go there. They should throw out Hussein if that's what the majority wants, and then get on with it, as we did.'

'They can't oust Hussein, they've tried it and he butchered them in thousands. They want the places they've always lived in.'

'Ah, I thought we should come to that! Their ancestral homes . . . Do you know how many of those who call themselves refugees now, came flocking in from neighbouring countries in the 'twenties and 'thirties when they saw what the Jews were making of this country, after their brethren had let it go to ruin and neglect?'

'That's not fair. In the first place it was the Turks who had let it go. The local peasants farmed as well as they could. It's not their fault they lacked the money and education the Jews had – later. The Jews made their own mistakes, early on. *Now* they talk about the courage of the men who drained the swamps and so on, but a lot went hopelessly wrong through sheer ignorance. Nobody ever talks about the abandoned settlements, the pioneers who ran back to Russia, or killed themselves, or settled down as landlords just as feudal as the Arab ones – '

'What the hell are you talking about? Do you know what they faced? The place was a wilderness! My grandfather was one of those ignorant fools you mention. When he came in 1905 he found the land barren, a few fields scratched out of the rock, herds of sheep and goats demolishing everything . . . No orchards, no husbandry, no thought for the future . . . It was the Jews who transformed this place. As for suicides, I know about those. My own grandmother tried it. My father heard the chair fall as he came through the door and grabbed her knees and held her up while she screamed at him to let her die . . . It was poverty and exhaustion that made her do it, but my father forced her to live. That's the first duty of a Jew. Dying is what they want of us, and what we don't give them if we can help it – '

161

'Who is this "they", Boaz? Do you mean the Great Them, the *goyim*, the entire rest of the world? Are you really as paranoid as all that?'

'Paranoia,' he said slowly, 'has its uses. It keeps you very alert.'

'It also prevents you from *ever* seeing ways out of a dilemma, because you start from the premise that there aren't any.'

'There actually is no way out of our dilemma in this region,' he said. 'That's what I'm trying to tell you. We live in it and with it, and we think about survival, and survival means strength. To frighten them, and if that doesn't work, to hold them off, and if possible push them back, to give ourselves a little more padding around us, fighting space for the next time. How shall we fight the Egyptians, next time? *Where* shall we fight them? You saw the Sinai after '73, littered with burnt-out tanks and rocket-casings and knocked-down aircraft – '

'And dead bodies.'

'Yes, and dead bodies. More of theirs than ours, thank God. But next time perhaps they won't be lying out there in the sand. If it goes badly at first, they'll be in Ashkelon, and Yad Mordechai, and Negba, and Beersheba. The populated areas will be our battleground because we've given the old one back.'

'That's the one good thing this Prime Minister's done. He gave it back for a peace treaty and all the benefits of – '

'Now we are back to Sadat's piece of lavatory paper that, when he next wants to shit on us, he will use to wipe his arse with.'

'That's what I mean, Boaz! Why start from the premise that he will want to shit on you? Is it so unreasonable to reckon that he doesn't want another war any more than Israel does?'

'Unreasonable! – it is blind stupidity, it is suicidal insanity. Do you see any of the other Arab nations rushing to join in this "peace" process? He's isolated. He has lost the leadership of the Arab world. He's lost face. Oh, you don't know them as I do, how can you understand? He'll have to get back his prestige sooner or later, and there's only one way. He will find an excuse – in a pact with another Arab country, or in some mythical "demand" of his people, half of whom are starving and expect to live no more than thirty-five years anyway. He, or his successor, will rouse them again to attack us, as he did in '73. Even if it is military lunacy, he will do it, because that is what Arabs do. It's the story of the frog and the scorpion. You know it?'

'Of course.'

Certainly she knew it. The scorpion asks the frog to take him across a river on his back. The frog says, no, you'll sting me and I'll die. The scorpion says, if you die, I'll drown, so why should I sting you? So the frog takes him on his back and starts to swim. Half-way across, the scorpion stings him. As the frog dies, he cries out: Why? And the scorpion, as he drowns, answers: This is the Middle East.

'A fine fable,' said Ann, 'invented no doubt by some clever Jew to explain the irrational self-defeating behaviour of the Arabs, who have consistently made the wrong moves from the outset. But what all such clever Jews don't ever seem to grasp is that the mantle of the scorpion has now fallen on to Israel, who, with her current policies, he is busy stinging *her* frog to death.'

'America, I suppose!'

'America, you suppose correctly. If you imagine the State Department is going to vote another twenty billion dollars for arms for us to fight another war which they see as being a direct result of our intransigence, you're deluding yourself – and without those supply-planes landing at the rate of one every three minutes as they did in '73, thanks entirely to Richard Nixon, the best army this country can raise couldn't fight for a single day.'

'The Jews of America would never allow any administration to desert us.'

'Boaz, don't count on that! The "Jewish vote", the "Jewish lobby" – they're part myth. American Presidents can afford to lose New York State, and one day one of them is going to find it out. In any case world Jewry is another frog that's getting distinctly nervous. They don't like the spectacle of Jews as villains instead of victims or heroes – they prefer the tiger to the rat, and they're conditioned to lose their nerve when the world turns against their figureheads. They won't support Israel one moment after it ceases to give them a sense of their own value.'

'America will support us even without the Jews because we're the last bastion of pro-American democracy east of Europe. They can't afford to leave us defenceless.'

'Have you ever heard of Diego Garcia?'

'No.'

'Well, you should. It's an island, well east of here. The British have leased it to the Americans who are busy turning it into another Malta against the possibility of Israel digging its own grave and jumping into it. Boaz, I'm telling you! In one more generation there won't be enough committed Jews in the Diaspora to keep this city in *parks*. Israel's got to be as near independent by then as makes no odds. And that she never can be, while most of her budget is going on defence.'

'Economic independence is a dream, like peace is a dream.'

'Like Zionism was a dream, only with the will of your grandfather's generation it came true. Because it had to. And if you want this country to survive, you've got to make the peace come true, because without it you can never achieve independence, and without independence the State will die, not with the bang of war but with the whimper of attrition.'

He gazed at her.

'And is this what you say in your lectures to the Jews who support us now?' he asked incredulously.

'No. Why should I preach withdrawal of support for this country, which I love? I tell them what I believe are the facts of the situation, which are that Israel must integrate into the Middle East, and that she can't until the Palestinians have a state of their own.'

'You are mad!' he said furiously.

'No, Boaz. If either of us is, it's you.'

'I've wished you would live here, because I wanted you. But now I'm glad you don't, except that you probably do more harm from outside. What this country is suffering from is a loss of collective nerve – a failure of will. It's being undermined by people like you. Your sort eat like a cancer at our sureness. I've watched it. I've watched the emotional depression growing, like a contagious disease fed from the Left. Don't you realise that spirit and will are everything, that every time you talk or write like that you are causing us to crumble further towards despair? Do you know how many are leaving, and why?'

'Hundreds of thousands. They're leaving to escape the stress. That's what I meant by attrition. How can the Americans go on caring about Israel to the tune of ten dollars a year per man, woman and child, when they see half a million expatriate Israelis in their midst, struggling to forget where they belong?'

'It makes me puke to think of them . . . money-grubbing, futile cowards – they're our life's blood, dribbling out of us – '

'Pouring, you mean!'

'It's your like who chew through the skin that should contain them!' he shouted.

'By God, Boaz, that's too much! It's not *my* like, but yours,

164

because it's you who keep this hopeless situation going and exacerbate it at every turn! Who can face a future of endless wars – perhaps even a civil one? It's all right for you, you were born a fighter, and you've got no children, no stake in the future – ' She stopped. She felt him gathering himself together and kept herself from cowering with an effort.

'You Christians – ' he began with trembling deadly quietness.

'I am not a *Christian*!'

'You Christians believe,' he went on, 'that the height of good-ness is to emerge from torment free of hatred, full of love and without bitterness. I call that *shit*. Shit mixed with vomit. I don't apologise for the hatred I have for my enemies. They hate us and want to destroy us, they've tried it again and again. There's neither sense nor justice in trying to come to terms with them. I accept – all the signs are there, one has to be blind or mad or set on self-destruction not to see them – that they can never be trusted nor appeased. It's not a question of a stake in the future. We have two ways. We can crawl away like trembling, greedy little mice to live in New York, or we can stay here and fight to be free Jews, and if I *had* a son I couldn't avoid knowing that, nor could I act differently. If you really regard Jews and Arabs as the same, with equal rights to this place, if you care equally for both sides, then it's pointless for you to call yourself a Zionist, and entirely pointless for me to give to you one more thought or moment.'

'Boaz, will you believe me if I tell you that it's not for the sake of the Arabs that I'm in favour of Israel withdrawing from the West Bank? It's for the Jews. De Gaulle didn't pull out of Algeria for the sake of the Algerians, he did it for the sake of the French. I want the Israelis to be *liberated* from those territories!'

Boaz watched her inscrutably. He was no longer excited. He was fully concentrated, fully engaged; they were embattled, their swords locked at the hilts. Ann, for her part, had forgotten their situation. She was thinking of nothing but the argument, of her overwhelming need to convince him at least of the genuineness of her own stance. The strange spectacle they must have made, kneeling there naked face to face, never struck either of them.

'Every word you've said has been an attack on the Jews. Every comparison, every argument, has been in the Arabs' favour. It's quite obvious you are not with us.'

'Wait – I've proved – '

'At best you're deceiving yourself. At worst . . . you're against us.'

'Will you shut up and listen!' she shouted suddenly. She had not really shouted till now. 'Your whole trouble is, you never listen, not properly – everything gets filtered through your own neurotic prejudices. Everything I've said has been to try to make you see that there's a parallel between the Palestinians of today and the Jews of the past, that their ambitions and needs, yes, and even their methods are similar. *No*, Boaz, *shut up*! You Jews wanted your own country. Everyone said it was a mad dream, but you had to have it – after the Holocaust, it became an absolute imperative. You worked for it and you paid for it and you fought for it, and you got it, because you felt yourselves to be a nation. Right? And nations need territory, to be independent on, to defend themselves from. Now, with the Palestinians, the exact same thing has happened. They've been subjected to a tragedy and to pressures which have given them the inner, dynamic conviction of nationhood. It's useless for outsiders to tell them they're not a nation, or that they never were a nation, or ask why they can't settle in other Arab countries – Boaz, can't you see the parallel for yourself? All those same things were said to the Zionists in the early days, but it was no use. They *felt* it, they were driven and impelled, they had to have a place of their own to be free in and nothing could turn them from it. To get it, some of them were prepared to do terrible things – '

'Ah! Of course. Like the PLO, I suppose.'

'Yes, very like the PLO.'

'Terrorist attacks on civilians abroad? Bombs on planeloads of innocent people?'

'Bombs in buses and markets full of innocent people, assassinations abroad, killing fellow-Jews who didn't see things the same way – what's the essential difference? Terrorism is terrorism. What matters is not which side you're on, but what drives people to it. You as good as said to me, last year, on the West Bank, that if you were a Palestinian now, you'd be a terrorist yourself, that it would be the only – '

'*I* said – '

'*Yes*! And you may have been right! Oh, Boaz, this is all peripheral really, you keep pushing me into corners where I have to appear to be defending Arab extremists. All I'm doing is trying to show you that you're deceiving yourself if you're using some – self-contrived sense of innate superiority of Jews in general over Arabs in general to justify ignoring their rights and their needs, treating them not just as enemies, but as – I don't know – some sort of barbarous inferiors.'

'I have spent thirteen years living with them and studying them and writing and thinking about them. I wouldn't put it as you just did, but there is no doubt they are entirely different from us, and if you push me to say it, I will say it: *we are better.*'

'That is a terrible, terrible thing to say or think. I don't have to remind you of the precedents, of people who thought they were better, and what they did to prove it which proved only the exact opposite – ' She saw his face pale and tauten but she was too angry herself now to stop, for she could not bear to hear such things from his mouth which had recently kissed her. 'So let's just see, shall we? Perhaps it's just a matter of terminology. Why is it heroism when young Jews assassinate civilian diplomats, at home and abroad – I'm talking about Moyne and Bernadotte of course – but when the PLO do it, it's murder? Why is it called "a security mishap" when Israeli espionage agents go to work blowing up American buildings in Cairo, but when the PLO carry out sabotage and admit to it, that's barbarity? Why is it an abomination if Palestinian infiltrators get into a village and blow up a school, or take hostages at Olympic Games, which result in the deaths of a handful of Israeli children or athletes, but it's "legitimate reprisal" when our Government orders retaliatory air raids on terrorist strongholds in refugee camps which result in the deaths of hundreds of civilians?'

Boaz now looked as if he meant to lay hands on her. His face had darkened with fury and she could easily have shrunk back in terror, but she threw one last dart at him to keep up her courage in the face of the threat she saw looming, without thinking of the inevitable result: 'Why are civilian deaths in a war situation always called a "massacre" if the Arabs cause them, but when the Jews do it – as in Deir Yassin – and Kibya – '

'*Enough!*' he roared.

She fell silent. They were both panting.

'Perhaps,' he said deliberately, 'the truth is, you were *not* fucked by some Jew you wanted. Or perhaps you looked at the camp photographs and thought – like some of your British Red Berets who were here – that we only got what we deserved. I saw what they wrote on our walls: "Bring back the ovens, Hitler was right". The worst kind of anti-semite, you know what they say about him – he's the one like you, who pretends that some of his best friends – '

Her hand flew to her mouth. The nausea was imminent now,

pushing its bile into her throat.

'I shouldn't have touched you,' he said. 'Because I knew. I knew what you really were. And you can say what you like about the Jews – one thing we don't go in for is fucking enemy women.'

CHAPTER 13

Jerking away from him so violently that she half fell off the bed, Ann got to her feet and blundered out of the room and back into the bathroom, banging her hip against both door jambs in her clumsy haste. She slammed the door with a crash, locked it and leant against it, grinding her teeth and stamping one foot on the tiles again and again until her leg ached and trembled. It seemed nothing but physical pain could assuage the outrage and agony of mind she felt.

Some part of her, nonetheless, was absolutely certain that he would come after her, force her somehow to open the door; that there would follow an explanation, a cancelling-out, a reversal of the last half-hour . . . He could not have meant what he said! The change from loving passion to passionate anger had been too hideously abrupt, too cruelly unlooked-for . . . Was he mad? Clinically, certifiably mad? Surely he must be! She'd known he had this rage which burned in him much of the time, she thought she'd allowed for it . . . She had longed to soothe and heal him, through love-making.

But now a terrible doubt came to her. Perhaps he had not made love to her at all. Perhaps he had actually fucked her – in the old meaning of the word, performing a crude act of conquest on her body for his own satisfaction, the satisfaction of some twisted thing in him which hated her for what she believed and stood for, and wanted to subdue her in the oldest way in the world. Only in Israel might it happen, because only here were beliefs, political beliefs, a matter of life and death.

Gasping with the effort to control herself, she listened. There was not a sound from the other side of the door. Trembling with tension she waited for him to come, but he didn't. He was not going to come . . . Pride? Or was the rejection she'd seen in his lion's eyes really the greater part of what he felt for her? Was that possible? She could have sworn he loved her . . . But if you love someone who represents everything you fear and loathe, then what? She suddenly felt she knew nothing about Boaz at all, except that he had insulted her past bearing and that she must get away from him.

She looked round wildly. Their clothes lay in two heaps on the floor, as if, standing in each other's arms, they had vanished into

169

thin air, consuming each other . . . Ann clamped her memory shut like a box of rats. She would not think at all. She would just act, step by step, as seemed best. The first thing was to get dressed and get out.

In trembling haste, she picked up her three garments and put them on, then her sandals. She needed to wash herself, but was in too much of a hurry to do more than wet her hands and wipe her face and the insides of her thighs. Staring at herself for a second in the mirror, she looked at the hair, hanging loose round her livid face . . . 'Your hair smells like a desert morning.' She clutched her body in a sudden agonising spasm of loss.

No. What mattered was the practical problem of her hairpins, scattered in his bed, unrecoverable. She could not go out like this. She found a comb and dragged it through her hair, pulling it back severely under her headscarf. Now she, like his wife, looked as plain and unwanton as a religious woman.

She turned to the door, took a deep breath, and opened it. She half expected, half hoped, he would be standing outside, but the house was silent, the corridor empty. Intolerably, she imagined him lying calmly on his bed, reading one of the many books which lined the room, having . . . disposed of her. On shaking legs she walked through the dark house to the front door.

There she stopped, because she couldn't go on. How could he bear to let her leave like this? But he had driven her, deliberately – he must want her to go – it was useless to stand there, willing him to come to her. She must be strong and resolute and go before she broke down completely and crawled to him. She had not known she had it in her to crawl. This was not one of the lessons in sexual behaviour that she had expected him to give her.

She got herself out of the house, not so much by a heroic effort of will as because she saw no option. As soon as she came out, the sun struck her and she felt dazzled and dizzy. The dog, sleeping in the shade, jerked up its head, then laid it on its paws again. Instinctively Ann looked at her wrist, forgetting that she had discarded her watch; she guessed it to be nearly noon. So much for the professor . . . What she would do about that, she had not the slightest notion, but it was surely a sign of sanity, of the operation of some automatic pilot system, that she could think of him at all.

She walked down the hill to the bus stop and stood there for an interminable time in the noon heat with a growing number of Arab men and women, some of them encumbered by market produce or huge ugly plastic shopping-bags. One or two of them looked at her curiously. One man seemed to look from her, back to Boaz' house, standing lonely amid its vines and citrus trees two hundred yards away. Was he smirking? She suddenly straightened herself and drew her Englishness round her like a cloak of inviolability. How dared they imagine she would do anything improper! She stared haughtily at the man. Outfaced, he looked away. She almost wanted to laugh, but the feeling verged on weeping and she crushed it down into safe numbness.

At last the bus arrived, a flamboyant, ramshackle vehicle with its engine exposed on one side where half the bonnet had come off, its bodywork decorated with bright paint and its windscreen bedizened with trinkets and artificial flowers. She joined the scramble and clambered on board, where, after paying her fare, she stood, squashed and swaying among the *abayas* and embroidered dress yokes, with one foot resting high on a sack of something across the aisle. No one took the least notice of her now.

At the Jaffa Gate stop she got off and found a taxi. Soon she was back in the New City, weltering in its habitual post-festal explosion of noisy activity. For Ann, it was like returning to earth from Mars; as they drove along Keren Kayemet she struggled to readjust, to get her mind into some frame of normality which would enable her to heal herself on the march, so to speak. Whatever she felt like, it must appear to Amnon and everyone else as if nothing unusual had happened. Sometimes when she was telling a good story Peter would say appreciatively, 'You've missed your vocation, darling. You're a born actress . . .' If she had any acting talent, she must use it now.

At Amnon's the iron street door was already hot to the touch, though the air was not yesterday's air and the heat, by comparison, was entirely tolerable. She walked slowly up the steps. It was only when she got to the top that she realised, with a painful shock, that she had lost her key. It was attached by an elastic band to the medallion she always wore on a chain round her neck. She had not the slightest recollection of taking it off at Boaz' but evidently she must have done because she was not wearing it. Christ! How could that be explained?

She rang the bell. Amnon opened the door and immediately threw his arms round her.

'So there you are! I've been dying for you! What a time I've had – what an adventure – and when I came back, totally exhausted, longing to tell all, you dared to be out! How is it that you are

171

always out when I need you?'

'I was in last night.'

He looked blank. 'Oh, you mean that stupid Zahal business. You know something, Ann, you're sweet, but you're crazy. I could be quite cross with you for going to so much unneedful trouble. It was not important at all. I phoned my officer this morning and told him I'd been out all night and he said he wished he could say the same, and any time this week will do . . . And now I have to go to all those people and explain I had a *meshugganeh-goya* in my house who insisted on waking them all up for nothing . . .'

'Sorry.'

'I don't blame *you*,' he said, squeezing her shoulder as he led her into the kitchen, where he was evidently in the middle of an elaborate solo lunch. 'But that Shachterman is a *tembel*. Why didn't *he* tell you it was just routine and that you should go to bed and forget it? Oh well, never mind. Have you eaten? No? Have some with me. Watermelon – *shemenet* – fresh rolls – cheese – I even bought tomatoes for you. "Red gold" we call them here now, they're so expensive. The shopkeepers are making millions on them . . . crooks. By the way, thanks for one thing, at least you were here to help Bob and Company. They were singing your praises at breakfast. The milk got spilt again . . . I think you were right about eating in the kitchen. That Mary is too beautiful for words. I've decided I can do without Sue-Ella, but Mary I must have. We haven't as many black girls here as you have in England, you know, they are apt to go to one's head until one is more used to them. Coffee? Help yourself, the kettle's just boiled, I would make it but I must rush. I only got in at about eight after a *terrible* night – it was my car that broke down in the end – I slept by the roadside. Yes, really! – somewhere between Massada and Ein Fashkha. I say "slept" – it's a lie. Every time I put my head down I imagined someone was looking in through the window. Or I heard footsteps . . . I never was so idiotically nervous in my life . . . Though there have been incidents along that Dead Sea road. They used to row across . . .' He put down the quarter-moon of watermelon skin he'd been avidly gnawing and gulped some coffee. 'You're very quiet.'

'I'm very tired. Where's the Circus?'

'Gone out sight-seeing. My God, they are non-exhaustible, Ann! If the performance shows half the energy of their tourist activities, we'll have a hit on our hands. A hit we badly need, by the way, as you saw last night.'

'Yes. Last night did have the kiss of death about it rather.'

'You can't imagine what it does to me when nobody comes. It's not just the money. It's the empty seats . . . I am in love with that place, you know . . . when the public spurn it, it's as if they insult a bit of me.'

'It wasn't the show or the theatre last night. It was the *khamsin*. Amatsia said so.'

'Did he? . . . We've had *khamsins* before. Why aren't you eating? Eat, *mein bubele*, eat!' He stood up and came round behind her to open the fridge, and then stopped.

'Look at your lovely hair!' he said in wondering tones. 'How it's long! I never knew about this. Why don't you wear it down all the time?'

'Mutton dressed as lamb.'

'What's "mutton"?'

'Very old sheep.'

He let out a chortle of delight. 'English is the most wonderful language! Mutton dressed as lamb . . . but wait. What's with "dressed"? Sheep wear clothes in England?'

'Dressed, as for serving at table,' said Ann, wishing she'd pinned her hair up somehow, anyhow. Now he was stroking it, and she found she simply couldn't bear to be touched.

She got up rather abruptly. 'Will you excuse me, Amnon, I have to make a phone call.'

'Well, there's the phone in front of you. I'll play with your hair while you're talking. Can I make a pig's tail?'

'It's a private call.'

'Oh,' he said, disappointed. 'Oh well.' He went out of the kitchen, but returned immediately, as was his wont. 'By the way,' he said, 'or rather, not by the way, because I'm very annoyed. Have you been making calls to England?'

'Me? No, of course not.'

'Well, somebody has been making enormous and expensive overseas calls. The phone meter has jumped about a hundred points since last night.'

'It wasn't me.'

'It must have been the Circus then . . . Oh, curse them! It's so sneaky and greedy! I give them the run of my house, like Bluebeard, with just one condition, that they don't make overseas calls without asking me and without paying. And the minute my back is turned – '

173

'Maybe they are going to tell you, and pay.'

'So why didn't they do it this morning?'

'They could have forgotten.'

'They didn't forget at all, because I noticed the meter then, and I asked them, and they denied it to my face.'

'Oh dear,' said Ann, remembering that Dill had talked about phone calls.

'Well? Well? Don't sit there! Advise me.'

'*I* don't know, Amnon. Forget it, perhaps?'

'Forget it! It's about fifteen hundred lira's worth! No, really, it's not the principle of the thing, it's the money! Do they think I'm Rothschild? I will tell them to leave. It's too much anyway, them all being here, I want my flat to myself. Except perhaps for Mary.'

'What about me?'

'Oh, you're all right,' he said fondly. 'Especially with all that hair. Do you wear it loose in bed?'

'No.'

'How, then?'

'In a plait.'

'Pity . . .' He looked at her speculatively. Flushed as she was already, she could blush no more, but she said to him sharply, 'Amnon, my call.'

'Banished. From my own kitchen – '

She phoned the professor, having first forced her brain to devise an excuse. The old man was obviously put out, having waited for her for two hours, and she was ashamed to ask him for another appointment. That left her with only one other today, a leftist politician who had been an army photographer during the War. She could scarcely imagine how she could gather herself together to go and speak to him in the Knesset. All she wanted in the world was to shut herself into her room, preferably with some strong sedative, and wipe the whole of the past fifteen hours out of existence . . . perhaps if she could sleep, deep and long, some of the rawest edge of pain and humiliation and anger would have been blunted by the time she woke . . . But her appointment was at 2.30 and it was nearly one o'clock now. She pushed away her plate and buried her face in her hands, trying to hold back tears. Boaz. It's not true, not a word of it – it's part of the syndrome, my dearest, the paranoid syndrome – deep down you can't believe I could love you . . . that's why you've twisted me and made me unworthy of being loved by you. Oh, what is it with you, what is it? I must know.

174

She reached slowly for the 'phone again, looked up a number, and was half-way through dialling when Amnon popped back. Ann's nerves were ragged and she jumped.

'Have you terminated?' he asked.

'Have I what?'

'It's my joke. You know, like in *For Whom the Bell Tolls* . . .'

'Sorry – ?'

'When they come back from making the earth move,' Amnon explained patiently. 'Pilar asks if they've terminated. It's my favourite bit.'

'Oh yes. I'd forgotten that.'

'Listen. I'm going to pick up the Circus at the Liberty Bell Gardens. Would you like to come?'

'Not now, Amnon, thank you.'

'I'm taking them to the Nat'am and they're doing their technical rehearsal. Then I'll take them somewhere for something to eat and sometime in between Dill has to have a rest. The show is early, it's at 7.30. Do you want to come?'

'No, I don't think – '

'I'm offering you a first night seat!' he said, hurt. 'Tonight we're full. Nearly. Well, all right then, I'll give you two seats, you can invite your favourite fascist.'

Ann stiffened. 'Who?'

'Shachterman. I suppose I owe him for last night, God knows why he bothered – it must have been for your sake, not mine.'

Ann sat still for a moment and then said, 'I don't think I will, Amnon. He wouldn't enjoy it.'

'No, perhaps not, too cheerful for him. I can't imagine him doing anything just for fun, can you? Did you get any Arabs out of him, by the way? At least he should be good for that.'

After a lengthy pause, Ann said, in a tone of surprise, 'I didn't ask him.'

'I thought that was the whole idea.'

'Yes. I forgot.'

'Forgot – about your book?'

'It seems I must have done.'

He said nothing and she felt him looking at her, narrow-eyed, guessing . . . She quickly looked up and said, 'May I ask someone else, then? – to the first night.'

'Yes, sure. Anyone you like. Listen, when do you think I should tell them?'

'Who? What?'

'The Circus! – that I'm kicking them out.'

'Not till after the show.'

'That makes sense . . . I'll book them into a hotel. Non-adjoining rooms. Maybe a *frum* hotel, just to serve them right . . .'

'No *frum* hotel would have Sue-Ella, or Mary either.'

'No, quite right too, much too distracting. I can't even pass the milk while they're about, let alone communicate with God . . . Well, I'm going. I'll give your tickets to Amatsia, he's doing front-of-house tonight. I'll be backstage, helping Sue-Ella onto the tightrope . . . Hope we all enjoy it more than last night, anyway. You know, your hair really *is* – *mashehu yotseh min haklal* . . .'

He bent and kissed the top of her head, giving her hair one more stroke. She sat still with the utmost difficulty. She still loved Amnon but today he seemed, somehow, like a humming-bird whirring round her head – unbearable to her. But she mustn't hurt him by jerking away or showing her eagerness for him to go, so she sat. But clenched.

He drew away and stood above her, rarely subdued.

'Are you all right?' he asked.

'Of course! Why not?'

'Indeed, why not. You are putting out spooky vibrations, that's all.'

'I'm tired,' she repeated inanely, knowing she was going to cry if he said one kind word more, probably even if he didn't.

'I can see . . . Can't you rest?'

'I've got to go to the Knesset.'

'Take a taxi.'

'A number 24 bus goes all the way – '

' – once an hour or so. Get a taxi. Don't be so mean.'

'All right, Amnon, I will, I promise.'

'*Ciao*, then.

'*Shalom*.'

When he'd gone, she let herself cry, and thought about the bottle of bourbon, but she'd bought this. Now she must pay for it. Drinking to ease the pain was not part of that. She blew her nose, cried more, used up another three tissues, washed her face and began at once to cry again. At last she dragged herself to the phone and made the call she had begun earlier.

'Allo, *mi ze*?'

'Shula, it's Ann.'

'Ann.'

'From yesterday.'

'I'm not losing my memory. I'm just surprised you called.'

'Do you want to come to an American circus with me tonight at the Nat'am?'

'No thanks, I'm not in the mood for circuses. Anyway, I hate them. For this you phoned me, after I showed you my door?'

'No, it was an excuse. I want your help.'

'Are *you* crying now? You sound it.'

'I've been crying. I thought I'd stopped.'

'What's the matter? Is it private?'

'Yes.'

'So tell me.'

'I can't, Shula, not now.'

'Okay, so don't.'

'Shula, don't be hurt. I want – I've got something to ask you. It's nothing to do with my book.'

'Nu? Ask.'

'You know a lot of people in Jerusalem. I wondered – do you know a man called Boaz Shachterman?'

There was a pause.

'Shachterman. Big, bad-tempered fellow – right-winger – lives out on the Beit Lehem Road somewhere. Very nice wife, poor thing.'

'Why is she a poor thing?' asked Ann, startled.

'Have I got the right man? It's been years since we met, maybe fifteen, twenty. Wasn't he in the 101?'

'The what?'

'Haven't you heard about the 101?'

'No, what is it?'

'It was a special unit, sort of commandos. In the early days. It was stopped, thanks God.'

'When was this?'

'In the 'fifties.'

Some instinct of self-preservation prevented her from pursuing this line.

'You were saying – about his wife – '

'Oh yes. I used to know them a bit. Years ago, when I was married. Before they moved out there in '67. When we all used to meet in the cafés. We all took a different view of things then, we were still – all in one boat, so to say, we were more tolerant. But anyone could see his wife was a *miscaina*.'

'In what way?'

177

'That type of man can never be easy to live with. It's the Rightist temperament. That's never just a matter of politics, you know, it comes into everything. A pattern. They order their women about, they bully their children. They train their dogs . . . "To heel!" *You* know. They can't stand any weakness, not even their own natural ones . . . They impose their private idea of order on everything and everybody around them. It's a known psychological condition, which goes with men like that. Author – what is it? – author – '

'Authoritarian.'

'Right.'

'You say he bullied his wife?'

'I won't say he was unkind to her. Just "do this, do that". To be fair, she would do it. She was very quiet – too quiet, we used to think. I used to wish she would stand up to him once, say, "Do it yourself, you big bastard". But she never did. She was just the right type for him, submissive. Like an Arab woman.'

'An *Arab* woman?'

'You know what I mean – slipping in and out of the room, fetching things, never say boo to a goose – is that the expression?'

'Do you know she left him?'

'No! Did she? Now that is a nice bit of gossip. Oh, how I used to love to gossip! Perhaps she got sick of him giving her too many orders and not enough pregnancies.'

'I wonder why they never had children.'

'The rumour was, if I remember, that he couldn't. Of course no one knew. But if so, foof! How it would drive such a fellow crazy. That his magnificent sperm should be infertile! Oy veh! Such a weakness as that he couldn't bear. He probably made her life a misery for it.'

And if, on top of that crucial weakness, he got an injury to his 'best' arm? So that he became an obvious cripple instead of only a childless man who might not be at fault? What would his wife feel, knowing what that could do to him, and to her? It might make her vomit with something quite different from physical disgust at his wounds.

Ann was aware that she was suffering some intense confusion, much more, though in a less violent way, than before. What she was doing now – necessary, vital as it seemed, and absolutely unavoidable – was a kind of spying. Eavesdroppers, she thought grimly, hear no good of themselves, and enquirers who lack trust and loyalty hear no good of their lovers. However, she couldn't

178

stop now; it was like some addiction, she had to know more and more.

'Shula, were you ever a friend of his?'

'Well. In a small way, I must confess I was.'

'Confess? What do you mean?'

'Just that obviously I am a little ashamed now of ever having liked him, considering that I knew all about him. I mean, there were no revelations, he was what he was. To be fair to him he never pretended or hid anything. Why should he? He was proud of it. It was only when I grew older, and – after '67 everything changed – one began to see things in a different light, and to draw away from people like Boaz, who were . . . how can I explain? They *were*, and they *represented*, a side of Israel which had been there right from the beginning but which, when we were all young and patriotic and united, we had chosen not to see, or to excuse.'

'What's now called the "fascist" element.'

'Right.'

'That word is used so much now – I'm beginning to use it myself, though I swore I never would . . . What does it mean, exactly?'

'Well, you know what is fascism. It's not just a rude word we use for our political enemies, it has this real meaning. It's thinking that anything you do is justified if it's for the State, that the State is a value. The National Religious Party think the State has a duty to control people's religion and morals – that's far-gone fascism, no other word for it. It's the same as with Hitler and Stalin, the State had to control education, I mean what was taught in schools, and that's what the religious parties want here too.'

'But Boaz Shachterman isn't religious.'

'No, of course not, but there are other ways to be a fascist. Boaz did things in the 'fifties, and from what I remember of him he would do them today – perhaps he does do them, in another way. Nobody knows exactly what it is he does for the State these days but there are rumours, and that's another reason why I don't meet him any more.'

'What things did he do in the 'fifties?' asked Ann, stifling a quailing sensation.

'Well, I told you,' said Shula quite matter-of-factly. 'He was in the 101. He was at Kibya. So – technically – you could say the man is a murderer.'

179

Ann sat motionless. She had always had the faculty of watching herself. Now she watched, from only a very short distance, how cravenly her inner self cowered before the oncoming of a black, nameless horror.

'You know about Kibya?' Shula went on with a kind of unintended remorseless persistence.

'Shula, I'm sorry, I'll have to – stop talking now. I'll . . .' Ann's voice stopped and she couldn't speak for a while. She didn't know how long it was – it was like a gap in time. When she came back to herself Shula seemed to have said, 'Ann? Are you still there?' several times.

'I must go,' Ann said, and hung up the phone.

She felt suddenly very ill. She wondered if she might manage to rid herself of the source of this feeling by the simple act of vomiting, but she knew the inimical matter was not in her stomach; the brain cannot so easily rid itself of its poisons. She sat quite still at the table under the neon, trying to fight the nightmare off, or alternatively to grasp it and cope with it somehow. After a while she felt a dull pain in her hand, and looked at it. There were toothmarks all down the side of her left thumb – she must have been biting it without noticing what she was doing. All desire to cry had left her. Crying was an immature remedy for immature emotions. Dimly she felt that she had just been propelled into a totally new dimension of feeling, for which nothing in her life had prepared her. She had wanted to turn, to face the slaughterer whose trade and products underpinned her life. She had not bargained on his having a face she loved.

CHAPTER 14

He was at Kibya.

It was not her era. She never remembered hearing of the 101. But she knew about Kibya. It was the biggest and harshest of the reprisal raids mounted by Israeli commandos in response to infiltrations across the Jordan border in the early 'fifties. It had ended in the deaths of more than sixty Arab villagers – men, women and children.

It was not Ann's way to drink to dull pain, but this was more than she could bear unaided. With the haste of someone with a gaping wound which would soon start giving intolerable pain, she jumped to her feet and blundered – much as she had blundered out of Boaz's bedroom earlier – into the 'seraglio room' and to the glass-fronted cupboard. Last night she had disapproved of Bob taking Amnon's drink without asking. Now she reached for the same bottle and poured a drink of the same size. But as she tried to down it, her gorge rose. She reached the bathroom somehow and fell on her knees by the lavatory bowl. She retched, with degutting violence, but nothing came. She sank back, tried once more to drink the whisky, became nauseated again, and again strained emptily . . . It was no use. There was to be no easy escape.

Feeling too wretched to stand, she lay down on the tiled floor with the glass in her hand. The very smell of the stuff mocked her. You asked for this, she thought. You wanted to experience everything, you wanted to be part of the human race. So here it is – a deep-dredger, opening up your shallow soul enough to enable you to participate in Jewish suffering. Of both kinds: the kind inflicted on them – pain, humiliation, degradation, disgrace. And the other kind, involving defiance, aggression, poison to the self-image – the suffering involved in discovering that the best way to avoid being a victim is to become an aggressor. Now you feel both. Keep them in your belly and don't try to dilute them.

She reached up and poured the bourbon away down the bowl.

She must open her mind to it, the way she had opened her legs this morning. The one involved the other, and it was no use pretending she hadn't known it. She just had not known the extent of it. Lying perfectly still with her face on the floor she thought, Now you've jumped away. All right. You're entitled to fight it off as long as you can. You can't be expected to accept a thing like that all at once. Eventually you must get close and look, but slowly. Slowly. Start at the outer rim of the matter, skirt round it first, before you turn towards the bone . . . You wanted to join him, to share his inner world. You went of your own will to the dark pool. But even he flung the grenade away when it fell at his feet, he did not hug it to his chest.

It's all part of the same thing. It's all to do with war.

Boaz had fought. He knew what war was like – for him it was not, as for so many in England under the age of fifty, a glorified reflection of other men's filtered triumphs. He had been wounded, in all senses of the word. Yet he looked with a certain equanimity upon the prospect of endlessly recurring wars. What did that make him? A bloodthirsty warrior like the Mamelukes, whose whole lives were dedicated to battle with its thrills and challenges and spoils? Was he one of those sorts of men who are never fully stretched outside the framework – the veritable rack – of war, for whom the imperatives of conflict – kill or be killed, win or go under, keep on your feet or be trampled down – are the only ones which meet their masculine strength and puissance with a sufficient challenge? Who was it who said, 'Even at the end of days, when the lion lies down with the lamb, I would prefer to be the lion'? Might Boaz not add, ' – And even then I might devour the lamb, if I felt myself growing slothful or bored'?

No. That was not it.

Technically, you could say the man is a murderer . . .

Not yet, not yet. Keep clear of that. I love him. I trust the judgement of my body's instinct. I have made mistakes in the love-search, but they were small, they were not grotesque, I have never been attracted to amoral men. I will come at it soon, and find the basic error, or if not that, the extenuation, or if not that, the root cause that will excuse him . . . I shall find it by examining the facts. About the incident . . . *Later*. First, about him.

Seven years ago when I first met him, what did I think of him, how interpret his eccentric choice of domicile, his all-absorbing concern for the Arabs of the West Bank? I thought him an honest scholar, a student. I wrote it somewhere: 'a sympathetic observer of the Palestinians' life-style, *moeurs* and values'. A sympathetic observer . . . *sympathetic* . . . Was that really what I thought? I had no particular reason *then* to want to think well of him . . . What led me to the conclusion that he was sympathetic to them? This illusion persisted a long time and was fed by observations of my own.

I watched him as he moved among them. It seemed to me then that he did not patronise or despise them. He approached them as equals. He spoke their language fluently. And their response surely meant something, no matter what Neville said. They received him with something more than formal courtesy. Traditional habits of hospitality would not account for the way they sat and drank with him, talked and laughed with him, opened their homes to him, shook his hand . . . Not if they had reason to suspect his motives. And did they not have reason, simply because he was a Jew?

Ann lay still. Yesterday in the *sharav*, when she had sprawled on the floor with Amnon in her unknowing innocence (it was like remembering a time before birth) the tiles had cooled her deliciously. Now they chilled her to the bone; her whole body was shaken with waves of shuddering. But she was hardly aware of it. She was remembering an occasion when Boaz had taken her – five years ago now – to the home of some Arabs in a village in the North. An unusual family in which both the father and the mother were schoolteachers. The wife was not like most Arab village women; she wore modern dress, gave her daughters freedom to use make-up and go out with young men, and was treated by her husband not as a sort of servant but as a partner. Ann found herself urgently recalling every detail of Boaz's manner and behaviour in that home, and the reaction of those people to him. Both sides were entirely relaxed, and if no friendship existed there, Ann felt she did not know what friendship looked like. As they were leaving – she remembered it clearly – the woman had shaken Boaz warmly by the hand, and the man had kissed him on both cheeks. Ann herself, her normal nervousness in strange milieus laid to rest by the atmosphere of friendliness, had been bold enough to joke: 'That's a funny custom, when a man gets kisses from a man and a handshake from a woman.' Boaz had shot her a warning look and she feared she had trespassed on some taboo, but no. The woman had laughed, and, standing on tiptoe, given Boaz a kiss.

Had he been hiding his hatred behind a façade of comradeship, worming his way cunningly into their confidence so that he could spy on them? Was he so profoundly devious? It was beyond Ann's power to believe it.

Technically, you could say the man is a murderer . . .

She curled up in a spasm as she lay on the hard floor, as if the words were a knife thrust. It was not so. It was not so! Boaz might embody the dark pool, but it was not a cesspit or a tarn of blood. She had asked, and been answered with, far more than she had wanted to know; but now that too much was, at the same time, not enough. There must be reasons, mitigations . . . If there were none, if he had helped to kill innocent people and come away unmarked, then there was a hole blown in her life that would leave her as crippled as he was.

She got up stiffly and went to her room. She had books beside her bed, in her suitcase, which she had brought with her – reference books, chiefly about the '48 War, but a couple of them were more comprehensive accounts of the Arab-Israeli struggle and might make some mention of the Kibya raid. At the moment her mind, when she let it off the tightest possible rein, strayed directly to the only comparable incident she really knew about – Deir Yassin. About this she knew all that anyone knew who had not been there. She had actually spoken to an eye witness, a Haganah officer, now a historian, who had gone to the engagement as an observer, and had witnessed the slaughter. 'A hot-blooded, not a cold-blooded massacre,' he had called it. That was the only extenuation he could find. He had said of himself, 'I am no vegetarian. War *means* killing; war *means* refugees. Those who start wars must accept that, and not cry afterwards.' But he did not condone these killings of defenceless civilians, over two hundred of them, by the two Jewish terrorist organisations which, on their own initiative, had attacked the village in the spring of 1948.

To differentiate Kibya from Deir Yassin – an official from a semi-official action, a reprisal raid from an unprovoked attack, in short, a necessity of war from a brutal massacre – became Ann's first concern.

With a sense of opening Pandora's box, she opened the books one by one and searched their indexes for references to Kibya or Company 101. One by one she discarded them. But even as she looked, she realised she was keeping one back, and suddenly she knew why. It was a book which, when she had first read it, she had tried to talk about to Boaz, believing at that time that they were sufficiently of one mind to agree about it. But he had burst into a passion of rage at the mention of it. Now she came to think of it, it was almost the first time she had seen him in that black mood, almost incoherent with anger. He had heaped his scatological curses upon both book and author, a young Israeli of the Left

184

who had written – in Ann's view – a most soul-searching and penetrating account of his country's history and his people's traumas. When she had tried to find out from Boaz why he hated it so much, he had refused to be specific, damning it in general as the work of a defeatist and a traitor. She had been astounded at the time, seeing in this reaction the first signs of a complexity of personality, a dark underside to his nature which the formality of their acquaintance, the facile assumptions she had made about him from the first, had prevented her realising till then.

Now she thought, There's some clue hidden here. Perhaps it is something to do with this incident. She looked for Kibya in the index; it was there. She forced herself to read the whole passage.

From the end of the War of Independence to the early 'fifties was a time of extreme insecurity for the average citizen of the new State. The elation of the Jews' first military victory for thousands of years soon withered in the corroding winds of day-to-day living surrounded by enemies smouldering for vengeance. The genuine hope that the armistice would blossom into full-fledged peace died hard, and both sides must bear responsibility for its death.

Infiltration, particularly across the border with Jordan, began immediately the war ended. What may have begun as a spontaneous need to renew contact with lost land, which banished farmers could still clearly see but were forbidden to till, soon developed into hit-and-run raids by guerillas, which over the years caused a large number of Israeli casualties. What was perhaps more serious, they caused a weakening of national morale.

The term used for these infiltrators was 'marauders', and the problem of dealing with them – since the authorities in Jordan were unwilling (or perhaps genuinely unable) to control them – fell to the Israeli Defence Forces. These, despite their triumph in 1948, were soon sorely in need of reorganisation, a boost to their self-esteem, and a revival of prestige within the country. In January 1953, Ben Gurion assigned this task to Moshe Dayan.

Dayan, headstrong, pragmatic and notoriously short-sighted, was tired of the demoralising failure of the IDF to stem the flow of intruders, and also of the one-sidedness of the United Nations, which tended to turn a blind eye on Arab raids into Israel. He therefore decided on a radical new policy, which he expressed as a belief that Arab governments *could* control their irregulars, but *would* do it only if the Israelis meted out such punishment in return that it would become clear that the theft of one cow from a kibbutz would hurt a whole Jordanian village, and the murder of one Jew would endanger the population of a sizeable area. In other words, two eyes for an eye; a whole mouth for a tooth.

Dayan gathered a small, select group of volunteers from various units for this task – not necessarily the most experienced fighters (many of them were still in their teens, too young to have fought in the War of '48) but those who had the will, courage and toughness to take the initiative. He groomed this group, which was known as Company 101, into a commando cadre, and with them mounted a series of vigorous and daring reprisal raids into Jordanian territory.

The grim climax of these operations came on the night of October 15 to 16, 1953, when a raid of catastrophic proportions and consequences was mounted upon the village of Kibya, eight miles from the border, following the murder by Arab marauders of a woman and her two children in the Israeli village of Yehuda. In the attack, the 101's blew up forty houses with their occupants, leaving some seventy dead. There was an international, and a national, outcry about this, and following an investigation the 101's were split up and reintegrated into various Parachute units. It is significant that both Moshe Sharett (then Prime Minister) and Ben Gurion denied Government responsibility for this raid.

While in operation, the 101's reprisals had the desired effect of putting the Arabs on the defensive and restoring the unity and confidence of the nation; but they had side and long-term effects which were not so healthy and which might have been foreseen. From the 101's – first famous for their daredevil courage, later notorious for their ruthlessness – stemmed a cult of toughness and violence which influenced a great many of the Israeli youth of the period and to some extent obliterated the more humane, one might say the hate-free approach to the enemy that had prevailed in their immediate predecessors, the Palmach. This earlier breed of commandos, in the course of winning a full-scale war against several Arab armies, had never descended to mass killings of civilians, nor had they ever regarded cold-bloodedness as an asset to them as fighters. The unfeeling ferocity with which the 101's drove on missions of destruction deep into the heart of Arab villages, over a period of months, with a callous disregard for the lives of their inhabitants, could not fail to produce in the nation which despatched them a new, unbalancing faith in militancy and aggressiveness to solve their problems with their neighbours – especially, perhaps, as the tactic was seen to be, in the short term, effective. (In the long term, raid and counter-raid inflamed antagonism and led inevitably to the Sinai War of '56.)

In a nation with a citizen army, service in which affects every family, leaders may be considered to have a duty not only to protect the population against sabotage and death, but to guard it from the disease of militarism. Those early days of fear, and the reaction to it, typified in its most extreme form by the 101's, laid the first layer of a shell over the Israeli mentality, which arguably did permanent damage to the national ethos.

Ann put down the book and sat, stunned. No wonder Boaz had been so incensed against it and its author. The equivalent in England, she supposed, would be a book which said that the pilots of Bomber Command in 1944 had been cold-blooded ruthless killers because they had gone out night after night to bomb civilian targets. Young men – Boaz would have been no more than eighteen then – who took hair-raising risks and bore in their very nerve fibres the burden of a whole nation's expectations, and the responsibility for a new kind of border warfare with few precedents to guide them – how could they stop to think what they were doing, to ask themselves if it was moral or immoral, if innocents were getting slaughtered with the guilty, or what effect their actions were likely to have on the country's 'ethos'?

At the same time, the horrifying brutality involved in blowing up houses with women and children in them stuck in her throat. Seventy dead . . . Seventy dead for the three in Yehuda . . . 'Two eyes for an eye. A whole mouth for a tooth . . .' For three Jews, seventy Arabs. 'We are better . . .' One would have to think so, to exact such a toll, and walk away, convinced you had done no more than your duty, and accept your due as a national hero . . .

'We are better . . .' Ann took out her notebook and leafed through her notes, searching for something she had recently read and jotted down as a salutary corrective to her philo-semitism ('Just as stupid,' Menachem had once argued, 'as the other thing.') It had been written by the old professor she had failed to meet this morning:

We Jews have among us every vice known to other nations. We have our share of murderers, thieves, rogues and adulterers. We can lay claim to any number of petty crooks and informers and traitors; we even have a few drunkards. Wife-beaters we have, and child molesters, and practitioners of unnatural vices of every description. We have in our ranks men who have undertaken every base action a man may perform in order to survive and cheat death – we have more of these than other races, because we have faced death more often and in more savage and degrading forms. There are cruel Jews and uncultured Jews and dishonourable Jews and ruthless Jews: Jews who push drugs and Jews who live off immoral earnings and Jews who terrorise innocent people . . . And of course we have plenty of fanatical, crazy Jews. In all these respects, we are not better – though let it be noted, no worse – than any other people.

But in one thing we are better. It can be shown statistically that we are, as a race, cleverer and more gifted. We produce more mathematicians and scientists, philosophers and inventors, more entrepreneurs and musicians and writers and Nobel Prize winners, proportionately, than any other comparable nation. We take great pride in that, with justification, for it is the gifted members of humanity which secure its progress and endow it with a sense of collective worth. But when you come to consider, does that make us, when all our qualities are set at opposite arms of the balance, better or worse than others?

From those who receive more, more shall be expected.

Ann stood up again. She found she was almost too tired to walk across the room; emotions, and the struggles of a mind faced with the unfaceable, are as exhausting as any physical exertion. She moved like a much older woman to the long windows and opened them onto the midday street. She stood on the narrow balcony, for the first time finding the noise of traffic, that bombardment of sound, a blessing, because it drowned out thought for a few moments till she got used to it.

She must get over him.

On all counts. First of all (though it shouldn't be first) he had rejected her, so she had no real option. But even if that had not happened, she had allied herself with one who, like Macbeth, had murdered sleep. The comparison with the Second World War, which had come to her so forcefully, did not entirely hold water.

Why not? Perhaps because of what Shula had said. The ability to kill at close range calls for a different quality than the ability to press a button and kill at a distance. The ability to kill in an instant when you are not threatened calls for a higher steel quotient in the soul than what Shula had done. To kill women and children, even if they are divided from you by walls . . . to throw instruments of death through windows left trustfully open on the night . . . actually to *see* it . . .

As *she* would see it, very soon now, if she did not clamp down on her imagination. She was not ready yet. Her stomach was not ready.

Her hands gripped the hot railing in a spasm like shock, and she struggled to come back to practical reality. She couldn't stand here forever, she had a life to live. The trouble was, she could not imagine how she was going to go forward. Someone must help her. She needed a friend now, someone who could grasp some part of it, who could share it with her . . . Ruth? Perhaps. Perhaps.

She backed out of the sunlight into the flat and groped her way to the phone in the kitchen. As she put her hand on it, it rang.

'Hallo, Lady Godiva, it's me – what are you doing still there? I thought you said you had to be at the Knesset at 2.30?'

'Why – what's the time now – '

'Quarter past – oh you are a nuisance – I'll have to drive you.'

'I'll get a taxi – don't you bother – '

'What if you can't find one? I'm only up the road, luckily for you I've got to bring Dill back for his rest before the rehearsal. Be outside on the pavement. Listen, why I phoned – did you see your letter?'

'What letter?'

'A letter from England, it came this morning, I left it in the postbox downstairs, and then I thought you might not think to look there . . . I'll be there in three minutes – don't keep me waiting, I wouldn't shlepp up to the Knesset on a first night for just anyone, you know.'

There was no time to phone Ruth now. No time to think, or do anything except gather up her things and go out. She picked up her letter from the tin box at the foot of the stairs. It was from Peter, and it was an actual letter in a long airmail envelope, not the usual weekly airgram. It was bulky. The sight of his writing – he affected a special brown shade of Quink, reminiscent to Ann always of old photographs – gave her a dull pang, and then a stronger one just because the first was not as sharp as it should have been. There seemed little room for him in her conscience just now; it was too crowded with other things. She stood outside the iron door on the narrow pavement, jostled by noise, heat and people. School had been out for some time and the street was full of children in shorts and t-shirts, all screaming and running or sauntering three abreast. Ann leant against a post near the curb and as the trucks shot by, felt the pressure waves buffeting her, scarcely more tangible than the one which had assailed her when she opened the door last night to Boaz . . . Oh, yes, the body knows its own! The mind dodges and struggles and thinks it can make choices, but the instincts tell you what you really are by telling you what you really want . . . Peter's fat letter lay in her hand, unopened.

A small, battered Volkswagen swerved in to the curb and stopped. Ann's heart stopped with it, but only for a second. The face hanging out of the window was not Boaz' face.

'Shula . . .!'

'I am an idiot.'

'Why – ?'

'You are waiting?'

'Yes, someone's picking me up.'

'Can I take you? Where do you go?'

'The Knesset.'

'I take you. Get in.'

Ann hesitated. Then she got out a bit of paper and scribbled a note for Amnon which she dropped in his post-box – 'Got a lift. Thanks anyway. See you tonight.' She climbed into the car and it nose-dived into the stream of traffic.

'Why did you come?'

'You need to ask? Because I was cooking myself a lunch and suddenly I stopped to think. It took time because most of my thoughts now are for myself. But good I was not too late to catch you. You want to tell me, or I tell you?'

'What are you talking about?'

'You have been in bed with that bastard. Yes? And then right after it, I tell you about Kibya.'

Ann stared ahead, numbed by this new assault. She could only see it as that. But perhaps 'circumlocutions' would have been worse.

'He's not a bastard,' she said at last, like a child.

'And I said all that about his wife, and about fascism, and God knows what . . . I am an idiot, fifty times over. I should have

190

guessed why you asked about him. I don't blame you. We all felt it, every one of us, in the old days. The pull of the man, like a bull, I remember it now.'

'Please, Shula. Don't. I don't want to be excused as – as some female animal is excused for falling prey to her mating instincts. What you say may be true, but there's more to it – the man himself attracts me.'

'You've got a strong stomach.'

'Hardly stronger than yours,' retorted Ann sharply before she could stop herself.

'Don't think I criticise. This is no place for weak ones, but then, the world is no place for weak ones. But for myself, I must say that I killed men. Soldiers with guns, face to face. Not kids asleep in bed.'

They drove round the rim of the valley, climbing steadily.

'I would like to ask you a hundred questions,' Shula said.

'I doubt if I would answer any of them.'

'I won't ask. But it would be interesting to know. I have my theory about the – what I said on the phone – the fascist personality. That it affects every action. I would like to ask how Boaz does it. I bet anything he would never let a woman take the top position. I bet he would make her bear her pleasure, or anything else he chose to give her, very quietly, like an endurance test he put her through. He would never show softness. Not Boaz! He would not say one loving word, but would want to talk politics the moment he climbed off – '

Ann had a childish urge to press her fingers to her ears. Instead she turned her face away and stared off towards the far side of the valley at the new housing developments and hoped Shula would soon, very soon, shut up before she began to hate her.

He wept. He drank my tears. He said my hair smelt like a desert morning.

'I am trying to put you off for your own good,' Shula said.

'So you're not sorry you told me about Kibya.'

'I am, because I like you actually, and I hate to hurt people I like. But I am not, because if you are mixed up with Boaz you had much better get unmixed before he hurts you far, far worse than I could, no matter what I said.'

After a moment, Ann said, 'It's over, anyway. He threw me out.'

Shula didn't reply at once, and Ann looked round at her. She was frowning deeply, with lines which were on her face already.

'Now you have surprised me,' she said. 'I hate his opinions and I hate his past, but I am very surprised that he fucks and throws. A whore, perhaps, but you are no whore. Did you do anything to him, to make him angry?'

'Yes. I said Jewish terrorism was like Arab terrorism.'

'Oh! Oh, well. That was asking for it. Though he will soon see you are right.'

'What do you mean by that?'

She shrugged. 'There will be things soon. Actions by us against them. Meir Kahane has called openly for it. The man is quite mad but he has followers. And there are others. Boaz will see. But he won't admit he was wrong, don't hope for that, not if there are bombs under every mosque in the West Bank . . . You must try to understand that when a man has killed people in an action like Kibya, he cannot turn around and admit those people are the same as his people, or that his deeds are as bad as the deeds of his enemies. You can't ask him to destroy himself for your sake. He is half-destroyed by himself already, he must hold on to the half that is left. Here we are.'

The guard at the turning-place outside the Knesset was waving them to a stop. Ann got out.

'Thanks, Shula.'

'For what? For half-killing you, I can see it. You were mad to go with him, to get involved with him. No, I won't tell anyone. Why should I, who do I see these days? Who can I bear to see?'

'Will you be in touch?'

'You be in touch. Come to my place and we might even get drunk. I've decided it's not so bad to get drunk if you are not in bad company. And listen, leave him alone. Don't go after him, don't pity him. Such men don't change, they just get worse. But don't abuse yourself. He is a *gever* and no woman on this earth would blame you.' She was silent for a moment. 'Is his arm a mess?'

'Yes.'

'Serve him right, pity they didn't blow it right off.' But her eyes were full of tears.

CHAPTER 15

The MK she had to interview was late. Ann sat on one of the padded seats in the press area waiting, wishing he would come so that she could concentrate on interviewing him and rest her mind for a while. She was quite familiar with her surroundings so there was not much in them to distract her, though she glanced automatically at everyone who passed. The doors to the press gallery were open, and if she could have roused herself to go into the office where they endorsed the passes for admission to the chamber, she might have gone in there and watched the session: that was what she normally did if she had to wait here. Not that her Hebrew was adequate to do more than grasp an occasional sentence or insult, but there was always something going on that she could react to. Once, after the '73 War, she had seen Golda Meir alternately weeping and thundering, as Opposition leaders accused the Government of causing young men's deaths through negligence. Now it was their turn to bear the responsibilities and receive the whips and scorns of their opponents.

Ann took out her tape recorder and plugged it into the two-holed socket under the curtains on the long window. She had her notebook out. Groping for the microphone she felt a packet and pulled it out of her hold-all. It was Peter's letter.

There was no excuse to delay reading it. She cast one last look all round in case her MK might be approaching, but there was no sign of him. With a heavy sigh of foreboding for the pangs she must reckon with now, she tore the flap open.

The letter from Peter was only part of the contents. Enclosed with it was a letter page torn from *The Times*, and two other letters, still in their envelopes, addressed to her through the newspaper in unknown hand-writing. She looked at the newspaper and saw, printed about half-way down, the letter she had written intimating that recent unsympathetic leaders about Israel and partial or selective reporting had some connection with the dependence of the press upon enormous Arab-funded supplements and advertising. Re-reading it she felt a thin shadow of the pleasure she would normally have got from having gained admission to those exclusive columns. Now it all seemed trivial and futile.

With a deep sense of reluctance, she unfolded Peter's letter.

193

Darling,

I didn't know about this effusion of yours. I was, as usual, rather dismayed by your vehemence. Some may call it intemperance, though I hope not, for your sake. I'm not unaware that often, after you've stuck your neck out in this way, the inevitable rebuttals sting you more than you care to admit. In a way I am proud of you for your gumption in speaking your mind (and struck dumb when you actually 'make' *The Times*, wish I could!) but at the same time, I sometimes wish that I could rein you in a little when you have one of these impulses. Surely you don't honestly think Auntie Times would kowtow to the kind of commercial bribery your letter hints at?

This may not be the moment to say so, but I'm not sure how much good all this Zionist lark is doing your career. I was talking to Mrs Wallorton in the village only last Friday. You know she's a great fan of yours and has read all your novels (now don't pooh-pooh her, darling, she's a very well-read old thing *and* discriminating) and she said, 'I wish you'd persuade your clever wife to get back to writing ordinary English novels that ordinary English people can identify with. I've nothing against the Jews at all, but she is getting to be a wee bit of a bore about them, don't you think?' You'll be gratified to hear that I went into a long harangue in your defence, saying how few novelists these days had commitments of any kind and that although I might not agree with all your ideas I would defend to the death, etc., etc. She was quite put out with me and went on her way tossing her head, a pity since I was about to ask her to lend me her Flymo (our old mower has packed up, this time for good, I'm afraid). But never mind.

The fact is, in my secret heart I think the old dear is right, and probably represents a lot of readers. It was all very well when you first came home from the kibbutz and wrote that first, very good, novel, because then you were, quite understandably, full of the whole extraordinary way of life and needed to get it out of your system. But practically every second book since then has had some connection or other with the Jews or Israel, and it's only natural if people get fed up with it. There must be plenty of perfectly good Jewish novelists around who know the background far better than you. And there aren't nearly enough writers around doing justice to the British scene. If any! They all seem to be hatchet-men.

It has occurred to me sometimes to wonder whether perhaps this passion of yours for the Jews and their destiny has something to do with your creative well-springs. Of course you'll say, with justice, that I know very little about that, being totally non-creative myself – one can't put books on insects in the same category as novel writing! But I've watched you at it over the years and it seems to me that a writer like you has a fundamental need of drama in your life. I remember the state you got yourself into during the Yom Kippur war. *You* thought it was a minor nervous breakdown. I played along, of course, because even self-induced mental states can give genuine pain; but now, so long afterwards, I wonder if you might be prepared to consider that you were getting yourself worked up in order to have a good excuse to go over there, at a high emotional pitch to match that of the Jews at the time, and then have a good wallow (sorry, darling, but I want to be quite honest, as I want *you* to be) – not out of self-indulgence at all, but for the good of your work.

What I'm trying to say is, could it be that you are fascinated by Israel for the simple reason that there is always tension there, and you need tension for your writing? I'm not lumping you with the primates but it's interesting to remember that quite a lot of species will deliberately provoke danger in order to keep themselves stimulated. Country life must be a bit dull without any admixture of adventure and 'kicks'. One woman writer I saw on the box the other evening said nobody can write without drinking. And somebody else once described the Jews as the lacing of rum in the world's weak tea. Well! Maybe they're strong drink to you! Do you think?

Ann looked up from the letter and glanced round again almost wildly, a look of appeal which nobody saw because there was no one near her and nobody on their way to rescue her. She had no recourse but to return to the letter.

Well, I suppose it's so much wasted ink (and my lovely brown Quink is getting too expensive to waste) to read you a lecture on that subject just now, but your letter in *The Times* made me want to reach out a restraining hand to your unbridled enthusiasms and remind you that, however exciting it all is out there, you're English, and you belong here. I know without you having to say it that your heart, wherever it may wander in its seemingly eternal quest of stimulation and an antidote to middle age and dullness, really belongs to me and to dear old England. I've known you (and loved you) so long that nobody could ever convince me otherwise.

Things here toddle along much as usual. Mrs Maylin hasn't been for three days because her daughter's had a miscarriage and so I've been looking after myself with my usual competence. The lettuces are holding up well and there's plenty of spinach and broad beans so I can open tins for quite a while and still not get scurvy! I've had very little time for the garden, though; business is brisk!

Yvonne dropped in for a chat last night. Seems there's a fuss because the new vicar – peripatetic, of course, we can't run to one of our own any more – wants to use the New English Bible instead of the King James. Poor fool imagines that if you take all the muck and mystery out of the Testaments, the churches will fill up overnight with eager new congregants who only stayed away before because they couldn't get the hang of passages like this: 'How doth the city sit solitary, that was full of people! How is she become as a widow! She that was great among the nations, and princess among the provinces, how is she become tributary. She weepeth sore in the night and her tears are on her cheeks; among all her lovers she hath none to comfort her: all her friends have dealt treacherously with her, they are become her enemies.' (I just picked that blind, with a pin – Lamentations – now no doubt freshly rendered, in the Newspeak version, as 'Poor old Jerusalem, left on her lonesome, boo-hooing all night because her pals did the dirty on her.') Yvonne's all for the change but when she saw me turn purple she downed her sherry in one and took her leave in some haste. There's something deeply depressing about people over sixty trying to appear trendy.

I don't know if you'll be interested, but I had a note from William with some quite striking news. It seems he's in line for a posting to 'your' part of the world. It isn't Israel, actually, it's Syria – near enough to intrigue you? He doesn't sound too thrilled at the prospect, though it's a step up to First Secretary; he says, 'Damned hot and dry, but at least not "dry" – not yet, at any rate.' For his sake, we'll have to hope the Ayatollah doesn't spread his baneful influence any further. Can't have poor old Will getting a public flogging and being sent home in disgrace – though I'm afraid even that might commend itself to him more than foregoing his pre-lunch gin and his evening noggin. The whole trouble with these Muslims, of course, is that unlike the Christians they have never gone through any form of Reformation or Enlightenment. They are still rigidly embedded in the Dark Ages and would cheerfully drag the world back into a sinister black hole of mediaevalism if we let them. I believe your Jews, or certain factions of them, are not so very different, although – and please note, my love, that I *do* give them a mark for neatness when due – some of them did pass through *our* Enlightenment and benefited accordingly.

Now there is just room left to tell you I love you and miss you, and not just because of the tins! I have learnt to put up with the empty feel of the cottage when I know I can get on the phone to you in London and hear your voice when I need to, but somehow that emptiness is a hell of a lot emptier with you three thousand miles away. I count the days, my sweet. *Don't* delay your return this time. Love ever, Peter.

P.S. Wed. Before I could send this off, a sizeable batch of letters arrived for you via *The Times*. You told me to open all your mail so I spent an interesting morning reading the reactions to your letter. I selected two only to forward which seemed a good sample of the polarities. Hope you have sense neither to be elated by No. 1 nor cast down by No. 2, which is not really typical of the negative ones. The poor old thing is all too obviously bonkers. You certainly do seem to rouse extremes of feeling in people! – well, who am I to wonder at that? P.

Ann didn't open the enclosures at once. She sat staring out at the expanse of sunny lawn beyond the Knesset windows. What in God's name entitled her to entertain feelings of *disappointment*? Was she disappointed that she had not been prodded by this letter into a greater sense of guilt than she now felt? Or was it that, deep down, below the expectation of guilt-pangs, had been another, of a different sort – a dim and undeserved hope of a hand reaching out, a hand, not of restraint, but of comfort, of steadiness? A hand like an anchor that might catch and hold on the shifting sea-bottom of her life?

Instead she struggled with a sense of irritation. Words, phrases, whole sentences grated. 'Your unbridled enthusiasms'. 'A mark for neatness'. 'Dear old England'. . . The loving part was complacent to smugness. The digs were disguised just enough to avoid the accusation of provoking an open confrontation . . . But the biblical passage rankled! Picked blind with a pin indeed! He must have combed the Old Testament for a passage that would give her such a sense of desolation . . .

He was fighting her commitment to Israel by stealth. She had never been able to induce him to fight face to face, all out, as she had with Boaz that morning . . . As well, perhaps. Evidence to the contrary notwithstanding, her marriage mattered to her. But perhaps (the odd thought occurred to her) if she had built up her spiritual muscles with Peter, Boaz would not have defeated her and put her to flight as easily as he had.

No. Give yourself some credit. Not easily. He brought out his big guns, he had to . . . You wouldn't have retreated for anything less than his calling you the enemy of his people. He threw you out in all but physical fact . . . But to be routed by such a lie! That was a source of pain all on its own.

How much more real Boaz was to her than Peter, even with the letter in her hand, and how readily, despite everything, she fled to him in her thoughts! It should be Peter she ran to, but this letter, for all its bonhomie, was inimical.

It was hard to imagine herself back in the cottage now, talking to Peter, sleeping with him (impossible!), making tea for the neighbours when they called to chat about the new vicar, walking the dog round the edges of the fields, being expected to care that Mrs Wallorton, well-read and discriminating in her genteel country retirement, was getting a wee bit bored with the Jews . . . She remembered how she had spent the weeks of the '73 War in front of the television set, watching the missiles seeking out the planes, watching the little winged shapes go down in smoke and imagining their contents so vividly that after a few days of it she broke and could no longer work or carry out her ordinary day's routine . . . Peter had been as sympathetic as he could but he shared none of it with her, he was a complete outsider; to him it was just another foreign outbreak. Then, when news of her air booking to Israel came through and she was recovering a little at the prospect of ending the terrible frustration of separation, she had driven into the village and walked round on shaking legs doing some essential shopping. Mrs Wallorton had been in the chemist's. 'Hallo, Ann. How – ' she had begun. Then her jaw literally dropped. 'My dear!' she had ejaculated, 'Whatever is it, you look positively deathly!' 'I haven't been well.' 'What was it?' 'It was the war.' 'The *war*?' asked Mrs Wallorton, looking completely blank. 'What can you mean, Ann dear? What war?' Oblivious . . . Ann had felt worse than alienated. People's indifference actually made her hate them. She had all but hated Peter . . .

I am living a dishonest life, she thought. The life of a national bigamist . . . Who had called her that? Ruth, of all people . . . 'You'll have to make up your mind one day. Or here, or there. With them or with us. Otherwise you'll tear apart.' Wise, wise Ruth! The *mot juste* – the precise sensation.

Ann was aware, through a gathering loneliness, of needing a cup of coffee. The cafeteria was downstairs. Once one had braved the complex admission procedure, all facilities were available. Maybe her MK was down there, having forgotten her . . . In a minute she would go. First, she would read the two 'poles' of reaction to her *Times* letter.

She opened first the one which Peter had numbered '1'. It was neatly typed and quite long. She glanced through it:

Dear Ms Randall,
     . . . Just to tell you what a boost to the morale is given by support from someone like you . . . In these difficult times, when once again the spectre of anti-semitism is raising its dreadful head, it is good to feel that a non-Jew in a public position is not afraid to raise her voice in protest against the obvious bias shown in every sector of the press against Israel, i.e. against the Jews . . . Your letter warmed my heart, as indeed do all your writings . . . You have a rare gift, expressing so cogently what so many of us feel but cannot say, nor would we get a hearing if we did . . . It is sad, and also strange, that there are not more like you . . . Surely it is obvious what is happening, the world's memory is too short, already people are saying none of it happened. As one who lost my entire family, it is almost past bearing. When I see the Arabs rising in their primitive power and arrogance and carrying all before them, I feel as if my parents and relatives are being starved and murdered all over again. Was it all for nothing? Only people like you among the *goyim* (excuse the word) give us a ray of hope . . .

Ann sighed and put it back in its envelope. She never knew how to feel about such letters. They distressed her. An honest partisan opinion should not call forth such effusive thanks; that it did, indicated a life lived over a bottomless bog of insecurity.

The other letter was shakily written on lined paper and bore no heading, address or signature. The postmark was a town in the North of England.

My friend showed me your letter and it just makes me sick. Well keep it up as long as you have your Israel it wont be forever. In the end it will be flushed down the toilet and you with it. You know what you are you are just a traitor to your country, and you know why its because you want to sleep with all the young Jewish soldiers thats all it is, it is just *sex*.

Oh God, one of those! thought Ann, and was about to throw it away when the next part caught her eye.

Let me tell you my son was killed by those dirty yids and his body hung on a tree like Jesus Christ who they also murdered only then they didn't have booby traps to put on his body when they came to cut him down. He was only doing his job and they caught him and hanged him like a common criminal. Well they will get what is coming to them and though I am over 75 years old God has promised I will live to see it and I hope you are there when it happens. I want to see one big hole in the ground where your Israel is today and if you are in the bottom of it in little pieces like my son I shant be sorry anybody who supports them with pen or sword is all as bad as them someone should make a bonfire of all your books like Hitler did he had the right idea about people like you –

Ann forced herself to read it to the end through a horror which had less and less to do with its contents. The root of the horror was that Peter had chosen to send it, and by the end a terrible thing was happening in her head – she could hear Peter's voice reading it, and see his blue, shrewd eyes taking little knowing glances at her over the top of it to see how she was taking it . . . And suddenly she knew.

Battle was joined. Open war. Whether he was prepared to admit it or not, he had had enough. He had set about to cure her of her Jew-loving obsession . . . He had sent as his first missile, not a *really* mad, obscene, anti-semitic letter at all (and there must have been a few of those, there always were) because she would be able to ignore that. Instead he had carefully chosen this, which no one with a shred of pity or honesty could toss aside, one that he knew would pierce her defences and embed itself in her conscience like a poisoned dart.

And it was not just living on tins and having to defend her to the village matrons, or sleeping alone, or feeling periodically alienated from her, that had caused him to do this. It was that thing in him that she had always just managed to ignore, but with this pitiable outpouring of grief and hatred in her hand could ignore no longer. True to his stereotype, Peter had, deep in his makeup, a streak of anti-semitism.

How to come to terms with this new-old, twisted piece in the jigsaw puzzle? Feeling a deep, fatalistic calm instead of the panic she might have expected, Ann unplugged her tape-recorder, put it back in her hold-all, got up and walked quietly down the wide polished corridors and stairway to the cafeteria.

It was half empty in the lull between lunch and teatime, but there were still a number of people sitting there. She glanced round at them. Even at this moment she was struck by the typically Israeli irony of the juxtaposition, at adjacent tables, of the handsome, white-bearded maverick left-winger, adopting a faintly heroic pose even though no one was looking, and the little virago who represented the far Right, with her dowdy 'rebel' clothes, dyed black hair and burning fanatic's eyes, puffing intensely at a cigarette and taking swigs of coffee as if it were brandy. They studiously ignored each other, and yet there they sat, at each other's elbows; one of them must have got there first, the other must deliberately have chosen to sit at the next table, and neither would give way . . . Each, to the other, represented an anathema more immediately deadly than any of the persecutors and destroyers of the Jews in the past; mutual hatred and contempt were personal and total. Fringe followers of the little ex-terrorist woman had threatened the peacenik with assassination, while he had publicly called her a threat to Israel's survival. Yet they had started from the same point. Both claimed sincere and passionate idealism. And he, too, had been a terrorist in his early years . . . What a mystery it all was, Ann thought. What a terrible, fascinating, all-absorbing, challenging mystery!

She got her coffee from the counter and sat by the long window. So. Now this. If Peter was an anti-semite, she herself was probably tainted also – a carrier of the disease she had always feared and despised. All this, perhaps – half her life, its most meaningful half – launched as a reaction, a response. What had Boaz said? – that she might have seen the photos of the camps and become the

201

Jews' champion? Nothing so simple! She had seen them all right. Would she ever forget it? Sitting in the cinema, aged fourteen, looking at it, life-size, intruding into her peaceful post-war environment, and *believing* in it. Why? What in all her life, safe, cushioned, loved, had made it possible for her to believe in that horror immediately, to recognise it, almost? Vivid images of the Catholic hell, dinned into her once by a dear little friend? Hieronymous Bosch? It was no less traumatic for her recognition of its truth and its likelihood.

And thinking: *We* did that to *them*.

Had she also thought – perhaps later – *They* must have deserved it somehow or *we* can never be forgiven? That thought might so have shamed her that she had pledged herself, in some deep place, to oppose the canker *in herself* . . . That it cut deep was certain. She remembered screaming from the wound – the next day it must have been (delayed reaction), eating tea and keeping very quiet while the images from yesterday's screen expanded, and subsided, and expanded again in her head, like a monster breathing deeper and deeper: the *mountain* of bodies that were nearly skeletons but not quite, the concave skin still in the hollows of their jutting pelvises, their gaping mouths and black eye sockets; and those others, just like them but wearing pyjamas and still, incredibly, walking about. Starved, stark, dead in all but fact, but *walking about* . . . It was that, not the overloaded pits or the dead children she had spotted tangled among the big corpses, which had finally exploded inside her head at the tea-table and made her throw herself onto the floor screaming, '*Beasts – beasts – beasts*!' Her distressed and bewildered parents, trying to collect her together between them as she threshed and raged: 'But darling, all that's nothing to do with us! You mustn't think about it any more . . .'

Oh, Boaz, see how wrong you are! One must let it come out. I let it come out, right out, I emptied myself of it and contrived never to feel it like that again. Such empathies are beyond endurance. That's why I can't feel Kibya, and you at Kibya . . . When that emptying happened thirty-five years ago I sealed up the place and why should I open it again and feel all that agony for either killed or killers?

But were you right about me? Am I, at bottom, the classic anti-semite with all the Jewish friends? All that self-abasement in the kibbutz, after I packed up the teaching; I thought it was just stubbornness, perverseness, I'll-show-them-if-they-won't-let-me-be-a-writer . . . But maybe it was something deeper.

She had sudden total recall to the morning she had gone to the office of the *sadran avodah*, the work organiser, and announced: 'I want to clean the lavatories. I want that to be my job from now on.' Blank stare – the *shikse*, the soft-handed urban intellectual with no Zionist background, cleaning the toilets? 'Why?' 'They need it.' 'No doubt. But why you?' 'Why not? Somebody has to do it.' He had gone on staring at her quizzically. 'Any conditions?' 'No. Unless I could request, at the weekly meeting, that the male members of the kibbutz lift the seat and correct their aim, and that the women use the sanitary bags I intend to see are provided.' He had laughed, and written her down as she wished. The story was all over the kibbutz by the evening. She was warmly congratulated by fifteen different people, and snubbed by as many more. ('The poor aimers, perhaps,' suggested Menachem.) Honours were even . . . She set up her dominion over the communal toilets and showers forthwith, and was pleased to be told later, only half in jest, that her work had made a notable contribution to the culture level of the kibbutz.

But that wasn't why she had undertaken it. Why that – the lowest of the low, the untouchable's job? Expiation? Oh, hell, she thought, what was the truth about *anything* . . . And did finding it out matter, or was it better to leave it all alone and just get on with living? She *thought* she loved this country. That ought to be enough . . . it would have to be.

Someone came and sat opposite her and she looked up at once, glad of some distraction. The face – the face was the same! The *sadran's* face from all those years ago . . . impossible! She stared at him incredulously.

'Hi, Ann.'

'It can't be! I was just this second thinking of you!'

'Why not? You saw me as you came in.'

'Did I? I didn't take you in . . .' She was struggling to remember his name. He was not Menachem's contemporary, but a much younger man, about twenty-five then, in his late thirties now. Tall, balding, good-looking, wearing sun-glasses. Not quite the 'kibbutz look', somehow, but attractive nonetheless. Ezriel – that was it. Phew. Awful to have forgotten.

'What are you doing here, Ezriel?'

'Can't you guess? I'm a Member of Knesset.'

'Good grief . . . Are you really? *Kol hakavod.*'

'A bit late for congratulations. I have been now since '77.'

'What faction – dare I ask?'

'Can't you guess?' he said again.

'Mapam?'

'A spent force. Lost without trace, *khalas*, sold its soul. No. I am with Shelli.'

'Shelli! You must be very high up the list – they've only got two members, haven't they? And one of them's sitting over there.'

Ezriel glanced at the white-bearded maverick. He caught his eye and they exchanged grins. 'Yes. And I'm the other – for the moment. After a time, we change with the next two on the list. It is called rotation. A very lousy idea in which we made a bad mistake.'

'Because you'll have to step down?'

'Not only. Because I will be replaced by someone less good.'

'You've lost none of your self-confidence.'

'Of course not. I have got more. One needs it in this place, and especially in my Party. The smaller the party, the more egoist one must be to maintain oneself.'

'Your English has improved.'

'I've been to the States.'

'But you came back.'

'I studied there two years and then, of course, I came back.'

'Good for you.'

'Why do you say that?'

'Because of all the ones who don't.'

'I am not a *yored*,' he said.

There was a silence. There was so much she wanted to ask, or rather, would have wanted to, yesterday. Now she just stared into her coffee. The reproach she had detected in his last remark had thrown her back into her earlier distress. Because of course she *was* an emigrant, a deserter.

'No one's had news of you for a long time,' Ezriel said. 'Except when someone in England sends one of your pieces of writing. You should keep more in touch.'

'Is the kibbutz still interested? After all, I *am* a *yoredet*.'

'But you were with us for a long time. A whole generation – the one below me – speaks good English because of you. That we don't forget.'

After giving herself a moment to savour the ridiculous feeling of pleasure this gave her, she asked: 'Anyway, who would I keep in touch with?'

'Menachem?' She looked up sharply. His inquisitive eyes were on her. 'On the other hand, perhaps not.'

'How is he?'

'He is . . . quite a lot changed, I think you would say.'

'In what way?'

'A lot of ways. A lot has happened to him. Especially lately.'

She waited, and he made her wait. At last she had to ask. 'So tell me, Ezriel.'

'Well, he got married.' A pause. 'Oh, not right away! Five years ago only. To a girl much younger than him, a *bat kibbutz*.'

'Anyone I know?'

'Yes, she was one of your pupils.' She stiffened. He was smiling now, and again he made her ask.

'Who?'

'Remember Devorah?'

She remembered. Colt-legged. Long hair like her own, only heavy and shining as only healthy young hair can shine. Cheeky. Beautiful. Not very clever . . . Incredible!

'Menachem . . . and Devorah?'

'Strange, eh? Everyone thought so. Everyone whispered . . . Father figure . . . You remember, her father was killed in Sinai, '56.'

'I'd forgotten. It was before my time.' She drank some coffee, wishing it was the bourbon. She could have kept it down for this. 'And? Do get on with it, Ezriel, don't make me ask everything . . .'

'Yes, they had kids. Two. A boy and a girl.'

So that was why Ruth had said, don't go back. Ann kept the pain off. It wasn't hard – there was so little room for any more. She tried to be glad for Menachem, and succeeded, far better than she would have done yesterday.

'So he's happy.'

'I didn't say so.'

'What does that enigmatic remark mean?'

'He is not happy at the moment, because his wife has left him.'

'For another man?'

'Yes,' he said, his chin on his hand, smiling into her eyes.

A strange notion came into her head.

'Anyone I know?' she asked again.

'Me,' he replied.

She reared back her head. 'Good God!'

'What?'

'How you smile in triumph as you say it!'

205

He shrugged. 'Why not? I love her.'

'And doesn't he?'

'The best man must win. He stole from the cradle before I stole from him. Besides, marriage is not ownership. She chose to leave him and come to me. She has the right.'

A burning, unreasoning sense of loyalty to Menachem – quite quixotic in the circumstances – took a sudden grip on her.

'I wonder if you'll smile when she does the same thing to you,' she said pleasantly.

He froze for a moment, but then relaxed again. 'It's nice,' he said.

'What is?'

'That after such a lot of years, you are still on his side. And in such a matter! *Kol hakavod.*'

She bowed ironically, her eyes on him. 'I'm sure you feel the "honour" is all yours,' she said. 'And the children?'

'You know in the kibbutz, it's not such a big problem. They're only small. They'll adjust to the new set-up.'

Searching for something safe to say, she asked, 'What are their names?'

'The boy is Bar, the girl is Shanit.'

New names. A new era. These were not the names *they* had discussed for their dream children, their might-have-beens . . . Thank God.

'I bet they're beautiful.'

He shrugged again. 'They're not bad. Mine with her will be more, though! The first is on the way.'

'You didn't waste any time.'

'I'm thirty-eight. I haven't any to waste. Tell me now about you. What brings you back to *Aretz*?' Ann told him, briefly. She had stopped finding him attractive. No wonder he didn't have the 'kibbutz look'. He was just another ruthless go-getter.

'A book about that old war, eh?' he asked. 'Well, would you like to meet *him*?' He indicated the maverick with his head. 'He had a busy war, and he loves to talk about it.'

'What about *her*?'

He glanced, scowled, looked away. 'Our little black devil? Yes, she was busy too. Her job was to broadcast polemical excuses for murder. She was good at it, I'm told – she believed in her work. She is very dangerous.'

'Still?'

'Now, even worse. Now she doesn't preach to kill people. Now she preaches to kill peace processes, by putting political knives in the back of Sadat. She has said she will do it, and you must admire her – what she says she will do, she will do.'

'How?'

'She will find a way. A political way. And if enough of us don't oppose it, it will cause a lot of troubles to Israel.'

'Her party is as small as yours.'

'Even smaller – not rotation, just two members.'

'And she's now the Prime Minister's sworn enemy. She won't get support, certainly not from the Opposition.'

'I hope.'

'But the Opposition won't support some extremist measure.'

'It depends. They dare not look weak, especially about certain things. The Arabs. The West Bank. Jerusalem. Jerusalem is our underbelly. If she is clever she will go for that, then everyone must rally.'

'Everyone? Not you?'

He shrugged. 'We too have to get votes. We won't support her. We might abstain. It depends what it is. To some extent we are all in the hands of our extremists.'

'Then there's no hope at all!'

'There's always hope! There's got to be. I'm going to have a son soon. I don't bring him into a hopeless world.'

'So don't abstain. Vote against.'

He glanced at the maverick, then back at her. 'Okay. If I haven't been rotated by then, I'll see to it.' He grinned.

He was facing the entrance, and now his attention shifted. The maverick's head had also turned, and the 'little black devil' stood up and looked round. Something like a charge had passed through the room.

'Excuse me,' Ezriel said, and got up and left her.

She turned. A group of men had come into the cafeteria, among them Neville Baum. Ann tried to catch his eye but he had already swept through the room, almost at the run, and was gone – on his way up to the press gallery, she supposed. She followed, catching Ezriel on the way.

'What's happened?'

'I don't know. Those were press people. Journalists never run unless there is something big.'

Ann knew it. Everything else was swept momentarily from her mind – the instinct for news was sharp enough in her still to drive all personal problems away. She took the shallow stairs two at a

207

time and caught Neville up at the top, where there was a bottleneck caused by the security officer inspecting each press pass at the entrance to the chamber. The journalists were jostling and jabbering like hungry starlings.

'Neville?'

'Hallo, Ann! Trust you to be in at the kill.'

'Kill? What's happened?'

'Haven't you heard? Someone tried to blow up some West Bank big knobs. Best bit of luck I've had for years! I happened to be *in* Beit Agron when it broke – just by chance, I could easily have been at home having a kip. I was actually by the telex when it came through! By God, I can't wait to see how the PM's going to tackle this one! He won't get out of this so easy – '

Ann had gone cold, without knowing why. Her mouth opened on another question, but then she turned and ran to the office, fumbling for her own pass. The girl at one of the desks was on the phone when she came in. Her face was white.

'Who did it? Have you heard?' she asked Ann in Hebrew.

'No – '

The girl bit her lips. She looked thoroughly shocked. She endorsed Ann's admission slip without appearing to know what she was doing, and immediately picked up her phone again and dialled.

Ann hurried back to the entrance. The security officer checked her pass, and looked in her bag.

'You can't take that in,' he said, pointing to her tape recorder.

'Can I leave it with you?'

'No.'

'Where can I leave it, then?'

He shrugged. His attention was on the chamber below, where there was a growing growl of voices.

Ann took the machine out, and all but threw it onto one of the padded seats. Two TV camera crews were falling over themselves unpacking their gear. A sudden uproar from the chamber made them pause, look up – they all made an instinctive move toward the entrance to the gallery, then, as one man, turned back and redoubled their efforts. Ann ran in past the security officer and down the three steps into the front of the crowded gallery.

Down below all hell seemed to be breaking loose. A tall, white-haired man appeared to be struggling with two or three others, one in uniform. The Prime Minister was on the podium, a dramatic little figure, striving histrionically to make himself heard through the bedlam of raised voices. The Speaker was banging for quiet, in vain.

Another security man came down the stairs behind her.

'*Asur la'amod sham*, you can't stand there,' he said brusquely. 'Find a seat.'

She looked round. The gallery – two rows of seats around three sides of the chamber – was already packed. Where had they all come from? How had everyone got wind of events so quickly? Neville was over at the far side. A local stringer, whose red beard she recognised from visits to Beit Agron, the foreign press centre, moved into one of the last seats and made a place for her on the end of a row. The TV crews were now crowding in above, setting up in feverish haste to record the riotous scene on the floor of the chamber, where the uniformed stewards were attempting to force the elderly MK either to sit down or leave. Suddenly his voice rose to clear audibility through the general hubbub.

'This is your doing! This is your fault!' he was shouting furiously at the Prime Minister. An angry roar from the Government benches met a cheer from some of the left-wingers immediately below Ann. Members all over the chamber were on their feet yelling at each other. The Speaker's gavel could be seen but not heard.

'What does he mean? Who is that?' Ann had to speak quite loudly to make the red-bearded stringer hear her.

'That's one of the Arab MK's – he's saying it's the Government's policies which have led to a revival of Jewish terrorism.'

Ann jerked her head round, ricking her neck painfully.

'What?'

'It's not definitely known. But everyone's made the same deduction. Of course it was Jews who did it. Why would Arabs blow the legs off their own Mayors?'

'Blow their legs off?' Ann repeated in dry-mouthed horror.

'One of them lost his legs, another a foot – or something like that. None of them was killed, anyway.'

'Where were the bombs put?'

'Under their cars.'

'Dear Christ! When was this?'

'This morning.'

Things were quieting down fractionally below. The Prime Minister had stopped trying to speak and was standing in a long-suffering pose, his dwarfish head, half turned away with his fingers lightly covering his bespectacled eyes.

'What an actor!' muttered the stringer. 'No wonder half of them hiss and the other half cheer! After every speech I feel like shouting "encore".'

'*I* feel like throwing rotten eggs,' said the reporter on his other side. 'Think what a lovely splat they'd make on that dome!'

'You'd only add another jewel to his crown of martyrdom,' grunted the stringer. 'He thrives on persecution – shut up, I want to hear – '

So did everyone else, to which end some sort of order was being restored. But the Prime Minister, as it turned out, had precious little to say on the subject of the outrage. He implored his listeners not to jump to hasty conclusions about the perpetrators of 'this dastardly crime'. He promised the fullest possible investigation. Then he passed rapidly to other matters, and made an impassioned speech, not one word of which had any bearing upon the tragedy and the disquiet in the forefront of everyone's mind.

'What the hell's he chuntering on about!' muttered the stringer. 'Let me out of here, I've got to file.' He got up and sidled past Ann, who was still watching the scene below unbelievingly. The reporter in the far seat leaned over to her.

'Baum wants you.'

She looked across at the opposite tier of seats. Neville was signalling to her – 'Let's go, this is a big yawn'. She ducked her head to avoid blocking the cameramen's view and followed the stringer out.

Neville met her in the press area while she was picking up her tape recorder. His round face was flushed and shiny with excitement.

'What do you make of that! He must've known about it for at least a couple of hours, you'd think he could have had something a bit more pertinent to say. Christ, won't there be fireworks now! I wouldn't stand in his shoes for a mint. The old terrorist having to mount a manhunt for his direct descendants ... What's the betting they never get caught?'

'Neville! What do you mean? Of course they'll be caught! With our Secret Service – an all-out investigation, he said. That means – '

'It means bugger all. It means they'll be told to go through the motions. You wait. This is one time our Mounties won't get their man!'

She stared at him. 'I don't believe it. You mean if they're Jewish extremists – '

'Oh, if they turn out to be PLO heavies doing a lean, they'll be under lock and key tomorrow, or over the border with a kick up their backsides. But it's not. Those mayors weren't moderates, they're all well known loud-mouths. And don't forget Hebron, the Gush had a debt to pay off over that little business. I'll tell you something I heard, the explosives and that were Zahal-issue, sophisticated equipment, and the attacks were well planned and co-ordinated, not the random stuff the Arabs tend to pull. No, these were ours all right and everybody knows it.' He stopped as if he'd run out of steam and stood, plump and panting, a sudden frown crossing his face. 'I don't know what I'm so chuffed about,' he said in an altered voice. 'It's bloody terrible.'

Ann said nothing. Neville was avoiding her eyes. It seemed suddenly to have come home to him as something more than a damn good news story. He reached abruptly for her hand and squeezed it, still not looking at her. 'Bloody hell,' he muttered with an air of surprise, 'when you stop to think of what it means – '

She had been thinking of nothing else. They stood there in the empty hallway, holding hands like children.

CHAPTER 16

It was no use expecting anybody to be interviewed now. The chamber was crammed and no one would leave it. Ann left with Neville and he drove her back into town. They travelled in silence.

'Where do you want to be dropped?' he asked in an unwontedly subdued voice as they approached Terra Sancta.

'Is there a Hertz office anywhere on your way?'

'Have you decided you need a car?'

'Yes.'

'There's a branch near the King David.'

He took her there. As she thanked him and got out, he asked, 'What are you plans?'

'I'm not sure . . . I'm supposed to be going to Amnon's first night tonight. I've got meetings laid on for the next week or so. It all seems rather improbable in the present circumstances. Why?'

'Jacqui wanted to see you. We were supposed to be coming to the show tonight too, but I won't be able to now, of course, and I don't think she'll want to come by herself. Maybe I'll send Eric – *Eppi*,' he amended with a grimace.

'I'll look out for them,' Ann said. His ugly little face, all woebegone, was peering up at her out of the car window. On impulse she leant down and kissed him. 'Don't feel too bad, Neville.'

'It's hard to be a yid,' he said with a sigh.

'Yes. Just bear that in mind.'

He saluted her wrily and drove away.

She went into the car hire office and went through the formalities, wondering, on the one hand, why she hadn't done this before, and on the other, why she was doing it now. She suddenly needed to feel she was mobile. As on several previous occasions in her life, she was acting, not precisely on impulse, but on intuition – her subconscious had some idea, some plan, which she was not yet aware of, which she felt compelled to act to prepare for.

She handed over the staggering sum of a hundred and ten pounds and was assigned a neat little two-door Fiat. It was hers for a week, with unlimited mileage and a full tank to start her off.

'May I drive this anywhere I like?' she heard herself ask.

'So long as you stop short of Damascus,' she was cheerily told.

' – The West Bank?'

'Of course, why not?'

Obviously he hadn't heard. Amazing – it must have been on the news by now. Presumably he just hadn't switched on the radio. A new breed of Israeli . . . in her day, everyone listened to every bulletin.

She drove back to Amnon's, rembering only when she was at the top of the stairs that she had lost her key. She was locked out. Please God someone was in! She rang the bell. A patter of tiny feet, and Dill opened the door wide. His snubby face lit up at the sight of her. 'Hi!'

'Oh lord, Dill – did I wake you?'

'Are you crazy? You don't think I can *sleep*, do you?'

'You're supposed to be resting, anyway. Are you on your own again?'

'Sure, why not?'

'You know, you should put the door on the chain before you open it. Don't you do that in New York?'

'Of course. Always.'

'So why not here?'

'I dunno. It feels safer here. Jews don't hurt people, only blacks and spiks hurt people. And junkies.'

There was a pause. Then Ann came in and shut the door behind her. She remembered how only last night, she had thrown the door open to the two soldiers. She would never do that again.

'Just the same. It's not a bad thing to do when you're on your own.'

'Okay, if you say so.'

'Go on, back to your nap.'

'Aw shit,' he said manfully. 'Can't we have a picnic, like last night?'

'No, you're supposed to rest for the show. Aren't you excited?'

'Naaaa. What's to be excited? I've done it a million times practically.'

'Never for me. I expect something special. And to be sure of being a good audience, *I am* going to have a nap.'

'*You* are?' he said, his jaw dropping comically.

'I am. I am a very, very tired woman.'

'You're not a woman. You're a lady.'

'That's all you know.'

She went straight to her room, hoping he wouldn't follow her – she couldn't keep the banter up for long – but he did.

'Can I take my nap with you?' he asked.

'Huh?'

'I sometimes do with Mary when she's in a good mood.'

'Thou wilt fall backwards, when thou com'st of age.'

His face was blank for only a moment. 'Yeah,' he said, 'I can do one now if you like.' And he startled her with a stunning back-over. 'That's just a sample. So can I? Nap with you?'

She heaved a sigh without showing it.

'Do you wriggle?'

He turned himself into a mobile corkscrew.

'I meant, don't, if you want to nap with me. My bed's too narrow for both of us, we'd better nap on the double one in Amnon's room.'

'Won't he mind?'

'No. He likes me to be near the phone.'

They went into Amnon's bedroom. The shutters had been closed and the room was blessedly dark and cool. Ann took off her sandals. She thought as she did so that she should shower – she should want a shower more than anything. It was still three-shower weather. And – surely – Boaz was something now to be washed off, washed away; she should be desperate to cleanse herself of him. Instead she lay down on the bed. Dill clambered on beside her. He lay still for about ten seconds, rigid as a corpse, then bounced up.

'Do you want to read to me?'

'No. I want to sleep.'

'Do you want me to read to you?'

'It's too dark.'

'I've got a flashlight! Shall I get it?'

'*No.*'

Pause.

'I'm an awful good reader. I'll read you to sleep.'

'I don't require your services, thank you. If you'll just kindly lie down and keep quiet, I shall be asleep in two minutes.'

They lay silently together for a long time. He really was very good. Perhaps he'd gone to sleep after all. She liked having him there; she didn't want to be alone. While he was beside her, it might be possible not to let her mind wander back to this morning's bed. She rolled on her side and lay, as she always did before sleep, with her face on her arm. Boaz was still there – on her skin – it was faint, but discernible. She drew in deep, slow breaths, inhaling the indescribably sensual fragrance of his hands as if her face were buried in hyacinths.

'Are you crying?'

She started. She could swear she hadn't made a sound.

'How did you know?'

'The bed's all trembling.'

'I could have been cold.'

'Oh sure! It's a hundred in the shade, and you're cold!' He moved till he lay close behind her and put his arm over her. 'Whatza matter?'

'A lot. Believe me. A woman my age doesn't cry for nothing.'

'A boy my age doesn't, either.'

She lay fighting her way through griping paroxysms of misery. He held her from behind, awkwardly, patting her on the arm with his little rough paw, calloused from hand-stands and trapeze-grips and clutching splintery stilts.

'Jeez, I'm sorry you feel bad . . . Please stop crying,' he said at last.

She put her feet on the floor, and blew her nose several times into Amnon's tissues. 'I'm sorry to do this in front of you,' she gasped.

'It's okay. Say, you know what you should do? Like you made me do last night. Take a shower to cool you off and then have something good to eat.'

She glanced at him over her shoulder and did her level best to smile.

'You know what? That's a damn good idea.'

He came and stood just outside the bathroom door while she showered. She used Amnon's rasping plastic sponge and washed herself thoroughly from head to foot. She cut her toe-nails and scrubbed her soles with a nail brush and rubbed softener on her heels. Then she put on a dressing-gown and let Dill in. He sat on the toilet seat and watched her while she shampooed her hair.

'Do you shave under your arms?'

'Yes.'

'Mary doesn't. She doesn't have to. Black people don't have much body-hair. Did you know that?'

'No.'

'Mary's beautiful. She naps with Daddy sometimes too.'

'Oh.'

'And so does Sue-Ella.'

There was a pause. Ann hung her hair over the bath and showered it clear of soap.

215

'Do you nap with Amnon?'

'No.'

'Whaddaya think?'

'About what?'

'My Dad screwing all those different dames.'

She peered up at him through the wet hair.

'What do you think of it?'

'I dunno. I guess I don't think it's so good.' He watched her making a turban of her hair in a big towel. 'I thought babies came from people screwing. That's what it said in that book Mom made me read.'

'So they do. But not every time.'

'Do you screw?'

'Yes.'

'Lots of different guys?'

She looked him in his honest child's eyes.

'What do you call lots?'

He considered. 'More than one,' he said at last.

That's not a polite question. That's none of your business. You shouldn't ask that. I'm too old for . . . I'm married . . . Don't . . .

'In that case,' she said steadily, 'yes.'

'So you think it's okay?'

'No,' she said. 'I don't.'

'So why do you do it then?'

She sat down on the edge of the bath and looked at him.

'The word "screwing",' she said slowly, 'is a bad word. I don't mean it's bad language. It's a bad description. It sounds sort of – careless, like – snapping your fingers, or dropping something, or eating a biscuit. It's not like that. It's magic. Good magic and bad magic. You can't imagine how powerful it is. If you think, when you're grown-up, that it's a bad idea to do it with more than one person, the chances are you're going to have to fight and fight with yourself. Sometimes it puts a spell on you – '

'What does?'

'Love. Sex. Wanting to do it. Sometimes it just – overwhelms you.'

'I never knew that.'

'What?'

'That it was that strong. I thought . . . That book said like it was just something people did.'

'It's something people do because they've simply got to. If you *just do* it, it's nothing.'

216

He went on looking at her for a moment. His eyes wandered over her face and she thought, he's noticing the lines. He's thinking, how weird, she's so old and she still does it. In a moment his little snub nose is going to wrinkle up in disgust, in spite of himself.

Instead he jumped up. 'Let's eat,' he said, and went out of the room.

Ann combed out her hair and then followed him. She was still profoundly tired and profoundly wretched, but there was something about Dill that lightened her heart. When she reached the kitchen he had put the last of the water-melon and an assortment of other fridge cullings on the table for her. They ate together companionably.

'Shall I make you coffee?' he asked professionally.

'If I drink coffee I shan't sleep. And I've got to sleep. I've simply got to.'

'Because you're sad?'

'And because I didn't sleep all night.'

'I didn't either.' Ann looked her question. 'Mom put that shitty quilt back on me.'

She heard herself laugh. Good God, she thought, how dare I! Still, she leaned across and kissed him.

'You're okay,' he said.

'You too. I'm going to set my alarm for seven. Please don't let anyone wake me. Good luck for tonight. I'll see you right after the show.'

Before she went to bed, she phoned Ruth, and asked her to go with her to the circus.

'Oh Ann! I'd love it – but I can't! Bronstein may come – he phoned now to Eli in the studio – '

'Is it definite?'

'No, of course not. Such people never bother to be definite, they think only *their* time matters. But Eli is excited, there were such big hints that he has made up his mind at last. I must be here if he comes, to help, to entertain while the business is talked . . . Oh Ann, if only he buys! *If only he buys!* It will be so wonderful. Eli will be like a different man, you don't know how he is changed when he sells something. He stands up straight and his face is all smooth – he just *glows*. Please, send your thoughts. *Will* that fat man to buy a big thing . . .'

'And if Bronstein doesn't come this evening, will you meet me at the Nat'am?'

'I will stay in and wait. He may come later . . . And if he doesn't come at all, I will shoot myself anyway, so don't expect me. I'm sorry . . . I love to go out, and especially with you, it's so nice to be with you, you are like fresh air after the *khamsin*.'

'Silly . . . Ruth?'

'Yes?'

'Did you hear – what happened? The bomb attacks on the – '

Ruth's voice changed abruptly. It became harsh and shrill.

'Yes, I heard. Ann, please, I can't think about it now. I want to think about Bronstein. I can't think about all that. Later I will think, please, don't talk about it.'

'All right. I understand – '

'No. You don't. But never mind. I'm sorry about tonight. Please phone tomorrow – or, no, don't. I will phone you if it goes all right. If you don't hear . . .'

Ann briefly considered phoning someone else, but there was no one she wanted or, indeed, could bear the thought of being with. She set the clock and fell onto her bed. Now her arm smelt her own again. Her thighs moved smoothly, drily across one another, the friction allayed by cleanness and fresh talc . . . She would recover. Anyone can make a mistake. In her exhaustion, she was able to deceive herself into believing it was merely a mistake of the flesh. As she had explained to Dill . . . She had fought, and lost, and been overwhelmed by the black magic. Now the spell was broken. She was – wasn't she? – chastened, humiliated by defeat, bruised, chagrined. But free.

A fine, soporific conceit, to be sure. At any rate, it took her down into all-too-temporary oblivion.

When the alarm dragged her violently back to consciousness at seven, she felt sick with reluctance and weariness.

I can't go, she thought. It's unreasonable of me to have expected it of myself, I've hardly slept for thirty-six hours. She lay there in the deepening twilight, steeped in the residue of sleep, longing to sink back again into an absence of thought. But now last night's empty theatre came back to haunt her. What if the horror of today's incidents on the West Bank should have put even first-night ticket holders off venturing into the Arab area? What if any Arabs who had planned to come to the Circus had decided to boycott it, or stayed away simply out of nervousness? A repeat of last night's echoing emptiness around the stage would be a nightmare for Amnon and Amatsia, not to mention Dill and the other performers. She would have to get up and go.

With a profound sigh she forced herself out of bed. The room reeled round her and she nearly fell over. Amnon Segev, she thought, I must love you more than I thought, to eschew a merciful oblivion for your sake at a moment like this. It was easier not to think of Boaz while she thought of Amnon, perhaps even at this moment desperately ringing up old friends and supporters of Nat'am to come and fill the breach. She put on a long dress – she wouldn't have to stand at the windy bus stop or wait on the pavement for a taxi now. She put on a London-heavy make-up and swathed her head in a silk stole. Despite these disguises Amnon's grandfather reflected an image of a woman ten years older than the one who had complacently admired herself against his black waistcoat only yesterday morning.

I only looked young here when I was enough of a non-combatant to be happy.

She let herself out of the flat after drinking a cup of strong black Nescafé. The little Fiat was waiting. There was comfort to be had from this little private mobile world of her own. (Why did she need it, one hundred and ten pounds' worth? She hadn't yet uncovered that.) She wished Ruth were coming. She needed to talk to Ruth, and she could, perhaps only to her whom she had known and loved for so many years, right back to Menachem, back to the beginning of the 'fundamental commitment'. She had barely fifteen minutes in which to reach the theatre but just the same she detoured to the top of Yemin Moshe, parked outside the Windmill and, hardly knowing why, ran down the steps to Eli's and Ruth's door. She rang. Ruth opened immediately, and only as she did so did Ann think: She might think it's Bronstein and be bitterly disappointed.

But Ruth's face did not drop when she saw Ann, since it was at rock bottom already.

'You came to get me,' she said flatly. 'You are a wonderful friend. You *know* things. Yes, I can come now. A minute, I'll get my bag and tell Eli. He was just saying, it was a pity that I told you no before.'

She vanished into the house for a moment, and then reappeared. She too wore a long skirt and looked as if she had dressed up for the theatre, but Ann, with a heart hardly capable of sinking further, had realised at once that she had dressed for the Bronsteins and that the Bronsteins weren't coming.

They walked in silence up the golden steps through the pools of lamplight. Ruth tucked her hand through Ann's arm and Ann squeezed it against her side. Ruth's head was high and her eyes glittered dangerously, with anger and with rigorously suppressed tears.

'Do you want to tell me . . .?' asked Ann.

'Yes, I'll tell you. It's short to tell. He rang about an hour ago. Pregnant with his great decision, which as he well knows is nothing to him and everything to us. He had to return suddenly to Miami and wouldn't be able to complete any deal this trip, but in any case he had decided to do something quite original. He would like to buy, not a picture outright, but the *rights* to a picture. A big oil of Jerusalem. He will subsidise having it reproduced into a number of thousands of copies which he will present to the Municipality. They will sell them for profit and promotion, and that is his gift to them.'

'Where does Eli come in?'

'That is a good question. Eli does not receive anything except a very small sum for the repro. rights of his picture, and then, if he is unreasonable enough to want more – a royalty on the sale of the posters and prints – he must negotiate for that with the Municipality. Mr Bronstein,' she all but spat the name, 'thinks Eli should be thrilled to know that his picture will be distributed or sold in big numbers, hung in embassies and travel agencies and offices of the Jewish Agency, rolled up and handed out to I-but-not-VIP's . . . He said to me on the phone, "Your husband's work will be seen and admired by thousands all over the world, it is wonderful promotion for him." He made it clear he did not think it would be good taste or sense for Eli to haggle with Yoni for some per cent of the profits because it is a promotion exercise and half the copies will be given away anyhow, he should be very happy and satisfied with the reproduction right Bronstein will pay him.'

'In other words,' said Ann indignantly, 'Bronstein gets all the credit, shells out practically nothing, and doesn't want Eli spoiling *his* generous gesture by bringing vulgar commerce into the deal at all by asking the Municipality for a royalty.'

'That's right, Ann. What do you think?'

'I think Mr Bronstein stinks.'

'I think more. I think Mr Bronstein is a big greedy fat cat and we are his mice. Whatever he does is to make his own fur shine. It is not for the Municipality or Israel . . . Do you know why I hate him worst at this moment? It is such a little reason! When he phoned, Eli was standing there waiting, and I said straight away,

"Do you want to speak to Eli?" But Bronstein said, very hasty, "No, no, Ruth, husband and wife are one flesh, right? And women are more practical. I'll talk to you and you can talk to him, you can make him see things in the right way." So I had to stand there with Eli's eyes on me and Bronstein's American voice like oil in my ear, knowing that when he had finished talking I would have to turn round and face Eli and tell him this – disgusting, insulting proposition, when he had been led to hope for a big, proper sale . . . Is this your car?' They had been driving already for five minutes. Ruth had only just realised where they were.

'I hired it. How did he take it? – Poor Eli! Oh God, how bloody, bloody rotten!'

'He took it like he takes everything. Everything he has ever had to take. Right back to the Germans. Very quiet. Too quiet. He just looked at me and listened and then he shrugged his shoulders and turned away, and the only thing he said was, "It's a pity you told Ann you wouldn't go to Nat'am, you would like it and I would rather be alone to work." You know there are men, artists, who would be put off working for weeks from such a disappointment, but my Eli is so brave he makes himself to work harder, and at once, like getting back on a horse when you fell.' She was crying now, but restrainedly, angry with herself for breaking down. It was soon over. She blew her nose hard and sat up straight. Ann took one hand off the wheel and found hers.

'I'm so sorry. I don't know what to say.'

'*You* don't need words, Ann. You had your instinct, which made you come. Now I am going to look at nonsense and enjoy it and it will make me stronger to go back and match Eli's strength and not let him see that I hate them, hate them, hate them!'

Courage, Ann thought. That is what I need too, that kind of *young* resilient courage. Ruth is not far short of my age and she has it still; she pushes her pain hardily away from her and blows her nose clear of the debilitating congestion of sorrow. With words, too, she gets it out of her system and then goes to the circus as deliberate therapy. Then on with life, on to the next challenge . . . Why can't I do that? Perhaps I can, if she can. Though mine is bigger . . . No, that's not true. Mine is merely more dramatic, more of a cataclysm. Hers is the long, grinding, corrosive agony that goes on and on. What is my personal suffering about Boaz, about Israel, compared with Ruth's in watching Eli suffer these endlessly repeated humiliations and setbacks which are so far from his deserts? At least I damned well *bought* what I got. But perhaps the therapy would work for me too.

But there was no time to talk now. They had reached the theatre. She parked the car as near to the front of the building as possible, under a lamp. There were, she was relieved to see, a fair number of cars along the kerb, far more than last night. She locked up carefully and they went through the arched portico. To her amazement, Ann noticed Ruth almost furtively touching the *mezzuzah* as she passed.

Ruth saw that she had seen. 'It's just for luck,' she said apologetically. 'Like you touch wood. An amulet . . . We're on enemy territory, after all, we need a little protection.'

The foyer was not as crowded as it should have been, but it didn't have the aching vacancy of last night. There was an atmosphere of tension. Ann looked round. There were no Arabs that she could see – not one.

'Ann! Hallo! You came!' said a loud, bright voice.

It was Jacqui Baum, flamboyantly dressed in a lime green and lilac silk trouser-suit. At her shoulder loomed an incredible young Adonis, in whose recently-acquired adult lineaments Ann could just discern the plump little Liverpool lad she remembered from her last visit to Neville's home two years ago.

'Good grief, this can't be Eric!'

Jacqui beamed and reached up – a long way up – to caress his smooth brown cheek with her red tipped and well-ringed fingers. 'Isn't he something?'

'He certainly is.'

'*Tishtoki*, Ima!' muttered the object of all this admiration bashfully.

'A mother he says shut up to,' said Jacqui with mock reproach. Then she turned to Ann. 'Do you think we're idiotic, coming here like this, tonight of all nights? I wouldn't have dreamt of it, but Eppi insisted.'

Eppi? Score one to the junior team. How long before it's 'My son the commando'? Ann wondered. The deep, primordial pride of womanhood in uniformed and gun-toting sons, in fierce, brave, aggressive male progeny, fulfilling a destiny – of driving off marauders – bred into them throughout the millennia of evolution . . . What price the tame option of a decent little semi in Calderstones, the lovingly packed lunchbox and ring-me-if-you'll-be-late-home, compared to the inner glory of that? The projection of fearful waits for news, the imagined horrors of death, maiming, or mutilation of mind or body – what are they in prospect when a boy's aspirations and ambitions tally with all that a woman is conditioned to hope for and expect of her men – the ultimate proofs of masculinity, the evidences that he is a young lion and not a young lamb?

'You think it's safe, then – Eppi?' she asked, turning to him.

He grinned at her use of his new name, but then his face sobered.

'I didn't say that,' he said. 'I just told Ima that we shouldn't stay away because of what happened today, it's like an admission of guilt, or an admission of nervousness. Whatever they do, or whatever they drive *us* to do, we have to deprive them of what they're trying to achieve.'

'Which is?'

'To demoralise us. Stop us living a normal life. Disrupt our patterns.'

'Yes, I see.'

'We had tickets to the theatre tonight, or rather, Dad did. Dad couldn't go because he's got to work, so he gave his to me. It's not that I go for circuses – kids' stuff. But I just asked myself, would I have gone, to escort Mum I mean, if what happened today hadn't happened?'

Answer: Not for anything on earth, you'd have stayed home and watched television, thought Ann with sudden insight. But the fact that there was an element of derring-do about it meant that nothing could have kept you away. You'll make a wonderful commando.

Amatsia appeared beside her. 'Thanks for coming, Ann,' he murmured. 'A lot didn't. Here are your tickets, they're front row.'

'Is everything all right?'

'Everything's terrible, but the show goes on.' He put his arm round her and gave her a quick hug, and his splendid black beard tickled her cheek in a way which brought the hot blood beating to her cheeks. And at once, desolation and dread assailed her. Would a million small things and large have power to bring Boaz close to her, this clearly? Yes, she thought, of course. It happened with Menachem and it will happen again. That is one of the symptoms of the illness of being in love. Free! What an absurd, what an immature hope! She would not be free for months, perhaps for years . . . nor should she expect to be. She had jumped in over her head and now must swim lengthily and laboriously to shore while the icy water of loneliness, rejection, regret and loss ate into her bones. How can one brush one's hair and start again while floundering in those arctic waters?

The bell sounded and they made their way through into the auditorium. As they went, Ann was poignantly aware of her feet slipping a little on the satin smoothness of apricot marble flags.

The show opened with a touchingly non-spectacular tight-rope act by Sue-Ella dressed in a long demure pink dress and carrying a frilled parasol. Dill had a sort of clown's rôle. The wire was strung between two posts about nine feet off the stage. Dill, dressed in knickerbockers and a sailor-top, entered bowling a hoop; stopped; gaped up at the girl strolling along the wire; and then circled both posts staring up at her from all angles. Then he walked under the wire till he was directly beneath her, still looking up. She reacted by gathering her skirt round her and, sitting down on the wire, swiping at him with her parasol. He dodged and stole one of her pink slippers, and then ran to one of the posts, shinned up it, and taunted her to come and get the slipper back. She climbed erect on the wire again, where she stood on one foot, balancing with apparent difficulty, threatening him. She tried to walk with one unshod foot but couldn't do it. Suddenly she did a heart-stopping drop from the wire, catching it just in time with her insteps. Then, hanging upside-down, but with her demure skirt still somehow caught decently between her knees, she inched her way along the wire towards him, her parasol held ready to chastise . . . At the last minute he grabbed the parasol away from her, set the slipper on the point of it, and dashed across the wire to the other post, jumping over her feet as they clung in defiance of gravity.

By the end of the act he had removed both slippers, her bonnet, her long skirt and her mutton-chop sleeved top, leaving her in a more traditional acrobat's one-piece garment which exposed her to the waist at the sides and to the navel in front. In the end Dill was caught, stripped of his knickerbockers and sailor-suit by some quick-release system, and chased across the wire, down the post and off-stage in a little G-string. Ann found the whole thing acrobatically impressive if in questionable taste. The rest of the audience loved it.

Next came Bob and Chloe who did a remarkable sad-clown act, again with Dill's help. This time he wore a costume suggesting some odd, mythical little creature, half bird, half beast, with a pointed beak and the little claw-like hands of some baby dinosaur, whom the gloomy couple hatched out of a large egg they found in an old trunk. They took turns to sit on it until Dill popped out and began leading them a hectic dance with his insatiable hunger and thieving ways. It was an inspired comic idea and Dill was superb, nimble, witty in his movements and full of what looked like improvisation. The long-faced couple ended up by climbing into the trunk to escape their demon-child – who closed the lid and stood crowing triumphantly upon it, while Ann marvelled at the fact that those two long, lanky people were somehow tucked in there. She had visions of them tied in knots like pieces of string. But when the applause roared out, and Dill raised the lid, they unfolded themselves and stepped out, unsmiling and also unknotted, for their bow.

'This is really good,' said Ruth as they clapped.

'Yes. I'm so glad you're enjoying it.'

'Why aren't you?'

Ann looked at her quickly. 'I am! I'm *kvelling* for the little lad, as if he were my own.'

'Still. You are as miserable as me. In the interval you'll tell me.'

'It would take ten intervals.'

When the interval came, after several more diverting items, the audience was clearly in a good mood. The earlier tension had eased; people were laughing and chatting almost as usual. Jacqui waved brightly to Ann across the heads of the crowd, and Eppi was grinning from ear to ear, clearly having forgotten about it being only kids' stuff. Ann caught sight of Amnon moving among the crowd, resplendent in his pale blue linen suit and vivid silk cravat, a vital little figure exuding energy and confidence. I could have stayed in bed, thought Ann, he wouldn't have missed me. But for Ruth's sake she was glad she hadn't. And a bit for her own. Dill was simply a boy genius.

Ruth led her out into the courtyard. It was a pleasure to be outdoors tonight: the air was cool and balmy, the scent of olive blossom caressing. The colourful clothes of the women offset the gentle neutrality of stone and wood.

Ruth found a small table for two and sat down at it.

'Sit,' she ordered. Ann sat. 'Now. I told. You tell me.'

Ann was very still. Hold it all inside, Boaz had said. Pain and guilt and other strong feelings should be kept in to 'do their work' . . . What work? The work his had evidently done, of twisting him and turning him into a man capable of his blinkered, self-defeating ruthlessness this morning? Or the constructive work of deepening, strengthening . . . Oh, to hell with all that! If that was the price of growing wise and strong, it was too expensive for her. But to come straight out with it, Boaz, and Kibya –

'First of all,' she said, 'why didn't you tell me about Menachem?'

Ruth dropped her eyes and sighed. 'You found out. Well. I always thought, if she wants to know, really, she will ask . . . It was the children I thought might hurt most . . . If I had said "he is married" you would be forced to ask. Yes?'

'Yes. You were right.'

'Who told you?'

'I met Ezriel in the Knesset today.'

Her face changed. 'Ezriel! And did he tell you the rest? His part?'

'Yes.'

'He was always like that – always. We used to call him *"Ma sh'ani rotseh akhshav"* – "What I Want Now". And he usually got it . . . The kibbutz won't say a word about what he did now, taking Devorah away from Menachem, because they are all so proud of him, getting into the Knesset, so Menachem will be put on one side. They'll say he shouldn't have married such a young girl, that she has done what is only natural . . . He will not get much sympathy. But he will be the one who carries most of it with the children, because *she* is straight away going to have one of Ezriel's – he made sure of that! And she'll be caught up with her new life . . . It makes me very upset.'

'You always liked Menachem.'

'Why not? He's a wonderful fellow. As you said yesterday, a real kibbutznik.'

'I said that?'

'In a way. You said Ephraim and Shimshon and the others reminded you of him. And *they* are the real, true types of the kibbutz.'

'Though they left.'

'Even though they left. They kept the same values, the same ideals. The same civilised, socialist outlook – you know what I mean. It is a quality of humanity, of humanism. Something I believe is the most important thing there is in the world.'

'More important than survival? More important than freedom and pride and independence?'

'The human conscience is more important even than these. If one is prepared to do anything for one's freedom, or to keep one's way of life, of course one is not worthy to keep it. Like in Orwell's *1984* when he's asked if he would throw acid at a child to destroy

226

his enemies. Menachem understood that.'

'How do you know?'

'You know the famous story about him in the War of Independence? He must have told it to you.'

'He told me a few stories. Very few.'

'This was one he might not have told you. You remember Avri
– little fat Avri?'

'Vaguely.'

'Avri went right through the war with Menachem, and once
they were dug in somewhere and they saw them, the Arabs, come
pouring over the hill and charging towards them. I am a sort of
pacifist myself but I would shoot then, wouldn't you? To save
your life? But Avri says when they got the order to fire,
Menachem shot into the air over their heads as they ran straight
at him. He chose in that extreme moment to be killed rather than
to kill.'

Ann stared at her. 'Menachem did that?'

Ruth nodded.

'You say Avri told you. That all the kibbutz knew it. Did they –
admire it?'

She shrugged. 'Some did, some didn't. But I did. Menachem was
ready to *die* so as not to kill. That's real courage, real integrity.'

But how is it that he's still alive? thought Ann. *Someone* must
have shot straight ... Little fat Avri, perhaps. Was he less
courageous, less of an idealist?

'Ruth,' she said suddenly, 'Do you remember Kibya?'

'Kibya?' asked Ruth in surprise.

'Yes. Does the name mean anything to you?'

'Why do you ask me about Kibya just now? Of course I remember it. What's it got to do with Menachem?'

'Nothing. I'm changing the subject. What do you remember
about it?'

'Well. It was in the 'fifties. Early 'fifties, '54, '55 – '

''53, actually. October.'

'Oh yes. It would be. I was about twenty-one then. I was in the
army. We heard about it. It was ordered by Dayan, you know?
And Arik Sharon was in charge under him. It was his group that
made that raid and a lot of others before, only smaller. He was
quite a hero to us in those days. It's a pity he went into politics.'

'He was a hero for raids like Kibya?'

'Of course! Till he organised those reprisals, things were terrible. We never knew what would happen next! We lived really in

227

fear a lot of the time. Our kibbutz . . . Well, you know where it is! Since '67 it's been right in the middle of the country, but then it was on the border. In what they used to call "the narrow waist". By the time you came, it wasn't dangerous, there was almost no troubles from infiltrators in the 'sixties and we could sleep at nights. But between '49 and those big retaliations in the 'fifties it was horrible. It's hard to be humane when you're scared.'

'But did anything happen, actually?'

'They used to come across the border and steal things and do sabotage, and sometimes there would be shooting near us. The border patrols chased them. But we knew there were never enough of them to guard us completely. We couldn't have faith in them. And there were counter-raids which failed – our soldiers ran. Okay, in our kibbutz was nothing so bad, but near us was Yehuda – you know? That was where they came in just before Kibya and murdered a mother and her two kids. Things were bad then altogether. People got scared. They were leaving. It was still austerity, we had rationing, Nasser was saying never never will we make peace with Israel – we were in very bad morale . . . And it was about that time that we began to realise that all the Jews of the world were not going to come flocking to Israel to join us, that the comfortable ones were just going to sit where they were and let us build their pride and their country for them. I remember so well the day my father suddenly knew it. He threw down the newspaper – it was teatime, I was home on leave, we were all sitting around my parents' little room – and he shouted, "They are not coming. Not now and not ever." It was some little item he had read, about some famous or rich Jew in the West, and it hit him suddenly. It was terrible for him. He really believed till then that he had done all he did for the whole Jewish people. To save them, to make them independent and proud and *normal*. And to find they didn't want it – !'

'But about Kibya.'

'Kibya? Well, Kibya was the biggest, that's all. It was a part of Dayan's strategy, to prove to the Jordanians that what they threw at us, we would throw back double.'

'Double? There were over sixty dead in Kibya, civilians.'

'You know how many people we lost altogether in those first years from infiltrators? Over five hundred! Very many of them were civilians, like the family in Yehuda. For me, when I heard about Kibya, I thought, Serve them right, let them leave us alone. And then, what a *scandale* in the world, in the UN – it was then that the pattern was fixed. When the Arabs do something – ignore it. At worst a little frown, a slap on their wrist. When the Israelis do something back, everyone throws up their hands and is shocked and threatens us with sanctions and tells us we are devils. It's not fair that we are expected to be so restrained and civilised when our enemies are doing whatever they can to destroy us or at least to spoil our lives. We have earned our right to be here, we are entitled to our homes and our futures, and if they keep on interfering with that, well, they must expect to get it on their heads from us and I am not against that they get it.'

'But those people in that village – they hadn't done anything to you.'

'How do we know? The army chiefs knew where to hit, where the marauders were coming from. They tracked them to the borders and our scouts found out where they came from and where they went to. If people who never sheltered them or helped them were killed – children, for instance, that is terrible, nobody is not sorry when kids are killed . . . But you can't pick and choose on a commando raid. And it worked, Ann. They stopped coming. You saw for yourself. Six years you lived quietly with us, *nahon*? '60 to '66. You lived quietly with Menachem in love and you enjoyed your teaching and you never had to take your pupils down to the shelters or be afraid that a Ma'alot would happen to you – that came much later. It was a good time, a quiet time. Despite recession and other worries, you picked one of the best times to come. You shouldn't complain about things that were done to make us safe there in the "narrow waist" where they could have cut our country in half if we didn't keep them away. Nine miles to the sea, that was all! When I think about that and remember how it felt to live just there, I can't always wish to go back to the Green Line. If we did go back to it, I would be afraid, I might feel just like we all used to feel – naked. Defenceless. When our commandos began really to defend us properly, it changed our whole feeling. It was the first time since the end of the War of Independence that we felt sure Israel would survive.'

The bell rang, and Ruth stood up. 'Good! Now we see the second half. You know, I'm so glad you asked me to come! And I'm glad we talked. It's important to remember sometimes those old days when we were so scared. What's a little Bronstein compared to being scared for your life all the time, scared your country won't last and that your army can't take care of you? That's one thing, our army can take care of us, they've proved it.'

'Ruth – '

She turned back. 'Hm?'

'I want to leave. I want to go somewhere.'

'Where?'

'I want to drive to the kibbutz and see Menachem.'

Ruth stared at her. The returning audience was pushing past them.

'How many years you didn't see him?'

'Fourteen.'

'And tonight you drive there and arrive to his door without warning?'

'Is it mad?'

'You still love him?'

She shook her head.

'No. I don't even know him any more. I need to see him and talk to him and I want to do it tonight. That's why I hired the car.'

The last people vanished and still Ruth stood there staring.

'Why do you need him?' she asked. 'Wouldn't I do? Or Eli? Or someone else?'

'I need *him* because I have a special feeling about him and because – '

'Well?'

'He's been hurt. And I've been hurt. And I remember he was wise and good. And humane. And perhaps he can heal me.'

'You haven't told me everything, have you?'

'No.'

Ruth came to her and hugged her.

'Go on,' she said. 'You can be there in an hour and a half, he won't even have gone to bed.'

'And you? How will you get home?'

'I will take some of the money Bronstein did not give us,' she said, 'and I will get a taxi. Because I am not leaving the circus before it is finished. I need it like you need Menachem.' She stood back, holding Ann's arms, grinned at her ruefully and then kissed her. '*Kol tuv*. Come back healed. Make it a good story to tell Eli and me to cheer us up tomorrow. Unless you decide to stay and live again in the kibbutz . . . I hear the *batei shimush* are not in such hygienic condition these days . . .'

'Oh, get away, you – ' But she could smile. 'If you see that chap with the beard, tell him I had a meeting.'

'I will.'

Ann turned back once as she went out through the empty foyer.

Ruth, in the act of waving, bent down to pick up a hairpin and as she did so a couple more dropped out audibly onto the marble floor.

CHAPTER 17

The drive was therapeutic. The car was as 'yare' as a good yacht, running fast and smooth and responding to a light touch. It was not too thirsty either, which was a good thing, as Ann discovered when she stopped for petrol on the outskirts of Tel Aviv. It cost twice what it did in England.

She grew excited as she turned off the Tel Aviv–Natanya highway to the familiar road leading to the kibbutz. Everything oppressive dropped, for a while, from her mind, which seemed to stretch itself and breathe deeply, relieved of its previous painful 'stitch'. Even Boaz was left some distance behind. At one point Ann had the odd conceit that he resented it and was chasing the car like some infuriated colossus, that glancing in her driving mirror she would see him pounding after her in seven-league boots, mouthing the words *You can't run away! You belong to me!*

The kibbutz was – almost to her surprise – just where she had left it. But there were changes which were instantly apparent. There was a tall wire fence round it now, lit by perimeter floodlights, and where the drive passed through it there was a gate which was closed, and a sort of guard-house. As her headlamps rounded upon it, a man stepped out. He had a sub-machine-gun hanging across his shoulder and as the Fiat approached he raised it a little and screwed his eyes half-shut against the beam.

She pulled up outside the gate and leant from the window.

'*Mi at? Mi at rotsah?*' He was clearly on edge.

'*Shmi Ann. Ann Randall. Ani mikhapesset Menachem Ginbar.*'

'Enn Rendell!' he ejaculated, peering at her incredulously. '*Rega!*' She waited while he hastily unlocked and unbarred the wire gate and swung it wide. He walked out to her and bent and peered through the window. He was a young fellow, about twenty-seven she guessed, half in uniform and half in civvies – good-looking with his curly fair hair and uncommonly wide grin.

'Enn! Don't you recognise me? I am Ehud!'

'Ehud!' The years rolled back. A little blond fiend, in vest and shorts, turning the lawn-spray so that it came through the window screen of the classroom, because she had had the temerity to throw him out of the lesson for persistent chattering . . .

'Ehud . . . Is it really you?'

'It is really me. Is it really *you*? Yes, I see it is. And you haven't changed!'

'Ehud – you're so big – I can't believe it – '

'We all grew up since you was our teacher.'

'*Were* our teacher – really, Ehud! If only you'd *listen* . . .'

He laughed. 'My English got pretty good now. You know I am married with an English volunteer.'

'Oh, so I get no credit?'

'Of course. Without you I couldn't ask her.'

They laughed. She kept staring at him. They would all be like this, all her children – grown while her back was turned . . .

'You come to see Menachem?' he asked curiously.

'Yes.' She was suddenly deeply embarrassed. If only there had been no fence, she had meant to park in a quiet part of the tree-bordered drive and sneak in, round the back way, finding her old route to the house they had shared . . . But perhaps he had moved. Veteran members moved into improved housing from time to time.

'I can't leave the gate. You drive straight in. Everyone will be very excited to see you.'

'Ehud . . . I don't want anyone else to know I'm here. I've only come to sit with Menachem for a while, then I'm going. I don't want – it's for his sake as well. I don't want a lot of silly gossip.'

'I understand,' he said quietly. 'He had enough of troubles,' and the spectre of the little blond troublemaker faded away and was replaced by an adult man with some sensitivity who might, even in a kibbutz, find it in himself to keep an interesting secret.

'Can I leave my car out here and walk in through the wood?'

'Sure. Put it just out of the way, over there.'

She parked it off the road and he let her through the gate. He was a head taller than she and she stood beside him for a moment just looking at him, getting used to it, the gap in time . . . He was smiling at her.

'You used to give me plenty of problems,' she said. 'More than any of the others. Why were you such a little villain?'

'Because you were a woman,' he said promptly. 'I never had a woman teacher. I couldn't let a woman to be my boss. I was very sexist then.'

'Oh, give me a kiss, you,' she said.

He blushed and bent to kiss her cheek.

'How is everyone? All the class?'

'Ayala died. You knew?'

'Ayala?' Russet hair, plump, quiet . . . Wrote beautiful poems and drew pictures in the margins. *'Died?* How?'

'In a car crash. And Shalom. In the army, Yom Kippur.'

The names were like triggers to the faces, the characters, even the handwriting. Shalom had been one of her pets. She swallowed. Grown up, killed, mourned for – and she, all unaware, with no share in it. 'What about the others?'

'Many left the kibbutz – most, I would say. But they are good. All married.'

'All?'

'All. We have between us from our class, twenty-one kids.'

'Good God!'

'They will be very, very sorry if I tell them you was here and you didn't stay to see them. A lot is here for Shavu'oth.'

'Then don't tell them. Please. One day I'll come back for a proper visit. I'll see everybody, you'll make a *kumsitz* for me . . . We'll catch up on news. Only not tonight. Okay?'

'Okay, Enn.'

She turned into the pine forest. It was dark and the way was foul with outcroppings of rock and underbrush, but somehow her feet knew the path. She actually found her foot feeling for a big boulder that *it* remembered, though she had long forgotten it. Her nose knew the night smells too and scented them, like an animal – here the pure lung-filling pine should be broken into by an acrid whiff from the sheepfold, and now, as she approached the backs of some gardens, by roses and African marigolds and the thick fragrance of sub-tropical honeysuckle . . . there it was! And soon she would find the path, and the path would lead, past two or at the most three lamps, to the house where she had been more sharply happy than she had been anywhere before or (until, briefly, this morning) since.

She found it. The shutters of the porch had been repainted, alternately blue and cream. A light stuck out over the screen front door which had not been there in her time, though she had often nagged the kibbutz electrician for one – perhaps he had only got around to it after she had left. Standing on the raised path she suddenly remembered the day they had laid it, pouring the concrete between the little wooden walls; there had been notices everywhere, *'Lo lalekhet al hamidrakhot'*. Not to *walk* on the paths, but it didn't say not to write on them, so Ann had taken a sharp stick and printed, just below their steps, their names:

She had not enclosed the words in a heart; that might have annoyed Menachem. In fact, she was anxious about what she *had* written. But when he came home from work and saw it, he had taken the three steps to the porch in one leap and burst in, shouting it like a battle cry: 'Ann! Menachem! Forever! *In English*!' He had embraced her and kissed her and then demanded, 'Where is the pencil? Now I'll write it in good Hebrew!' She gave him the stick but the concrete had dried and it was too late.

She looked down. It was still there. *Ann. Menachem. Forever.* She could see it clearly in the lamplight. How many people, visitors or newcomers, might have noticed it since and asked, 'Who was Ann?' But she felt sure, at the same time, that Menachem no longer lived here. How could he have brought his wife across such a pre-empted threshold? There was a light in the house. She knocked on the screen door. Someone would have to direct her to Menachem's present home. She hoped that whoever came would be a stranger.

But it was no stranger. It was Menachem.

So changed. So very changed, her beloved, her darling! Oh God, don't show it, don't let it show in your eyes how he has aged, what that pretty little slut and that ruthless young buck have done to him . . . he is nearly bald . . . his eyes are embedded in shadows . . . but his lips are still full and his shoulders still broad. Stand up straight, Menachem! Snap your fingers and show you don't care . . . But you do care. How you care! You never could hide your feelings. You showed me you loved me from the first, you showed me your pain when I left you, you never could hide anything. You are not like Boaz! With you, everything was open and straight, not buried and twisted . . . And you don't know me. You don't recognise me. So Ehud was lying, and I must have changed too.

'Ann. *Ze lo yekholiot . . .*'

'Yes. It's me.'

'Eneni yekhol lahamin . . .'

'Believe it, Menachem.'

'Come in. Before anyone passes and I have to share you.'

He took her through the familiar porch into the familiar, now shabby and unlived-in-looking, room, the 'room' of the 'room-and-a-half' that these old style veterans' dwellings consisted of.

The half-room that had been their bedroom was curtained off; not the same beautiful sea-coloured curtains she had brought from England, but a single dull brown one, utilitarian, limp. There were books on the old bookshelves, but no houseplants trailing their softening leaves round the ugly black metal pipes that held them, no batiks and paintings on the walls given to her on her birthday by pupils, no green glass jeroboam filched from outside the school lab. and stood in a corner filled with bulrushes and peacock feathers . . . It was very stark, very bare. Very austere. The apartment of a single man who has no heart for his surroundings. She turned, overwhelmed by feeling.

'Menachem, I heard. Only today. I heard from Ezriel himself. I got it all – compressed – your life of the last years, all in the space of a cup of coffee. I had to see you.'

'To tell me you are sorry for me?'

'No. Though I am, sorry and angry and jealous and a thousand other feelings . . . I had to see you for my own sake. Something's happened to me and I need you to help me.'

He smiled at her, the old smile. 'May I hold you first in my arms? Then perhaps I will believe.'

They embraced without kissing. It was a sort of agony. The same, but entirely, totally, fundamentally different. (And no arms should hold her but Boaz' arms, no hands touch her but Boaz' hand-and-a-half.) Yet the years fell away and the shock renewed itself when she drew back and looked up at him and again saw him, old and hurt and changed. The merciless female animal in her which had chosen Boaz over Peter suddenly forced her to understand Devorah.

'I've never quite got over you,' Menachem said.

'Nor I you. How could we?'

'Come on. Sit down. Chairs of a sort I have. Not like our old ones . . . Remember when we got our first real armchair, and you hated the colour of it, and I tried to re-cover it? I was no upholsterer!'

'I never heard you swear so much.'

'You were not supposed to understand. For that I swore in German, Yiddish and Arabic.'

'Cursing-out sounds the same in any language. When you got on to the armchair's mother's origins and morals – really! At least in England we stick to what our inanimates do in lavatories.'

'Oh, we are being silly! What a rubbish we're talking, after all these years when so much has happened . . . But you make me

236

laugh. You always made me laugh, that was why I adored you. We *yecces* are not so strong on humour. Look, two minutes you're here and tears already – ' He wiped his eyes with a handkerchief, spotless but unironed like all kibbutz handkerchiefs. 'I have not cried from laughter since you ran away from me.'

'Menachem, don't! I ran away from the kibbutz, not from you. I ran away as young boys used to run away to sea, only with me it was writing.'

'You have done well at it, too. I've read all your books.'

'How did you get them?'

'What do you mean? I bought them. There they are, on the shelf where we used to keep a mix of plant-cuttings and your Penguins . . . When you went, I must say I missed Joyce Cary and Graham Greene almost as much as I missed you! But there were so many empty spaces in my life . . . I remember getting more plant pots to cover up the holes on the shelves, more clothes that I didn't need to fill the cupboards – I never had so many sweaters and shirts and trousers, the *communa* got suspicious, they must have thought I was keeping some relative in clothes! But the worst space I couldn't fill. Not for many years.'

'Nor me.'

'But in the end, we both did, *nahon*?'

'*Nahon.*'

They looked wrily at each other.

'I hope yours worked out better than mine,' he said.

She didn't answer.

'You're still married?'

'I don't know.'

'*Ma zot omeret?*'

'It means that something has happened just now that may break my marriage.'

'Is that what you came to talk to me about?'

'Partly.'

'Tell me.'

How? Quick and straight – she always could, with him.

'I am in love.'

She was moved to see his face change, as if she still belonged to him; the reflexes still jerked, as hers had this afternoon when Ezriel had made it clear that Menachem had been hurt.

'The man I love is not like you. He . . . his views are rightist. And he was in the 101.'

Menachem sat motionless, looking at her with his chin on his

237

hand for some moments, and then turned his head away.

'Why should you say, "he is not like me", implying that I am in some way better?'

'What do you mean?'

'You say he was in the 101, as if that condemned him. As if my unit was essentially less guilty. You think I never soiled my hands? You think we always stuck to the purity of arms? In war – any war – men turn into animals. I know, I saw it, and I was not immune.'

Ann smiled. 'I can't believe you did anything very terrible, Menachem.'

'Because you lived with me and it would damage you to think so. I did terrible things. They didn't seem terrible at the time; they seemed necessary, inevitable. History will judge us. But my own personal judgement is already given.'

'What did you do that gives you such a feeling?'

'We drove Arabs from their villages. In the North. It was called Operation Broom, and was supposed to clear Arabs from strategic spots only, but the orders were – shall we say – interpreted freely by some local commanders. Ours was an immigrant from an Arab country; he hated them. He didn't care too much whether the village was on a vital crossroads or not. He would say, "Let's get rid of them, they'll only make trouble. They should be glad we don't kill them." And not one of us protested or said a word . . . We rounded them up and took their rifles, which to them is something like castrating them, and marched them to the border. Later on some villages were totally destroyed. Obliterated. We planted forests on them. Now our kibbutz has its Independence Day picnics in such a forest. I used to go with the others and sit under the trees, and if I sat on a rock or on a broken bit of a house made no difference to me. Now I don't go any more.'

'At least you didn't harm them.'

'What does that mean? We let them live, but we ruined them. We broke their lives.'

'You never told me.'

'That's the worst thing of all, to me. I didn't tell you, not because I was ashamed, but because I didn't think of telling you. I didn't think it was important.'

'When did you decide it was?'

'Lately. Only the last few years.'

'Why?'

He hesitated. 'Perhaps the children . . . How does one explain

238

such actions to one's children? Of course they have worse to face before we come to that. What is happening now with me and their mother. They are so small, so – sensitive. The vine's tender grapes. Now I must watch them suffer, and that is . . . There is no worse in the whole of life. *Much* I would rather, at this moment, that I had not been selfish and had them. I can't bear to think of it, how it must affect them . . .' He turned away from her.

'But Menachem, she's not going away.' There were many cases in the kibbutz, of divorce and remarriage – it was better here than outside because the children kept both their parents, they saw them all the time, and living in their 'groups' cushioned them. Their peers were so big a part of their lives. 'You should be glad at least that you live here.' She was still thinking of William, how his mother's desertion had damaged him for good.

Menachem shook his head.

'I have seen what happens. If it is worse outside . . . Well. I can't see how it could be worse for the children than what happens here. To see your mother living with a man not your father, to see new children coming and her walking through your home place with them in her arms . . . Here, there is no escape from all that, and from the whispers around you. A kibbutz is made of whispers.'

'No it isn't, Menachem, it's made of solider stuff. The whispers are just a nimbus.'

'I hear them everywhere. I move through a fog of them.'

'My dear, I'm so sorry! It must be hell for you.'

'I am not sorry for myself. I have asked for it in a way. But they are innocent. God help them.'

Ann frowned. She never remembered hearing him speak the word 'God' in that tone before.

'You said that as if you meant it,' she said lightly.

He glanced quickly at her. 'I did mean it,' he said.

'Menachem! What are you saying? Don't tell me you're coming back to religion!'

He replied oddly: 'Don't tell me you are not.'

'Certainly not! You freed me of the last traces of my conditioned Protestantism. I would no more go back to it than put my soul back in to prison.'

He smiled a little. 'You may find you'll change,' he said.

'But how can you possibly be religious, here? The whole of the Movement is ideologically against it.'

'I am not the only one who begins to see we threw out the baby with the bathwater. Wasn't that one of the expressions you taught me?'

'I never thought to hear you using it in this context!'

'You are disappointed in me.'

'Menachem – ! I wouldn't presume to be. I know nothing about the pressures you're under. But I am surprised. How has it happened?'

'It was not from those pressures, as you call them. It began long ago. There is a man here, an old man, a professor – '

'A professor here? In the kibbutz?'

'No, no. He lives in Jerusalem. He is a great man, a great thinker, and though he's an Orthodox Jew I can agree with him on many political things. For instance he says we must give the West Bank to the Palestinians, not for their sake but for ours. And he says the National Religious Party is a fascist party because they coerce people into practising religion whether they want to or not. About that there is no doubt in my mind. But he also says that Judaism is the root from which we drink our nourishment, and that man's whole business in this life is to consider his stance before God. I've been very much influenced by this man, I can say I am his disciple.'

'Menachem . . . You taught me to live independently of God, to cope with life without saying "Please" or "Thank you" or "I love you" or "I hate you" to anyone but human beings.'

'I was wrong,' he said simply. 'Without God, we Jews are the same as those who have always despised us, we are like animals, or plants, creatures without a spiritual dimension, living through our lives on instinct alone.'

'How can you *possibly* say that, living here with atheists who for forty years have ordered their own lives without reference to religion or religious ethics or prohibitions, who contrive to live upright and productive lives, without crime, without polluting the earth or their own bodies, without exploitation, without cruelty? With mutual respect and mutual support? Doesn't that *prove* – '

He was shaking his head slowly as she spoke. 'It's all gone wrong.'

'What?'

'It has all gone wrong, Ann. It's not what we meant it to be. The idealism, the joy has all gone out of it. Don't you see why? We are nothing so special, as we thought we were. We can't be anything more than greedy, selfish, fallible human dross while we deny the existence of God.'

'Menachem! Is this you talking?'

He looked round the little room sadly. 'This room,' he said. 'This room is for me a symbol. Were you surprised to find me still here? But of course it's not "still". I have lived in two other veterans' apartments. The last one, which I shared with my wife, which I left when we divorced so that *she* could still live there and receive the children there, that was the latest, the most *luxus* that the kibbutz provides. You should see it. A worker in town should have such a flat. What we didn't have . . . a kitchen with everything, a stove, a big sink, pine furniture, expensive formica surfaces, expensive curtains, expensive wallpaper – yes, wallpaper, Ann, with little bumps and stripes! And in the main room, teak, and glass, and art tiles, and cupboards, such as you and I never dreamed of. Remember when we moved in here from the single room and porch I had as a bachelor? How we were excited to have a room and a half, two rooms really, instead of just one, how we planned it and arranged it and decorated it and spread our few possessions to fill it, how each new thing we got we rejoiced in and gloated over? And do you remember how we began, from that time, to be less and less happy?'

'No . . .' she said blankly.

'Yes. It was so. In one room we were happy, and I remember, years before, being even more happy in a wooden hut, and happiest of all in a tent . . . Or, I would have been, if I had had you there.'

'Speak for yourself. I would have hated a tent.'

'No, you wouldn't. Because in those early days we prided ourselves on living the simplest way, with the fewest possessions; on sharing everything, owning nothing of our own. God still breathed on us then, because of our enterprise . . .'

'Or perhaps He hadn't quite realised you'd abandoned Him.'

'You're laughing at me.'

'I assure you I'm not.'

'I think God was giving us our chance, to go a little away from Him, to try life without Him but with another ideal, which He approved of, a life of dedication, a renewal of Eretz Israel . . . But then as the years went by and we began to say, You see, it can be done, we can live without God, He grew angry – '

Oho! she thought. And isn't He the one that wrote *that* book! Thou shalt have no other God but me, not even Socialism, which is every bit as bad as a golden calf any day! I think I get the idea.

241

When He saw it was actually *working*, that you were all making out – not in a material sense, but that you were all presuming to be *good* without Him, that really got Him hopping mad. So He injected a bit of the old Adam into all of you and made you want more and more *things*. He saw to it that you all got private radios and electric kettles and *fridges*, *noch*, and when you didn't get the message then and come back into line He lost all restraint. He made you work harder and harder until you could all have *televisions* in your rooms and that was His way of opening the ground under the feet of the kibbutz movement, the way He did under the children of Israel in the desert. Private property crept in, and with it of course inequality and soft living and foreign travel and loss of idealism and direction. He helped this process along by making a few wives leave their husbands, He changed your perspective about your wartime exploits, and He killed a few of the children. And on top of that, you know what He did, Menachem? He made all of you grow older. He slowed you down, He diminished your vigour and your dynamism and your zest for life and your belief in your brave cause. And then He did something very clever. He found a wise old *tsaddik* in Jerusalem and combined in him all the political ideas a kibbutznik never really sheds however old he grows, with good old-fashioned Jewish fundamentalism, and He gave His wavering little atheists a guru they could follow without really having to about-face completely. You've got to hand it to Him, Menachem. That God of yours knows what He's doing. He knows the heavy stuff doesn't work any more, it drives away more Jews than it frightens into good behaviour. After the Holocaust, anyway, he'd about shot His bolt in the direction of chastisement for His Chosen, I should think – even *His* omnipotent imagination must have boggled when *that* didn't stem the anti-religious tide, and in fact considerably swelled it . . . So now that brute force has failed, a little real low cunning is needed. And I'm sorry to see that on you at least, it's working.

He was staring at her across the room as if he could read her thoughts. Perhaps he could – it had been known. She met his eyes for a long moment, watching the pain in them almost coldly, but then let hers fall. Remorse seized her. How dared she – *she*, in her situation! – berate him for his natural weakness, his 'fall from grace'. . . But it was he who had made a good atheist of her, he had been *her* guru, and now he had stepped voluntarily back into the bog of reaction, of dependency, of woolly mysticism . . . She felt bitterly angry with him.

'About taste and smell, there is nothing to discuss,' she said ironically, quoting a Hebrew saw.

'And about religion. It is like being in love.'

'Which is a mental illness. Quite.'

He smiled.

'I do not feel I am mentally ill. On the contrary, I think I have been spiritually ill until recently. I couldn't have stood against what has happened with Devorah if I had not had that to fall back on. It's given me great strength, and I mean to give it to my children.'

'Does Devorah know about that?'

'She is not my business now, she is Ezriel's business. I shall give my children what I think they ought to have, I am not bound to discuss this with her.'

God help them indeed, thought Ann. A born-again Jewish father and a rational humanist mother. Not to mention a pragmatic bastard step-father . . .

'What am I thinking about?' he said, getting up abruptly. 'You have driven here in the middle of the night to see me and I haven't even offered you something. What? – coffee? – tea? And I have some cake. My neighbours – the female ones – are making a fuss of me. They make me cakes as a payment for having something new to talk about in the *communa* and the kitchen.'

Ann was hungry. She drank the coffee and ate three pieces of the cake, which was not the same cake she remembered. It was a sophisticated cake now, with apple, glazed with jelly – and was she mistaken or could she detect a *soupçon* of some exotic liqueur . . .?

'The new kitchens have improved home fare, anyway,' she said. 'Yellow ring-cake from the *wundertop* was never like this.'

'Yours was always good. How does it feel to be back in this room?'

'Strange. There's nothing left of me here. Yet it closes me round as it used to. Is the view the same?'

'No. There's no more view. They built directly behind.'

'They didn't cut down our trees?'

'Yes. Now they will build on the football field. They build everywhere.'

'The football field? What madness! Whose idea is that?'

He shrugged. 'The young people take over now. They want bigger houses. They want to live indoors. The sun is too hot for them.'

'And don't the older members go to the meetings any more? As I remember, these things used to have to be voted on.'

He replied with a shrug.

'Perhaps you're all too busy praying,' said Ann.

'I'm sorry you're so angry with me.'

'I've no right to be angry, Menachem. Not with you and not, certainly, with the kibbutz. I left those young people . . . I'm not saying I could have changed anything . . .'

'You opened doors for them. Some of them used them to go through, out into the wider world.'

Ann stared. 'Am I really blamed for all my pupils who left?'

'It is mentioned sometimes, as a factor. But it is nonsense. I always say so. The doors would have opened anyway – the volunteers from America opened them after '67. That was when the rot set in. You only gave them a liberal outlook. You stimulated their creativity. You also made them competitive . . . that's true. Remember the fuss when you began giving them *marks*! Oy veh . . .' he moaned in mock horror.

'I stopped when I saw they didn't like it – '

'Oh, but they did! They liked very much to compete with each other, to boast that they got a gold star . . . It was their parents who saw in it the seeds of the beginning of what must end in exams, in universities, in mass exodus . . .'

'You're not seriously suggesting the kibbutz is finished, that it's a spent force? All this building must mean growth, not stagnation.'

'It will remain, as a village. An ordinary village. As a kibbutz it was finished from the time the kids stopped doing the *hora* and started doing rock and roll.'

'Menachem . . . really! Die-hards were saying the end was nigh when the first private showers were built.'

'They were right. A slow death is a death nonetheless. We should have gone on showering together, listening to a single radio in the dining-hall in the evenings, wearing communal clothes . . .'

But Ann, at the words 'showering together', had stopped listening. He went on for a long time talking about the old days and where things had gone wrong and she thought, I came here to talk to him about Boaz and Kibya and Peter and England and I can't talk to him about anything that matters because he is lost. Not just to me, that was to be expected, but to himself. Peter is older than he is but at least he knows who he is and he is not a broken

244

man. On the other hand, what has Peter started, what has he built up that had power to break him when it began to change, to modify, to become a distortion of his dream?

Menachem was working his way gradually round to the political situation. With difficulty Ann came back to him. Her accumulated weariness was beginning to overcome the second wind she had got when she forced herself out of bed that evening. Contemplating the long drive back, even over empty night roads, was enervating. She was losing way . . . She had come here for something for herself which she did not deserve and was not going to get. On the contrary, she was getting a sense of misery that would exhaust rather than revivify her . . . She wished she hadn't come, but what use was that? She was here now, she must make the best of it.

'. . . So you think there'll be another war,' she said flatly.

'And another, and another. There will always be wars. We will continue to win them on the battlefields and lose them in the forums of the world. But here at least we die fighting. And at last,' he went on, in a completely matter-of-fact voice, so that she didn't at first register the full meaning of what he was saying, 'When the day comes that they are stronger than us – when they take us *here* – ' and he laid his open hand against his throat – 'then we will go out with the biggest bang this world has ever seen.'

There was a long, an endless-seeming silence.

'What do you mean by that, Menachem?' she asked, carefully, at last.

'You know what I mean by it.'

'You mean that Israel should use nuclear weapons to commit mass murder and mass suicide if she is pushed to the wall. *Is* that what you mean?'

'That is what I mean.'

'The Massada syndrome. You are reverting to true zealotry. Well. You always were an all-or-nothing sort of man.'

She stood up.

'I must go.'

'Tonight?'

'Yes. Right now.'

'Why don't you stay?'

'Because I don't want to.'

He stood up, and looked at her with his sad, shadowed eyes. 'Things change in fourteen years. People change.'

'They certainly do,' she said.

And even more, my once and not future love, do they change in thirty-two years, since the day when – all reliance on God bravely abjured, alone in the universe with nobody watching but little fat Avri – you fired into the air at the risk of your life to avoid killing a fellow human being.

CHAPTER 18

It was getting on for midnight when Ann reversed the Fiat and drove out of the kibbutz drive and back to the main road towards Petach Tikva. It would have been a great deal better, she reflected, if she had stayed in her seat at the theatre with Ruth and watched the end of the Circus, and then gone backstage for the inevitable first-night party which was part of the Two Alephs's tradition. Ruth would have enjoyed it too, and then Ann could have driven her home and perhaps had a chat with Eli which might have taken him out of himself a bit. Ann could never tell with Eli, whether he was sad or happy. Ruth evidently could – what had she said, that he 'glowed' when he had made a sale? Oh God. Why couldn't just something have gone right for somebody that day? Maybe it had . . . Amnon at least must be feeling good. The show was obviously a success . . . Dill was an extraordinary performer. She had been aware of feeling quite ridiculously proud of him, as if he had been hers in some way. Well, one needn't be somebody's mother in order to feel proud of them, just their friend.

She was aware of keeping her brain busy on fringe matters, of fixing her eyes on the headlamp-lit tarmac ahead as a way of preventing her mind from swinging backwards. But it was impossible for long.

Could it happen to *her* that she would sink back into some form of superstitious belief, out of sheer misery, exhaustion or despair? She remembered a crucial test she had passed, back in the early days when she had first cast off the habits of faith. Menachem had developed erysipelas on his foot and been in awful pain, and the doctor had injected him with penicillin without checking to make sure he was not allergic to it. He lapsed into a coma and, for several nightmare hours, hung between life and death. Ann had stood at the bottom of his bed (in that same room – he had not been taken to hospital) and stared at him, her whole being willing him back to life and at the same time picturing him dead and herself alone, knowing him to be nowhere . . . And the temptation to send up prayers, the automatic prayers of childhood ('Please let him live!') was inordinately strong. But she had thought, no. And she had not prayed. She had checked her brain at every attempt to say 'Please,' to say, 'Let,' to say anything

247

which suggested any hearer other than Menachem's struggling will for life in his unconscious body. It was very hard, she remembered, and in a strange way even harder to resist dispatching thought waves of gratitude heavenward when he won his battle.

After that she was never even tempted to lapse back into the old, superstitious ways. In her trials today she would as soon have placed a dish of rice and flower-water before some towering idol, or fasted, or made a blood sacrifice, as put out calls for help to the heedless and incomprehensible deity of her childhood – let alone to the savage being Menachem had elected to crawl back to. The only vestiges took the form of a muted defiance, which, she was aware, had showed itself all too clearly in her silent outburst to Menachem . . . the determination to show that one could manage alone, and be good, without the divine carrot or the divine stick.

Good . . . Well. A relative term, after all. She glanced irresistibly into the driving-mirror. Nothing but other headlights followed her along the dark road. Perhaps because she was heading back towards Boaz, geographically at least. He had no occasion to chase her . . . Talk about superstition, talk about irrational ideas . . . But she could feel the pull. That was real enough. As real as a spring, stretched to breaking-point and now slowly easing . . . She felt the icy waters lapping round her neck, the suck of the black mud on her feet, and became aware of a great, and novel, loneliness. Menachem had always been with her. For fourteen years she had held him in a secret place in her heart, an image of the perfect love, the 'very parfait knight'. . . That was now abolished. And not alone by him. By her . . .

And suddenly a horrible feeling of shame seized her, the same emotion, and to the same degree, that she had felt after physically attacking William. *How could I have done it!* Menachem, like William, was a *miscain* – an unfortunate, life-damaged, someone to be cherished and protected. The surge of love and protectiveness which had assailed her when she had first seen him that evening, and seen what the years had inflicted, rushed back on her, too late. For, knowing his vulnerability, aware of it with the deep empathy which still lay between them, she had struck out at him with her mind as she had struck at William with her hands and feet . . . And now she felt the pain she had inflicted, as he sat there watching her so quietly, seeing her contempt, and felt almost sick with it, and with helpless self-directed anger . . .

It's in me, she thought, horrified. That violence, that need to assert myself, to the point of cruelty . . . Who am I to judge Boaz?

Or anyone?

She pulled up suddenly. Where the hell was she? She remembered passing through Petach Tikva and seeing a sign to Tel
Aviv . . . Had she turned right, as it directed, or left? Or had she
gone straight ahead? Surely if she had turned right she would be
in a more brightly-lit, populous area, instead of this narrow dark
road with small patches of twinkling lights away off to the sides
and ahead, instead of the steady reassuring yellow glow of modern street-lighting . . .

She took out her road map of Israel and her pocket torch. The
map, unfolded, covered the steering-wheel and dashboard. The
finger of light probed the folds. She found Petach Tikva, through
which she had recently passed, and then the finger traced the
minor road to the east which she must unthinkingly have taken.
A few tiny villages with Jewish names were marked – other
kibbutzim, perhaps. Then the lime-green colour of the plain
blended into pale brown, indicating foothills. The secondary road
– a thin red line – wound on for a matter of eight or nine miles,
and then split into two. There was a town at the point of the
division.

At first the name meant nothing because it was spelt Qibya.
But suddenly it registered. She was within ten miles of the place.
She must be very near the old Green Line, the border formed by
the '48 fighting and nullified by the Six-Day War. Having lived so
close to this border – an uncrossable barrier then – during the
early 'sixties, it seemed uncanny to her that she could now cross
it just by driving on, that in ten minutes she could be in the West
Bank – enemy territory, as they used to call it. And as it still was,
she realised, particularly after the events of today. It would be
madness to go there, at night, alone, in a car with an Israeli
number-plate – West Bank cars bore distinctive ones and could
be recognised at once by security forces in Israel proper; but by
the same token, Israelis venturing into the Arab hinterland could
be spotted by the inhabitants. How else had the man who threw
the grenade into Boaz' car identified his target?

She switched off the torch and folded the map. There were no
street lamps here and the only light now came from her
headlamps. She turned them off to test her reaction to darkness
and loneliness. She found there was also a profound stillness and
silence to contend with, broken only by the chirping of crickets.
She thought, If Boaz were with me now, I would drive on. He
wouldn't know where we were or where we were going, and

perhaps, when we drove into the town, he wouldn't recognise it and he would say, 'Where are we?' and I would say, 'Oh, this is some little village, I think it's called Kibya,' and – like Hamlet and the players – watch for the reaction . . .

But it was her own reaction she really wanted. She wanted to see the place. But it was folly to indulge this longing. It was dangerous. Boaz never crossed to the West Bank unarmed. Much better not. Or – 'if, already' – then obviously it was much more sensible to come by day. Only she knew somehow that it was now or never.

She switched on her headlights and drove on.

The road was poorly surfaced and twisted more than appeared on the map, and the ten miles took nearly half an hour to cover. Possibly, also, because she was driving very cautiously. She was as nervous as a cat.

The headlamps showed her a strange, desolate region, a weird contrast to the well-lit, built-up, densely cultivated area she had left behind. All was stone and scrub with a few olive groves. The road itself was the sole sign of civilisation, a civilisation of a past age, abandoned long ago and fallen into the pot-holes of neglect.

She passed through one village, a slumbering jumble of houses and debris almost indistinguishable one from the other; the buildings were without plan, their corners turned all ways, like the blocks of a giant child thrown down in a heap. Then more road, more wildness and strangeness.

There were no other cars at all, though she did pass two men on bicycles, neither with lights. Both riders were Arabs and both looked at her curiously as she passed. She felt herself to be a trespasser, or worse. Though she knew she meant no harm she did not expect them to know it, or believe it. Her underlying sensation, as she drove up into Kibya at last, was one of guilt and furtiveness.

It was an Arab village like the other, with the narrow road running through houses of all sizes and shapes set at odd angles along branching, unmade lanes. There were yards enclosed by low walls, containing fig trees and vine trellises. A few shops and a café stood at a cross-roads with a stack of green plastic beer crates and a jumble of stools prosaically outside.

An elderly night-watchman was sitting outside one building smoking. She had planned to draw up near the centre of the town, but that was where he was; he half-rose from his stool as her dipped headlamps caught him, but sank down again as she changed gear and drove past. She switched off her engine at the top of a rise in the road, and coasted down toward the far end of the village, letting the car pick its own stopping place.

She switched off the headlights and shut the windows as the car came to a halt, and sat quietly, letting her eyes get used to the dark. The night was perfectly silent, perfectly peaceful. It, and the village, were like a stage set, a backcloth upon which her imagination could freely play. Now was the time when she must come to it, the heart of the matter. She had sheered off it for over twelve hours, but for what had she brought herself to this place but to turn now and face it?

How would it have been, if one had been living here – then? Would there have been any defence? A Legion patrol, perhaps . . . No, or the raid would not have succeeded so completely. Home guards, no doubt, none too alert or well-trained, armed with old British or even Turkish rifles. For the rest – sleep, until suddenly –

What would they hear first? Would the commandos come mechanised, or on foot? On foot, almost certainly, for the sake of silence and surprise. A shot? Perhaps . . . And next?

At Deir Yassin the intention had been to warn the villagers by means of a loudspeaker, though in the turmoil of battle it went unheard. Would there have been warnings here? – Would the awakener have been the harsh unnatural bark of a human voice crudely amplified, the unsynchronised swift drubbing of heavy running feet . . .? Then, assuredly, shots, a whole volley, perhaps the timpani rattle of a machine-gun. Shouts. Other cries . . .

Did the people run? Which would one tend to do, leave one's home, still half-stunned by shock and sleep, and flee through the bullet-bored narrow streets (where to?), or to huddle in the false shelter of a familiar place? Which would be the instinctive course – to carry one's children out into the deadly, noise-filled darkness and away, or to conceal them – under a mattress, in the roof space, inside a grain silo or an indoor well? Ann knew which she would choose.

And then would come the detonations. If one had not left one's house by then, might those explosions not paralyse the mind with terror? What would it be – dynamite laid to the foundations, or, as at Deir Yassin, hand grenades thrown through windows? Had there been more – gunfire raking the rooms, pistol shots at fleeing shadows? Who knew? Seventy dead . . . Could that be merely an unavoidable accident of war?

251

Imposed on the innocuous sleeping silence, Ann heard sounds, produced with marvellous efficiency by that organ of her brain which enabled her to conceive plots and create characters, and which now, at her conscious bidding, turned torturer. She could hear the shots, the muttered orders, the running feet; a sudden deafening explosion, another . . . the stutter and crack of gunshots. Fire . . . Now she cringed inwardly, trying to rein herself in, but the screams had already begun. Against the darkness she saw the corpses of the defenders, sprawled on the dusty roadway. The roof of the house before her collapsed inward, and another blew out, hailing lethal chunks of pale stone. She heard the choking and the cries. And, perhaps clearest of all, she smelt the smells: masonry dust, cordite, fresh blood, and the stench of human terror to which all animals react.

And the soldiers. Purposefully going about their task, shouting now that there was no further need of silence . . . setting the charges, running behind a wall, running to the next place, the next doomed building . . . She witnessed it as she sat there, a stinking hell of violence and suffering, the kind which reaches forward and goes on for years; cries whose echoes ricochet on and on, individual spurts of blood which flow together into rivers, tears running down small bewildered faces which time transubstantiates into a corrosive poison, pouring out in all directions . . . She felt it reach her, and it burned so badly she wanted to scream her own lungs out.

But there could be no relief in weeping and raging now. There was no kindly, uncomprehending mother or father to ease the pain by assuring her, however falsely, that it was nothing to do with her. Now she must sit up straight and absorb it in stillness and silence, because she was too old to deceive herself into supposing that if she sank down and wept it would undo one single second of that horror, or alter by one iota its cause, its results or its perpetrators.

If Boaz was here, he was here, and if not, if the faces beneath the helmets were all anonymous, what of it? They were Jews. They were Israelis. They passed her in the streets, they drove her about in buses, or served her in shops. She had not slept with any of them and that must make some difference, but not all that much, if she were honest. If she could stop caring for Boaz, if she could teach herself to hate him, thrust him far away from her, pretend she had never seen him, what would that change? Would it cancel out a line of what the moving finger had written across the walls

252

of this sleeping village?

Yet, how peacefully it lay now under the myriad visible stars . . . How easy to comfort herself by thinking, Look, here it is, rebuilt, repopulated, reborn, a phoenix . . . The nightwatchman puffs his cigarette, not a light shows, not a child cries in his sleep. Just so might one sit in the purlieus of St Paul's, or the heart of Dresden, or among the towering new office blocks of Rotterdam or even Hiroshima, and salve one's heart with the balm of the human talent for regeneration and resurrection. No Christly miracle – no single act of revivification – could compare with the wonder of any of these. And just because this is a little village in which a mere seventy people died instead of hundreds of thousands, it is no less of a marvel – as their slaughter is in one sense no less of a crime, since each man can die only once, and each heart suffer only so much sorrow.

Menachem had said there *were* villages which no longer existed. They had been annihilated, bulldozed into the ground, their foundations smothered and their sites obliterated. One could search in vain for Deir Yassin on a modern map of Israel . . . There was no main street there where one could sit in one's car on a silent night and recreate, against a safely rebuilt backdrop, a scene of slaughter for the good of one's soul, or contemplate the miracle of human regeneration. And there were others, in the south, in the north . . . expunged, their populations scattered, each site an overgrown graveyard without markers or any reminder to passers-by that within living memory they had been living places. Kibya, compared to these, was one of the lucky ones. At least, in the unending story of the scorpion and the frog, it had been stung only once, and been allowed to survive.

Ann felt she was as much a part of that story, now, as any of them. She too could assume both rôles: the idealistic, trusting frog and the perverse and cruel scorpion calling down its own damnation. Sometimes she, like all others concerned, could play both parts at once . . . and not just because of what had happened that morning. It had started long ago when she first began to identify herself with this country, when she first discovered her 'fundamental commitment'. She leant back and closed her eyes. How easy it is to support a pure cause! Not just easy; it is the joy of joys, life's most sublime satisfaction. What a lovely war that must have been, in '48, with everyone so sure. Nothing sullied, nothing spoilt, no doubts, no schisms, or at least none that could stand against the tidal wave of certainty and conviction. All on the side of the angels . . . Ephraim was not the first to tell her of the sense of uprightness, the purity of spirit of the young fighters of the time. She had imbibed a sense of it during her kibbutz years. It was familiar ground. She was conditioned to accept it as a fact, not to question it. And it was easy to love men like that, to feel proud of loving them – those who had kept their integrity, and who were visibly suffering now from all that had happened since . . .

She had thought those men with the 'kibbutz look' *were* Israel. But they were not. Not any longer. They fought their honourable war to give the Jews independence and a place of their own after millennia of persecution and betrayal and helplessness, and then retreated to their kibbutzim and lived their decent hard-working lives, voting in perpetuity for their old party even after it had ceased to exist as an effective force, gradually slipping into old age, wondering why things hadn't worked out as expected, what the recurrent sacrifices were for, what had gone wrong . . . While a new generation – which began with Boaz' and could now be seen embodied no less in the young man who had tried to rob her, and the younger Gush settlers, then in Eppi Baum and Ehud – picked up the torch and ran off with it at a tangent. So who was Israel now?

This morning she had thought Boaz was. Brave, stubborn, virile, ruthless – but crippled, abandoned by his friends, nursing terrible determination and terrible secrets. A man of war, with singleness of purpose and the strength of his convictions, but – sterile. *Sterile* . . . No, he was not Israel! She would not believe it. And if, at times, he did seem representative to her, it was because he matched her in some way. Even now, sitting here in the village he had helped to mangle twenty-seven years ago, she knew she was still linked to him, more drawn to him than ever. Did her very body and soul then counsel despair, that she could still regard her love for a man like that. not as some aberration to be rigorously repudiated, but as the essence and symbol of her passion for this place and these people? Was the dark pool spreading to swamp the whole forest – was a single tress not enough, that she felt ready to leap in and immerse herself completely?

Perhaps that woman, the mother of the murdered British sergeant, was right. 'It's just sex, that's all it is.' Crazy people, as Shula had said, must also be listened to. Or perhaps Peter knew better, and all she sought here was tension, stimulus, drama. Or was it all just her own subconscious reaction to some guilt-laden awareness of anti-semitism in herself, as Boaz professed to believe?

To think that any of these might be true was somehow more terrible to her than contemplating the participation of the man she loved in a massacre. And what did *that* mean? God knows . . . She was no nearer the heart of the matter now than she had been this morning, when she lay under Boaz, throwing chastity and self-respect and Peter's trust and every decent, uncomplicated facet of her life away for the single moment when he pierced her. Did the frog die in ecstasy? she wondered. Did the scorpion withdraw his sting and somehow struggle to the shore? Or would the sting not come out, and did they fight their way to safety locked together? Was only the frog in pain?

A shadow fell on her out of the lesser shadows. She felt her heart lurch with terror, and then calm itself. A man stood outside the car, an Arab, looking in at her. Her instinct made her hands and feet leap to the controls of the car to start it and drive away, but something stopped her. Instead she rolled down the window and leaned out.

'*Sholem aleicum,*' she said. It was the only Arabic she knew.

The man stared at her. His eyes, in the hard, lined face, glared through the darkness. He said something to her in a sharp, gut-tural burst of sound. She smiled and shook her head, spreading her hands to show both that they were empty, and that she did not understand.

He was not armed. They were not allowed to have weapons, these Arabs who, Menachem had said, regarded rifles as symbols of masculinity. This man now had to face her – an intruder, a woman, an enemy for all he knew, enclosed in that other virility symbol, a vehicle – emasculated, powerless to drive her out. And by refusing to pay him respect by showing fear, she was emascu-lating him further; she saw it in his look of angry bafflement.

She pitied him. She almost wished he *had* a gun, so that they could be more equal, so that she could feel threatened and by some evidence of it restore the manhood which his whole situa-tion as a West Banker undermined.

Boaz always stressed the 'otherness' of these people. He behaved as if only someone like himself, who had intimately studied and lived with them, could understand their alien *moeurs* or make meaningful contact with them. Yet suddenly she felt it was all nonsense; she wanted to communicate with this fellow human being before her, and she could.

'Do you speak Hebrew?'

After a moment's hesitation, he nodded. How strange! That the 'enemy's' language should be the link!

'I wanted to see your village,' she said.

He continued to stare at her. She leant a little towards him, keeping her hands in plain sight on the window edge.

'It's very pleasing.'

'*Yehudiah*?' he asked.

'Yes,' she said. It was the first time in her life she had claimed Jewishness, lied about it. Why had she? Because, in relation to this man, it was as nearly true as it could ever be, and much simpler than the real truth.

'Were you born here?' she asked. He nodded. 'Were you here – '

Dared she ask? If ever there were a taboo, it must be this . . . Boaz, the Arab expert, would be appalled. He was, she had often observed, peculiarly touchy on their behalf, exaggeratedly careful that their sensibilities and customs should be respected.

Perhaps the man could sense her genuine wish to reach him through the intangible walls that divided them. He prompted her.

'When?'

'When the soldiers came. In '53.'

He nodded, almost eagerly it seemed.

'I was a boy.'

'But do you remember it?'

'Yes. They came at night.'

She waited, her eyes fixed on him in the faint starlight.

'They came on horses,' he elaborated, quite unexpectedly.

'*Horses?*'

'Yes. And they had big guns. Cannons. They destroyed the village with cannons.'

'The whole village?'

'The village.'

'How many died?'

'Many. Hundred. Two hundred.'

'Of your family?'

'No.'

'You know others who lost people?'

He was silent for a moment.

'My friend told me once his uncle was killed then.'

'Are there still signs?'

'Signs?'

'Ruins.'

256

He shook his head.

'All the houses were rebuilt?'

'Yes. Fine houses. You can see.' He gestured behind him.

'And do your people still talk about it?'

He shrugged and shook his head.

'The old men. *We* don't. There are today's troubles. Enough!' He laughed.

'For us too.'

'Do you want coffee?' he asked suddenly.

Startled, she said, 'Where?'

'At my house.'

She knew from Boaz that the man might well have misinterpreted her visit. The morals of unescorted women were automatically suspect. Yet she might nevertheless have gone with him, if it had been day, rather than show distrust or seem discourteous.

'I should like to. But it's late. Please excuse me – you were kind to invite me.' Then she lied again. 'My husband expects me home.'

'You are married?' he asked, incredulously.

'Yes.'

He shook his head, puzzled, but he smiled. It seemed natural to put her hand out, and he shook it and released it quickly.

'Shalom,' he said.

She returned his salute in Arabic. He smiled again, perhaps at her mispronunciation. She started the car, turned it round in the narrow street. As she drove back, past him, she lifted her hand. He did not return her greeting, but stood silently by the roadside, empty-handed, watching her go.

CHAPTER 19

She 'backed out' of the West Bank and drove the rest of the way back to Jerusalem by the main road, arriving, excessively weary, at two in the morning. She spent the last part of the journey keeping herself awake by imagining Amnon's wrath when she had to wake him up to let her in, after his sleepless night near Massada, followed by a stressful day, topped up with a hectic party. The doorbell didn't sound very clearly in his bedroom. She hoped he would hear, or that somebody would – but of course there would be nobody else in the flat, unless he had changed his mind about banishing the Circus. He probably had; it would be characteristic of him to flare up and then, in the excitement and satisfaction of a good opening, have forgiven them.

She parked the dusty Fiat round the corner and walked back to the iron door. Amnon usually made sure it was properly closed before he went to bed, but tonight it was ajar. She mounted the steps and rang the bell. The light Amnon normally left on in the kitchen when he was out or asleep was not shining. The balcony was in darkness except for the indirect radiance of the street-lamp; the eucalyptus trees in the small yard below, which last night had been tossing nervily in the wind, were limp and still. It was almost cold, nonetheless. Ann shivered as she stood there waiting.

After ringing the bell four or five times she concluded that Amnon had not yet come home. That must mean the party at the theatre was still going on. Well, tired as she was, there was nothing else for it – she must go there.

She returned to the car and backed it out again into the main street, and then drove to the theatre. The floodlighting on the Old City walls shone on in the cool, unpopulated night . . . odd, you would think it would go off at a certain time to save fuel. It gave Ann a curious feeling, like a play being acted to an empty house.

The streets of the Arab sector, leading to Nat'am, had lost none of their menacing quality since she had noted it in the taxi the night before last. Then at least there had been lights and noise and people. Now there was utter emptiness and stillness. Somehow even the dark silence of the broken road leading to Kibya had not struck her as more sinister . . . It must be tiredness. God Almighty, how tired she was! She would get the key from Amnon

258

and go back to the flat at once; nothing on earth would persuade her to stay, even for one drink, except – if Dill were still there – just to give him a kiss and tell him how good he had been. But of course, he would be in bed hours ago.

As she turned into the street where the theatre was, a figure stepped into her car's headlights. It was a young soldier, with his arms raised to halt her. Did he want a lift, or what? She stopped within a couple of yards of him, and leant out of the window.

'Where are you going?' he asked her in Hebrew.

'To Nat'am – the theatre.'

'*Asur.*'

Forbidden? 'Why?'

He straightened up and looked up the dark street behind him. Now she saw the road block up ahead and another man in uniform – an officer, she thought – walking towards her. He joined the soldier beside the car.

'Who are you? What are you doing here?' he asked her.

She gave her name. 'I'm staying with the director of the theatre. There's a party there tonight – ' And she stopped.

Something in the look which passed between the two soldiers gave her her first indication of something wrong. Their presence here, even the road block, would not have done it, because such things were commonplace in times of tension. But they looked at each other, and the look spoke of her ignorance of some circumstance, peculiar to this place, this moment and her destination, which filled her with a nameless anxiety.

The officer made a sign to the soldier and he walked away along the road in the path of the headlights. The officer bent again to the window.

'Something happened here,' he said. She stared at him without breathing. 'An explosion. The theatre was damaged. Did you have friends there?'

Her mind went blank. Friends? Who? What were their names? There were a lot of them – a lot – who were there, whom she had left there, in that building? No names and no faces came.

'You had better go to the hospital,' the officer was saying.

'Hospital – ?'

'That's where they took them. You know where it is?' He pointed the general direction. 'Are you all right?' She nodded again, but did not move. He stood there beside her. Once he straightened and looked all round. Then he bent down again, waiting for something. Waiting for her to move off, or – to ask –

259

'How – ' Her lips moved, her breath burst through, but no sound came at first. It was as if she had forgotten speech. 'Were there – many – '

'Casualties? Yes. The bomb went off during the show.'

She made a little sound and bent over the steering wheel. He reached in and touched her shoulder. 'You'd better go,' he said. 'Can you drive all right?'

She sat up. She couldn't think. She had to go somewhere, to learn what had to be learnt. Her brain, crouching numbly on the brink of panic, fled homeward. For a moment the road block in her headlamps vanished; she saw a moving design of rooks swirling behind the branches of a dead elm, and heard Peter's dog barking after a rabbit.

She looked at the controls of the car, wondering what to do to make it move. Suddenly she heard herself saying, 'I want to see.'

'The theatre? I'm sorry. There's nothing to see anyway. The front's still there. You wouldn't know. And we can't let anyone inside.'

'The front is still there?' she asked stupidly.

'Yes, I said so.'

'And the *mezuzzah*?'

'The *mezuzzah*?'

'On the doorpost.'

'I don't know, *g'veret*, I didn't look.' His young voice was stiff and she understood he was impatient for her to go.

She suddenly remembered how to start the car, and she did so, so sharply that he jumped back. She forgot to say goodbye or thank him. She did a U-turn and began to drive. She had no idea where the hospital was, but she drove in the direction he had pointed in, up through Sheikh Jerakh, and quite soon she saw it. A big building, faced with golden stone, but dark now, dark with her dread, though the entrance was lit.

She found herself walking up the steps and into the reception area. At once she was participating in a scene in one of the anterooms of purgatory. Men and women, and several children, were sitting or crouching or walking about. Some clutched each other, some moaned, some held back sobs with their hands. Others sat or stood alone. The anguish was patent and tangible and she felt it thrill through her like the hideous vibrations of an old-fashioned dentist's drill.

Suddenly she saw Neville. He saw her at the same moment, jumped to his feet and ran straight towards her. His round fat face was grey mottled with red, and contorted with something akin to indignation.

'They've killed him!' he burst out shrilly as he reached her. 'They've killed my little boy, Ann – ' He spoke with shrill earnestness, as if he were registering some serious complaint with her. 'That's what they've done. He's dead and gone. They told me just now – '

His face crumpled. Numbly, feeling only the vibrations, still purely physical, she put her arms round him. He tried to hold in his sobs, reducing them to strange sounds like a creaking door. After what seemed to Ann a long time, during which her eyes, over his shoulder, raked the large, crowded hall in vain, he pulled away and looked at her. She thought she had never seen a face so ugly and so wrenchingly pathetic.

'Jacqui – ?' she forced herself to ask. The names were back now. Jacqui. Amnon. Ruth. *Oh, Ruth! Not Ruth!* Amatsia – the Circus –

'Jacqui's in here somewhere. She's alive. I'll have to tell her. I wish *I* was dead. I wish I was. How am I going to stand it? The rest of my life, with such a burden! And her – she's hurt bad – but she'll wake up soon – I'll have to go and tell her. I was in Beit Agron, y'know – just the same place as this afternoon when the news came through about the mayors – standing there beside the telex – it just started clicking and the tape came up right into my hand – and I thought to myself, I thought – hey-up, here comes another good story, if I hurry I can catch the second edition . . .'

'Neville, don't . . . don't!'

'Are you telling me to stop talking, to keep quiet, not to think about it? Do you think I can help myself? I've got to live the rest of my life with that moment, just a split second, when I thought – bomb in theatre – ten dead – that'll make the front page – '

'*Ten dead!*'

'That was then. It's more now. Another five at least. And a lot of injured. They were bringing 'em up here in a fleet of ambulances for two hours, digging 'em out of the rubble. The roof fell in on them – '

Lumps of Jerusalem stone cemented by lumps of shit . . . Thus Amnon had found it. Now the stone had other cement.

'Have you seen Amnon?'

'Who?' He looked at her blankly.

'Neville – forgive me – I must know if he's all right – I'll come back to you in a minute.' She had caught what she thought was a

261

glimpse of pale blue in a far corner, which could be Amnon's linen suit. She left Neville standing alone and almost ran between the groups of people, her heart jerking thickly in her chest.

Yes. *Oh thank God!* – there he was – sitting on a bench, covered with dust and blood-streaks, his head buried between his arms. She flung herself down at his feet and threw her arms round him.

'Amnon! Oh Amnon – thank God you're safe – '

He jerked upright as if waking and stared at her with his mouth gaping. He, too, had been crying, but not for some time it seemed. His eyes were swollen but not red, and quite wild, like the eyes of an insane person.

'What shall I do?' he asked her immediately. She couldn't speak. She just knelt there on the floor between his knees and held on to his arms. 'It's all broken. My theatre. It's full of dead people.'

'No, Amnon. It's empty now. It's all cleared now.'

'Did you see it?'

'No. But everything's quiet. They're guarding it. And the front's – still there. Tomorrow we'll go together, you and me and Amatsia – it can be rebuilt – '

But he was shaking his head like someone in an ague.

'No,' he said. 'No. It's all gone. Amatsia's gone. I saw. He went under. The arches caved in. Big square stones. They poured on him. I saw them take him. On a stretcher. His face was covered but I saw his beard under the side of the blanket. There was blood. There was blood everywhere.' He sat motionless, staring at her as if he didn't see her.

She stood up and walked to the central desk, where a uniformed girl sat. She had lists in front of her. Ann stood there stiffly until she looked up. Her youthful professionalism was clearly being tested to destruction.

'Excuse me,' said Ann gently, as if she feared to disturb that fiercely retained detachment. 'Ruth Gilboa?'

The little nurse bent to her lists and her trimmed filbert nail moved downward past the pairs of Hebrew words, each a forename and a surname . . . it stopped.

'You are a relative?'

'No. A friend.'

'Yes. She was admitted.' She looked up and managed a smile. 'She is in Ward Eight. Her husband is with her. She's not hard-wounded. She's sleeping now. Come in the morning and you can

262

see her.'

'Could I see her now for a moment?'

'The hospital is in a state of emergency. As you see, there are so many people – relatives – if we allow one, then . . . Please. Come back tomorrow.'

'Thank you.'

She went back to Amnon. He was still in the same position, his mouth slightly open, his eyes glazed.

She crouched at his side. 'Come on, Amnon. We're going home.'

He got up obediently. She put her arm round him, and led him through the crowd to the main door. He had been just her height; now he had shrunk. Once he stopped dead, and looked back, and round, as if seeking someone. But a gentle tug set him going forward again. Ann looked for Neville. He had gone.

In the Fiat Amnon said, in a puzzled tone, 'This isn't the right car.'

'It's all right,' she said. 'We'll find yours tomorrow.' They drove through the night. She glanced at him every few seconds. His eyes were open, but apart from that he might have been unconscious.

She parked the car where she had parked it before – before she knew. Before everything changed, yet again. Before everything dropped down onto a new level, into a new dimension. Her relief at having Amnon, at least, no matter in what mental condition, was so acute that as she switched off the headlights she turned and took hold of him and held him.

If I'd had to come back here without Amnon – with nothing, with no one, with death and horror and no hand to hold – I'd have run to Boaz – I want to now – I need him to hold me together, to protect me. *He* is still alive, still as whole as he was this morning – he is not lying in a hospital bed like Ruth, or sobbing in my arms like Neville, or leaning against me shocked to dumbness like Amnon . . . Take strength from that! He is somewhere. I want him. I want him! But I have Amnon. I have to take care of Amnon.

She helped him out of the car, through the iron door, up the steps. She found the key in his pocket and led him into his own place. Home has a healing power. He straightened and looked about him as if surprised to find himself there. He walked by himself into the kitchen and sat down at the table under the bright neon. Ann stood looking at him almost fearfully.

'What can I give you?' she asked.

He shook his head.

'Something. A drink.'

'No.'

'Have you any sleeping pills?'

'What? No . . . No.'

How are we to get through this night?

'You must sleep. Come to bed.'

'Sleep?' he said incredulously.

Suddenly she remembered. The hashish – if it was still there . . . She went through into the central room, and, stooping, groped under the mattress. Her fingers touched plastic. She took it back into the kitchen where Amnon still sat as before.

'Amnon – '

'Yes.'

'Do you know – about this?'

She opened the bag and showed it to him, brown, crumbly stuff like rotten wood.

'It's hash, isn't it?' he said dully.

'Take some.'

He looked at her. Then he reached for it.

'Yes. Good.'

'How . . .'

'You can eat it.'

'Eat it? Amnon, are you sure? I thought it had to be smoked.'

'It's stronger and quicker if you eat it.'

He suddenly put his face down on his arms as if some image had entered his brain which was too terrible to be borne.

Ann put on a kettle and made some instant soup from a package. She was afraid of the hashish; it was a drug, and she knew nothing of drugs except that they could be dangerous. But she must help him to escape. She put the bowl of steaming soup before him with a spoon and then opened the plastic wrapping.

'How much?'

He took some soup in a spoon and crumbled a small lump of the stuff into it and swallowed it. Then he did it again.

'Amnon, not too much . . . Please. Don't . . . go away from me.'

'You have some too.'

She hesitated, but only for a moment. She took the spoon from him and did as he had done. It was as if he were getting on a train and she, left on the platform, terrified, jumped on the footplate rather than be left behind.

'How long does it take?'

'Not long. Just sit still. Try not to think.'

They sat for quite a while. Then Ann said, 'I need to lie down. I'm so tired.'

'Let's lie down on my bed.'

They went hand in hand to his bedroom and lay down together. Just like babes in the wood, she thought foolishly. Like children. Lying with him was as comforting and innocent as lying with Dill.

'Did you find them a place?'

'Who? What?' said Amnon after a pause.

'The Circus. You said you'd find them a new place.'

There was another long pause. Then Amnon said, 'It's beginning. Can you feel it, in your toes? They say that's where it always begins.'

'No. I don't feel anything yet.'

'Don't fight it. Relax. Let everything go. Amatsia says it's marvellous stuff. He gets his from an Arab he trusts, in the Old City.'

But Amatsia's dead. Blood on his beard, that beautiful, flowing patriarchal symbol . . . Beards keep growing after you're dead. She remembered her father. He lay in his coffin for three days and when they nailed down the lid he needed a shave.

'Do *you* feel something?' she asked.

'Yes, oh yes. It's lovely. It's lifting me away. It's lifting my outer skin from my inner skin. Puffing out . . . it makes padding. All round you. Amatsia always listens to music when he's on a trip. He says it is something beautiful. It gets inside your head. It strokes all your senses.'

'Music of the spheres.'

'What is "spheres"?'

' "There's not the smallest orb which thou behold'st, But in his motion like an angel sings." '

"Lovely! We had a company once,' he said dreamily. 'Five people, they acted whole Shakespeare plays on that stage of ours, without costumes or sets, taking all the rôles . . . They even did the horses' hoofs . . . with their cupped hands, on their chests . . .' His voice tailed away.

'I don't feel anything yet,' said Ann. 'Shall I get up and put on some music?'

'No. Stay here.' He took her hand as it lay at his side. 'Amatsia says it's good to have a woman with you on a trip. He says you feel her softness and smell her sweet flesh in a different way. When they picked him up he was still alive. I saw him move his hand. I couldn't get to him. There was madness. Smoke, and dust, and thousands of people, all crying, but I saw his hand move . . . Like this.' He moved his fingers against her wrist in a gesture of love and death. 'As if he was trying to wave.'

There was a long silence. She turned her mind this way and that with a little steering wheel. She saw Dill crowing on the trunk in the distance and turned towards him.

'It was a good show.'

'Yes, oh yes, it was. The audience loved it. Why did you leave? You are never there when I want you,' he said pettishly.

No, she thought detachedly, that's true. I've always avoided the bad things. I missed the '67 War. I missed the '73 War. And where was I tonight, when I was needed?

'I wanted to go and see someone. He's lost his hair and got very sad and gone back to the God who punishes the Jews. Amnon.'

'What?'

'I thanked Him when I saw you. As if He cared!'

'Never mind. It was a figure of . . . thought.'

'And I drove to Kibya.'

After a long pause he asked, 'Why?'

'Because it was there that it happened.'

'Not *only* there,' he said. Their voices had become uninflected, slow. There were long pauses. His fingers gently caressed her palm and wrist.

'I know. But it was bad. Wasn't it bad, Amnon?'

'In a way.'

'Ruth didn't think it was so bad. She said it worked. She said they had to do it.'

'But why Nat'am? Ann? They didn't have to do that! It was for them, too.'

'Perhaps that's why.'

'Perhaps.'

Ann saw the scorpion clearly, but she knew it wasn't real.

'My toes are still all right,' she said, 'but I'm falling asleep.'

'Don't fall asleep. Stay with me.'

'Cuddle up, then. We'll fall asleep together.'

He rolled over very slowly and she held him with his head on her shoulder. He put one arm over her as Dill had.

'You did find them a place, didn't you? A nice place?'

'Who? What?'

'The Circus.'

He didn't answer. He seemed to be asleep.

266

'Amnon?'

'I didn't have time. I was going to let them stay.'

Things went black, as if she had sunk down, over her head, in the dark pool, and then slowly and with reluctance (for she wanted to drown) she came up to the surface again.

'So where are they?' she asked in a clear, sharp voice, like an angry teacher.

'H'm?'

She shook him. 'Amnon? Where's Dill?'

'I'll tell you tomorrow. Don't spoil the trip. You feel so good. Where's your hair? Let it down. Do you want me to love you?'

'No.'

His hand, which had moved to unpin her hair, moved away again and lay limply across her waist. She turned the steering-wheel as sharply as Boaz had. Dill, in his costume as the little egg-born creature, was left behind, still crowing, fainter and fainter.

'Oh . . .' She said suddenly, with a note of academic interest.

'What?'

'I've just remembered. Amos Oz's fourth example of . . . what was it?' There was an indefinite period of silence. 'Communal creativity. I've got them all now. Settlements. Jerusalem. The Hebrew language. And the *army*. Isn't that odd? That was the fourth one.'

'He died,' said Amnon slowly.

'No, he did not. He lives in a kibbutz.'

'*And* Sue-Ella.'

She shut her mind with a crash, like the iron door.

'He was hurt in a car smash,' she said firmly, 'but he survived. And he says the army is an act of creativity. And he's a novelist like me and he believes . . . what we do. You do still believe it, Amnon? About peace, about living at peace with them?'

'I'm going to South Africa.'

'What?'

'I've just decided. South Africa. I've often been invited. I've said no, but I will. They may let me show them how to run a mixed theatre. That proves they're not so bad. And they help us. We've got to have friends.'

'Amnon, don't go there.'

'Why not? What does it matter? There may be more hope there.'

'There isn't. Don't go. Don't. Don't go.'

267

'I can't bear it,' he whispered suddenly. 'I can't bear it.'

'I can't either. But don't go. Wash the cement off the stones and build again.'

'They didn't find much of Dill at all. It went off almost under him. It was against one of the pillars. Walking on his hands . . . He leant one knee against the pillar . . . The way you lean your elbow . . . It was funny. The audience was so happy . . .' After a pause during which Ann drove her mind furiously in circles, twisting and turning, Amnon said, 'Yoni will come. He'll be sorry now. He liked Amatsia really. Amatsia said, "Yoni's all right, done wonders for the City. Trouble is, he's not growing old gracefully." But it will be a proper funeral, Yoni will see to that.'

'Yoni might help you rebuild. The City might help.'

'No. But he will come to the funeral. And he won't say "I told you so". He is still . . . rather graceful.'

There was a silence. The tears ran down the sides of their faces. Then Ann said, 'He noticed the bed tremble.'

'It's trembling now.'

'Yes . . .' Her nose was running. 'Amnon . . .'

'What?'

'What will happen tomorrow? When the trip's over?'

'I'll go to South Africa. And you'll go to England.'

'Will I?'

'If you've any sense. And you'll never come back. So let me love you.'

'No.'

He lifted his hand from her waist and she thought he would put it on her breast. But instead he laid it softly on her face as if to shut out the world.

CHAPTER 20

It was not the doorbell that woke Ann very early next morning. One couldn't hear it well from Amnon's room. It was the footsteps, heavy and deliberate, walking through the flat from room to room.

She lay perfectly still on Amnon's bed, with Amnon in her arms, his head still pillowed on her shoulder, his arm across her. She was still wearing the long dress she had put on for the theatre, and her silk stole was coiled round her body and his like a winding sheet. Her hands tightened on him. He was heavy with sleep. She could have moved him, with an effort – thrust him away, jumped up, run out of the room . . . Because she knew. She knew who it was. She knew the weight and consciousness of those footsteps, and it was clear to her immediately what had happened.

He had turned on his radio to catch the early news, and had heard. He had instantly – on impulse, as she herself might have acted – picked up the medallion, with the key attached, which she had left behind and which, no doubt, he had never intended to return; had got into his car and driven here, rung – once – and then let himself in. And in about five more seconds he would conclude his search of the flat in this, the furthest room from the front door. He would stand in the doorway, there, where her eyes were fastened, and he would look down and see her lying on the bed with Amnon in her arms.

And why didn't she move? Why didn't she leap up instinctively, run to meet him, to head him off – to circumvent whatever terrible consequences must follow his seeing her thus with Amnon, of all men? He could not affect indifference to her, not after rushing here to see if she were safe. He loved her. To see her like this would do him harm, and in return he might harm her, harm Amnon . . . Yet she didn't stir. And when the seconds had duly ticked away, the footsteps came across the tiles to the door, and it opened, and he stood there, looking down into her eyes.

The relief on his face was unconcealed. His injured hand made an aborted movement towards her and his eyes closed for a moment. When they reopened they flicked to Amnon, lying like a child on her breast. Then they came back to her. She lay under his gaze, and waited for the lion to leap, for the violent assault, whatever form it took, to be launched against her – or, if not that, for him to turn on his heel and leave her for ever.

She gazed steadily at him, holding her passionate terror and love tightly in the tendons of her arms and belly so that nothing would show, that he would see only in his own reflection in the steadiness of her gaze. And after an immensely protracted moment, he said in a low voice, 'Get up. I want to speak to you alone.'

He turned and walked out of the room.

Gently and carefully, she extricated herself from Amnon's embrace and laid his head on the bed. He didn't stir. She got off the bed and stood up. Her head was clear – score to hashish over alcohol. She had not even taken off her shoes last night but for some reason she took them off now and walked bare-footed across the cool, dusty tiles to find Boaz.

He was not in the flat, which didn't surprise her. She discovered him out on the balcony. The sun had risen and the traffic had started its morning racket; it would have been better to talk in the quiet of the 'seraglio room': but she understood what it had cost Boaz to enter Amnon's house at all, that nothing but the most urgent concern for her could have induced him to do it, and that now she must face him out here. She also knew that he was not going to hurt her. Not in any way. The relief of this knowledge unmanned her far more than her previous fear.

They stood looking at each other. The sun filtered through the eucalyptus leaves and flickered on their faces, and the scents of a Jerusalem morning – eucalyptus and pine, dust and fumes, coffee and bagels and a million flowers – floated about them. She put her hand on the warming stone wall, feeling its delicious harshness. Like Boaz's hand, which now reached to touch her. Every sense was heightened by his presence, far more than by the drug she had taken the night before. The grief and the horror of yesterday's events were heightened, too. Nothing was swept aside for this meeting; it was all there, crowding in to be felt, invaders of her peace.

His hand had grazed her cheek and passed round to hold her by the back of the neck. His expression was bemused, fierce with emotions no longer quite under his control.

He shook her a little and his teeth showed in a grimace.

'Come with me,' he said.

'Come with you?'

'I want you to leave everything you've ever been tied by, and

270

come and live with me. I want you to reject your English husband for whom your body evidently feels nothing, and your country, to which your mind was unfaithful from the day you first set foot here . . . You can't live forever in this state. If I am paranoid, you are schizophrenic! I want you to realise that you belong *here*. It is wrong and weak to shuttle between the two, writing your articles and books, making little speeches – never mind now what you say in them, it doesn't matter – what matters is, you are keeping all you are really committed to at arm's length. And you're not built for that! I know a woman when I've tried her body. You can accept challenge, you don't shrink from pain or roughness. You enjoy pleasure to the full. It proves what I always knew. You are like me. You thrive on intensity. All that – English flatness and blandness and safety – that's not for you, there's no challenge in it, it demands nothing. Israel makes demands, it hurts the flesh, it fills you as I filled you – it makes you weep, as I did, and drinks your tears, and forces you to know you are alive.'

'The land that eats its people.'

'As they say.'

'I would say rather the land whose people eat each other, as you might eat me, if I'd let you.'

'I ate you yesterday, but today you're still here.'

'And so are my beliefs.'

'I don't care what you believe! No, that's not true. I care deeply, but not enough. Yesterday I heard you walk out of my house and I determined never to think any more about you. But for all the hours in between I have thought about you and wanted you. When I heard the news this morning, and thought you might be crushed under weights of stone, or wounded by blast, or dead, I knew it was no use. Whatever you are, whatever you believe, whatever you fight for, you're a part of what I am, and we must somehow live together. Because my honesty is all I have left. I can't live an honest life without you. I think it's the same for you.'

'But I'm afraid of you, Boaz.'

'I know. You are right. And I can't promise not to frighten you by shouting at you and attacking your ideas and trying to change you. Or more, by being what I am. But you're strong. If you're my enemy, you're a worthy one, and I prefer to spend my life struggling with you than struggling without you.'

'And what about my preferences? Perhaps I prefer a decent blameless life with a decent blameless man.'

271

'Is it? Is *he* – decent and blameless? Your country is no more innocent than this one, if you look at its history, and probably your man has his hidden guilts.'

'Not like yours, Boaz. You broke your resolution about me when you thought I might be dead. But you've killed people in that same way – under falls of stone – by blast, by fire – women – '

'I did that. Yes. I make no apology.'

'Shouldn't you? – However silently and inwardly?'

'No. We were soldiers. We followed orders. The orders were to give warning, to check that the houses were empty.'

'But you didn't.'

'We couldn't search each house. There was no time. We expected a Legion border patrol at any moment. But we gave a loudspeaker warning in Arabic outside every house. And we'd seen many of them run, after the village fell to us . . . We thought they were all out. We shone flashlights through the doors. It was only later, when we heard the numbers, I thought of all the places there were to hide.'

'And did you lose sleep?'

'It was a bad feeling. But that's war. It happened. And that village wasn't chosen at random. It was where they were coming from. We had to stop them coming. And after Kibya, they stopped.'

'You were very young.'

'Don't delude yourself, or insult me with slop like that. I would do it today and worse, if Israel was threatened. I told you, my way of fighting is only clean if it is able to be clean. I can be the tiger, or I can be the rat and the wolf. I don't believe in the purity of arms, only the effectiveness of arms.'

'Would you use nuclear weapons?' she suddenly asked.

He hesitated.

'Would you agree to their use? Would you, Boaz?'

He looked away from her. There was a long silence.

'No. I would fight to my death, I would do many things. But I would not destroy everything. This place must stay whole.'

Ann gazed at him. Menachem, godfearing Jew with the kibbutz look, would: Boaz wouldn't.

'And would you expect me to live with you in that house, in an Arab district?'

'Yes.'

'Your wife couldn't stand it.'

'My wife hated and feared the Arabs. You, I understand,' he

said, ironically, 'love them.'

'I don't hate them, that much is true. But I don't feel at home with them. I doubt if I could enjoy living among them, and especially not with you, who do hate them and whom they have reason to hate.'

'Who told you I hate them?'

'You did.'

'No! I told you I hate our enemies. I don't hate the people I live with and work with – what am I, a masochist? I get on well with them. I help them when I can and they help me when they can. And that's not a function of hatred.'

'So why did they try to kill you?'

His eyes narrowed. He indicated his arm. 'Is it your understanding that they did this because of the old actions?'

'I was thinking more of contemporary ones.'

'You'd better tell me what you mean.'

'It's common gossip that you're some sort of spy.'

He threw back his head and gave a snort of derision.

'Is that what they say?'

'Is it true?'

'If I say yes, will that end it between us?'

'Very probably.'

'Are spies not a necessary part of any country's defences?'

'Possibly. And I accept my share of the spoils of their work. But I don't want to live with one. If that's cowardice, or squeamishness, I plead guilty to it.'

'Come here.' He drew her towards him by the elbow and looked closely into her eyes. 'Now listen and believe me. I am not a spy. Not in the way you mean. A small part of my work is to keep an eye on things, and if I hear anything which is useful to the military establishment of Israel I tell them, just as you would. I hope you would. But the Arabs know all about that and they generally take good care that I have nothing to pass on – they are not idiots. Unless of course it is something which they want the authorities to know. You understand, of course, that many of them go in fear of the PLO more than we do. They also fear the retaliations that we make against them if they make us problems. If they have a strike and close their shops, we open them by force. If they make a riot, we send in troops to put it down. If a leader opens his mouth and shouts, "Down with the Jews! Up with the PLO!" we kick him across the border. All these things and others you and I can quarrel about at our leisure. The point I'm making is that there are Arabs on the West Bank who have no more interest in these upsets to their lives than we do and they sometimes drop us a hint, and sometimes the hint falls on me, because I am around and they know – in a way which you can only understand if you know them – that they can trust me. They know exactly what I do and where I stand. They also know that my chief work is studying them so that I can write about them. I do this for myself, and for anyone else who is interested. My dissertations are in the libraries of all our universities. I am writing now a book – you must help me with it, by the way, because it is in English – which I hope to get published abroad. I want very much to get to the bottom of these people, to understand them fully, even though I know quite well it is impossible. They are like an onion, layer under layer and no hard core of absolute integrity that I can discover . . . But they fascinate me, and you must understand that I fascinate them – I am a patriotic Israeli Jew who speaks their language and lives among them and I have no horns and no tail and they are forced to the realisation that they can relate to me. I believe I do more for good relations than all your peaceniks with their marches and speeches and treasonable cloak-and-dagger meetings with PLO leaders.'

She smiled suddenly and took a deep, pain-free breath.

'Are you satisfied with my explanation?'

'For the moment.'

'*Nu?*' He shook her arm.

'I still have a husband, whom I love and who loves me.'

'You belong more to me after three fucks than to him after ten years.'

'You have a crude way of looking at things. My roots are in him.'

'Pull them up. Plant them again in me. I will nourish them better.'

'You don't know what they need to settle and grow. More than fucking and fighting, Boaz. If I leave Peter and come to you, you're stuck with me and my problems and guilts, as I am with yours. You think yourself a better mate for me than he is: but are you good, kind, faithful, patient, supportive, generous and tender?'

'No. I am selfish, ill-tempered, moody, rough and often ruthless. But I will feed your body and mind as he has never done.'

'You'll also bully me. And I won't stand for it.'

'Good. I've told you, I like a strong resistance.'

'A woman, just like a man, has her irrational passions to

contend with. Perhaps, now my lust is satisfied, I am ready to throw you away and go back to my real life.'

He looked from one of her eyes to the other and then released her arm and stepped back.

'Go, then.'

'Do you mean it? You'll let me go, without a fight?'

'Yes. Only you can judge which is your real life.'

'I have. And I've judged wrong.'

She stepped up to him and kissed him, embracing him fiercely, feeling the power of her own renewed sexuality and delighting in it. But it was just the raw material of a partnership. How could they build it into a life together, a life worth what it must cost, to Peter, to themselves? How long could such a relationship possibly last?

She broke from the kiss to ask, 'Would you try to stop me seeing other people, loving them?'

'I might try. I wouldn't expect to succeed.'

'I love Amnon.'

He gave a grim half smile. 'So I saw.'

'I thought you would be mad with anger.'

He looked away from her, over the railing, into the garden.

'Sometimes,' he said, 'I have been to women . . . women I would not normally go to. After Kibya I went with a woman just because she was a comrade, she had also done dirty work. She didn't love me and I was not even attracted to her but I went to her then because I needed a woman who understood one thing, the feeling you have after killing, the feeling that now you deserve to die, that you can't pity yourself any more if you die. She comforted me without a word, with her body, and I went away next morning and she went back to her husband and children. She gave me back my wholeness.'

'Perhaps it's my· wholeness that attracts you. But you may destroy it.'

He looked at her. He was holding her wrist tightly, keeping a physical link between them. He said, 'You mustn't allow me. You must stop me by every means. Except by leaving me as you did yesterday. When the door closed and I found it was not in me to surrender, to go after you and bring you back, I suffered a death in myself. You must understand I will say terrible things, that I will fight you and that something in me may try to destroy you. After all, your mind and ideas are alien to mine. You can't give your "yes" to half my life. You can be a danger to me and to what I

275

care for. But whatever I say or do, you must fight back, and never run away again.'

There was a silence, and then suddenly she began to cry. For the first time he took her in his arms, not as a lover but as a friend.

'What – what is it? Do I ask too much?'

'Yesterday – in the theatre – ' she sobbed, ' – people I loved – a little boy – '

She cried against him for along time, and he held her close and comforted her. It was all still there, waiting for her – Ruth's injuries, about which she still knew nothing; Amnon's despair and desire to run; the absolute necessity of going to see Bob and Chloe and sharing with them her last memories of Dill, mourning with them, throwing herself wholly into their bewilderment and loss to lessen the pain as much as she could. Neville and Jacqui, too . . . But people here lived with that, it was always happening. She had learnt in the kibbutz, when that boy was killed, how to come close to grief-stricken people and help them. It was a *mitzva*, and it was part of being here. Part of what she was to undertake. But how did these people bear their losses, when she could feel like this about a little boy she scarcely knew?

Boaz was waiting for her first spasm of sorrow to end. How fortunate, she thought, that he doesn't despise tears! I'm going to shed so many. He even had a rather grubby handkerchief to lend her.

'Listen, Ann. I pay your grief this tribute. I won't use this against you. I won't use what happened to your friend's theatre to point out the lesson of the people who planted that bomb.'

'How good of you! After yesterday's earlier events, you had much better not.'

His face changed, but then he nodded slowly.

'*Touché*,' he said quietly, and kissed her wet eyes.

They stood embraced while the traffic noise from the other side of the iron door grew louder. At last she stood away with a heavy sigh.

'I can't come at once.'

'Of course not,' he said immediately.

'You understand I must be with Amnon?'

'You can't leave a wounded friend on this bloody battlefield, who would not understand that?'

'So you know he's a friend, not a lover?'

'If I had really thought you would let anything happen between you – '

'Oh! I thought you were being so noble.'

'I am not noble. Never. Don't hope for it. I'll wait for you. If I can do anything, telephone me.'

'I love you, Boaz.'

'That's not a word I use.'

'It's one you'll have to learn.'

She walked down the steps with him to see him off. Coming out through the iron door into the street was like emerging from the dark pool and the satanic forest, to enjoy – at least till night drew her to its dank edge again – her daytime hours in the hot golden sun.